A TALE OF
TWO NAVIES

A TALE OF TWO NAVIES

Geopolitics, Technology, and Strategy in the
United States Navy and the Royal Navy, 1960–2015

ANTHONY R. WELLS

NAVAL INSTITUTE PRESS
ANNAPOLIS, MARYLAND

This book was made possible through the dedication of the U.S. Naval Academy Class of 1945.

Naval Institute Press
291 Wood Road
Annapolis, MD 21402

Library of Congress Cataloging-in-Publication Data
Names: Wells, Anthony R., author
Title: A tale of two navies : geopolitics, technology, and strategy in the
   United States Navy and the Royal Navy, 1960–2015 / Anthony R. Wells.
Other titles: Geopolitics, technology, and strategy in the United States Navy
   and the Royal Navy, 1960–2015
Description: Annapolis, Maryland : Naval Institute Press, [2017] | Includes
   bibliographical references and index.
Identifiers: LCCN 2016034115 (print) | LCCN 2016034270 (ebook) | ISBN
   9781682471203 (hardcover : alk. paper) | ISBN 9781682471210 (ePDF) |
   ISBN 9781682471210 (ePub) | ISBN 9781682471210 (mobi)
Subjects: LCSH: United States. Navy. | Great Britain. Royal Navy, |
   Sea-power—United States. | Sea-power—Great Britain. | Naval strategy.
   | Naval art and science. | United States—Military relations—Great
   Britain. | Great Britain—Military relations—United States. | Geopolitics.
Classification: LCC VA58.4 .W45 2017 (print) | LCC VA58.4 (ebook) |
   DDC 359/.03094109045—dc23
LC record available at https://lccn.loc.gov/2016034115

25 24 23 22 21 20 19 18 17   9 8 7 6 5 4 3 2

This book is dedicated to the men and women
who served in the US Navy and the Royal Navy between 1960 and 2015,
a tumultuous fifty-five years that witnessed dramatic political and strategic
changes during which the seascape of the world played a dominant role.
This book is their story.

In memory of all those who lost their lives in the service
of the US Navy and the Royal Navy—the last lines of
"Ulysses," by Alfred, Lord Tennyson:

Come, my friends,
'T is not too late to seek a newer world.
Push off, and sitting well in order smite
The sounding furrows; for my purpose holds
To sail beyond the sunset, and the baths
Of all the western stars, until I die.
It may be that the gulfs will wash us down:
It may be we shall touch the Happy Isles,
And see the great Achilles, whom we knew.
Tho' much is taken, much abides; and tho'
We are not now that strength which in old days
Moved earth and heaven, that which we are, we are;
One equal temper of heroic hearts,
Made weak by time and fate, but strong in will
To strive, to seek, to find, and not to yield.

Contents

Illustrations

Photos

TABLE

CHRONOLOGY

Acknowledgments

I would like to thank my beloved wife, Dr. Carol Evans, for the painstaking creation of the index. In a book with such complex technical detail this was indeed a labor of love, combined with considerable resilience and great professionalism.

Introduction

This book is about naval thinking: its impact at every level of naval activity and interaction with national defense in its many complexities. An attempt has been made to select themes that are relevant and most topical for current issues, providing a framework for thinking through where both navies need to go in the future and why. Perhaps most of all it seeks to encourage thoughtful discourse on how to steer a successful course through what is often a minefield of opponents, skeptics, fellow travelers, and those with ill-conceived agendas or who simply have little or no knowledge of both navies' rich maritime heritage or of the basics of maritime strategy. The book wants to provide guidance and stimulation. It will attempt to answer key questions, as a Socratic response. Most of all it aims to encourage thoughtful dialogue with readers so that individually and collectively they may contribute to the debate and actions needed to keep both countries' naval strategies deeply rooted and focused on well-reasoned fact, intellectual integrity, and rigor. The past fifty-five years provide us with bedrock experience that can help us shape the future.

The US Navy and the Royal Navy have a unique relationship within the "special relationship" between the United States and the United Kingdom. The special relationship was forged during World War II by President Franklin Roosevelt and Prime Minister Winston Churchill. At its heart lay special intelligence sharing at the most sensitive levels, much of it focused on naval matters. Parallel to and coupled with intelligence activities ran a continuous thread of maritime strategic planning and execution that bonded the two navies throughout World War II. This golden thread that contributed so significantly to ultimate victory in 1945 continued in the postwar period. By 1960, when this story begins, this special relationship and the destinies of the United States and Royal Navies had become entwined, and endured thereafter.

The fifty-five years from 1960 to 2015 have seen extraordinary challenges and changes for both navies. They have been as demanding as World War II and of comparable strategic significance. One critical factor lies at the root of the strategic underpinnings of the past fifty-five years: the combined and shared national self-interests of the United States and the United Kingdom in preserving and protecting the values and interests that sustained them during the darkest days of World War II and for which they fought. This story from 1960 to 2015 reflects those very self-same Anglo-American values, which have been preserved to this day. The United States and Royal Navies together represent the enduring values that unite both countries in common goals.

This book is not a formal history or an anthology and does not follow a strict chronology. It is more a discursive analysis of selected key themes across time, as well as of how the two navies interacted in distinctive ways. I aim to engage and challenge the reader's own knowledge and experience in a Socratic way, so that the reader may form his or her own ideas and conclusions, as a result of what I hope are stimulating and illuminating observations. This book does not, therefore, aim to be definitive in any sense of the word but rather a discourse between the author and readers whereby they may collectively form clear and reliable ideas about not just what happened in this critical fifty-five years but also how it will shape all our thinking about the future. Professor Sir

Franklin D. Roosevelt and Winston Churchill at a church service on board HMS Prince of Wales *during the Atlantic Charter Conference, August 10, 1941, in Placentia Bay, Newfoundland*   US NAVY

Michael Howard, the father of the Department of War Studies at King's College, University of London, has stressed that the past is not necessarily always a true guide to the future, that lessons learned may not always be applied to future events or scenarios or for formulating plans, policies, or programs, and certainly not to grand strategy. However, he does conclude that understanding why things happen in military institutions and their ultimate engagement in war has value, that such knowledge and insight can help address a way forward. The past should not be prologue but instead used to anticipate change and formulate future endeavors based on a didactic interchange between the past, the present, and the foreseeable future. For example, both navies are currently involved in what is the most expensive defense program for each nation, the replacement of the submarine-based ballistic missile, the keystone of both countries' nuclear deterrence strategy. The history of both navies' nuclear-powered ballistic-missile submarine (SSBN) forces is a study in strategy in its own right. The Cold War era has transitioned to the post–Cold War period. Both navies now witness the growth of Chinese naval power and the reemergence of a Russian navy that looks a lot different from the one US Navy admirals visited in the heyday of post–Soviet Union perestroika in the 1990s. Given the massive investment and the opportunity-cost choices confronting both governments, what do the past fifty-five years tell us? What is the interaction between the US–UK SSBN forces' strategic underpinnings, program elements (technical, operational, force structure, and financial) and other choices, and the past? The continuity of institutionalized naval thinking may be challenged in ways that were simply not present when President John Kennedy and Prime Minister Harold MacMillan signed the agreements that shared US submarine nuclear technology with the Royal Navy and led to the creation of the UK's Polaris submarine force. Political will and funding interact with both navies' concerns about lost programs and diminished force levels as a result of the inevitable high cost of SSBN replacement. Based on our knowledge and experience, what is the best outcome for both countries and their navies?

Bookshelves and e-systems are full of outstanding works on both the US Navy and Royal Navy during this period. This book will not attempt to replicate what is easily available elsewhere. For example, the technical details of both navies' force structure down to the unit level, in extraordinary fine and accurate detail, can be found in works like *Jane's Fighting Ships* and the myriad publications of the U.S. Naval Institute, by distinguished authors such as the late Royal Navy captain John Moore and the American civilian author Norman Polmar. The histories of all the main conflicts, local wars, and other engagements are well documented and analyzed in multiple sources. Where this book hopes to contribute and stimulate is in the nonquantifiable domains that relate to the question *why*. In particular, it will cast light on themes where the author has unique knowledge and insight, hitherto unexamined and highly relevant areas. To illustrate from the past, the British government only released in 1974 a limited amount of information of the Ultra secrets of World War II and the Enigma code, together with the existence of Bletchley Park. Within a few years the data, which was released very slowly, changed completely our understanding of World War II, as exemplified by Sir Harry Hinsley's masterful volumes published by the British government on the history of British intelligence in World War II. The point is self-evident. There is much that naval professionals and those associated with the political-military process do not know or consider. This is no one's fault. It is the nature of the way security-conscious navies conduct business. What is key is to ensure that all salient factors are considered. When either navy engages in a critical event like a national strategic defense review that will lead to resource allocations and changes in national defense priorities, policies, and programs, there is likely to be generational impact. Here is an illustration. The British government decided in the 1960s to not replace the Royal Navy's fleet aircraft carriers, thereby ending major carrier-launched fixed-wing aviation (with the exception of the three small, 20,000-ton, *Invincible*-class Harrier carriers or through-deck cruisers). Two new *Queen Elizabeth* fleet carriers will enter service in the early 2020s. There has been a gap of over forty years since HMS *Ark Royal* was decommissioned. The consequences of decisions made in the 1960s were witnessed in the Falklands campaign and more recently in operations off Libya.

The themes are selected for good reasons. They are based on criteria that reflect what drives change at all levels: from the high-level institutional and organizational aspects of political-military decision making down to the effects of hugely significant technical changes that in due course impact policy making and operations. A few obvious examples of the latter are nuclear-reactor technology in submarines; underwater cruise- and ballistic-missile launch; multispectral missile and warhead seekers that permit precision strike to within CEPs (circular error probabilities) of just a few feet or less; unmanned stealthy, long-range reconnaissance vehicles; distributed, real-time intelligence systems; and Aegis-like combat systems. The list is huge. All make a significant difference, some make quantum leaps. Fifty-five years have witnessed monumental technical changes: the digital revolution alone is in retrospect quite mind-boggling. When Allen Turing made his revolutionary applications of basic computer technology at Bletchley Park in World War II, he was in the van of technologies that will see no slowing down beyond current "cloud," cyber, and digital communications and signal-processing technologies in the coming decades. The questions for readers that will be posed as this book unfolds is how should we best exploit these emerging technologies for the strategic and tactical benefit of both navies and that fit optimally the national security needs of the United States and United Kingdom.

The dialogue that occurred in our period of interest between the various editors of *Jane's Fighting Ships* and US and UK intelligence officials was responsible and collegial. Retired Royal Navy captain John Moore had been a head of one of the United Kingdom's intelligence agencies when he was a serving officer and later, indeed, regularly visited your author to discuss content for his annual volume. What this says is that many of the publications that readers are familiar with are simply outstanding and do not require embellishment or updates, certainly not replacement.

The structure of this book has been determined by its key themes, and these are reflected in the chapter titles. The themes cover the important relationship between both navies, manifested by their intelligence organizations, technology developments, political-military restructuring, selected key operations, and their joint and overarching reactions to the various global threats that they faced from 1960 to 2015. The abiding thread that connects these themes comprises the core issue, concepts, and furtherance of a global maritime strategy to protect the vital national interests of the United States and the United Kingdom.

A Tale of Two Navies draws on the unique knowledge and experience of the author, who had the privilege of serving in uniform with both the US Navy and the Royal Navy while working closely with their respective intelligence agencies. As a result, the substantive material that forms the basis for this book is both selective and focused; there is no intent to cover the waterfront, across each and every domain of naval activities that the two navies embraced. Thus, the author does not review all the major US and British naval operations, technology developments, or details like orders of battle and weapon capabilities. There are bookshelves of excellent sources that cover these topics. What you have in the following twelve chapters is the author's insider perspective of critical themes that will endure for the foreseeable future. Please do enjoy the dialogue, for the goal is to provoke your own thoughts and opinions, for you to carry forward to support an enduring US-UK global maritime strategy.

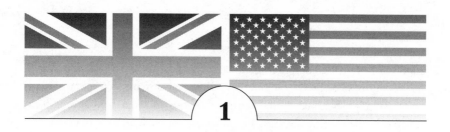

Organizational Change and
Strategic Priorities Impact
the US Navy and the Royal Navy

In 1960 the US Navy and the Royal Navy were emerging from a fifteen-year post–World War II period that had solidified the Cold War in geographic, political, military, and economic boundaries. Both navies underwent major organizational changes in ways that have influenced their development ever since.

Before exploring the detail of the various postwar organizational transformations, it is important to understand and evaluate some fundamental differences in the political systems of the United States and the United Kingdom and how these impact their navies. The United States is a republic with separation of powers between the executive, the legislature and financial provider, and the judiciary. The United Kingdom is a parliamentary democracy in which the legislature and the executive are one and the same thing, with a cabinet system of government. The executive is formed from the winning party at election time, with the elected leader of the winning party becoming prime minister after Her Majesty the Queen invites that person to form a government—a constitutional nicety at one level but part of the United Kingdom's unwritten constitution. The monarch is the titular head of state, the head of the Church of England, and also, significantly, the Lord High Admiral of the Royal Navy.

By contrast, the elected president of the United States, after the popular state-by-state votes have been converted to Electoral College votes, nominates his or her selected cabinet officers for confirmation by the Senate—not always an easy experience for those nominated and by no means automatic. The relevant committees of record will decide whether the person nominated to be Secretary of the Navy and the Under Secretary and Assistant Secretaries of the Navy will be voted upon for confirmation by the full Senate of the United States. Once confirmed those appointed officials report through a well-defined chain within the Department of the Navy and the Department of Defense to the president. For their part, British political officials within the Ministry of Defense are members of the House of Commons or, much less often nowadays than previously, of the House of Lords. They answer through the secretary of state for defense to the prime minister, but, and this is very significant, they also answer directly to Parliament as sitting members of the House of Commons or House of Lords.

In the United States, the House and Senate Armed Services Committees and the House and Senate Select Committees on Intelligence are responsible for approving all expenditures for all defense- and intelligence-related activities. In the United Kingdom, the sitting elected members who are also appointed to political positions within the Ministry of Defense present their budgets and programs for confirmation in the House of Commons as part of the defense vote within the UK parliamentary budget process. This is a completely different process than that of the United States. As a result, there are very considerable differences in budgetary and military outcomes for the two countries' navies and in how they are politically managed and financed. US Navy political appointees have to cross the Potomac River from the Pentagon and answer to the above House and Senate committees of record for their budget needs and also for the execution of funds across all naval domains, from personnel to acquisitions, force levels, and the underpinning strategy that is the argued basis for the annual budget process.

Committee staffers are critical in this process—the men and women who support the committees as professional staff members and in the offices of each individual representative and senator. The latter have direct interests not just at the national level, in terms of the proper funding and execution of US defense policy, but also with respect to the crucial impact on individual districts and states (for congressional representatives and senators respectively). Defense and intelligence budgets affect local jobs, bases, repair facilities; these staffs are concerned that large acquisition programs offer contractor employment in as many states as possible. The sensitive dialogue among both committee and representatives' and senators' staffs and Navy officials is therefore very subtle and important, totally unlike how the Ministry of Defense and the Royal Navy do business in the United Kingdom. Until very recently postwar US defense funding was characterized by what is colloquially termed "pork barrel" funding, whereby individual representatives and senators secure projects for their home districts and states. From a solely political perspective, sitting on one of the powerful defense subcommittees (parts of the all-powerful House and Senate Armed Services Committees) is a major political advantage for politicians whose home areas have significant or growing defense work, bases, or infrastructure.

The impact on the US and Royal Navies of the above major differences significantly affects how the senior uniform leadership interacts with the political and ultimate controlling arms of government. The Chief and Vice Chief of Naval Operations and the Commandant and Assistant Commandant of the Marine Corps appear regularly before the key congressional committees to explain and support their funding requests alongside the political appointees—the Secretary of the Navy himself and his assistant secretaries. They may be also called to account for any other relevant matter that Congress determines appropriate. Three- and two-star US Navy officers regularly appear before both full committees and subcommittees to explain their plans, policies, and programs. The Congress has many ways to influence the US Navy, and its toolbox is full of subtle political means to influence programs and outcomes.

The United Kingdom has very different processes. Elected ministers represent Royal Navy interests in the houses of Parliament (the House of Commons and the House of Lords), and senior officers are expected not to interact politically at any level unless specifically instructed by the appropriate elected minister. Senior Royal Navy officers do not have working relations with members of Parliament similar to those of their US counterparts. The British civil service supports ministerial positions and budgets with inputs from the senior naval leadership. During our period the permanent secretaries in the Ministry of Defense and their large civilian staffs (career civil servants selected by open competition and trained at the national level) yielded considerable power as the key interfaces with ministers, as the elements of continuity in policy and programs, and sources of key ministerial guidance that in the case of the US Navy is provided directly by the staffs of the Chief of Naval Operations and the Commandant of the Marine Corps. This is a very significant difference. A four-star admiral in the Royal Navy has nothing like the political influence, access, or interaction that his equivalent does in the United States. In our fifty-five-year period, British First Sea Lords and Chiefs of Naval Staff have rarely been seen to exert their rights of access under various constitutional niceties that devolve from Her Majesty the Queen being the Lord High Admiral. One of the most significant consequences for the Royal Navy is the inability to exert direct political influence on the budgetary process and resulting programs. It has nothing like the access that the US congressional committee structure affords the senior leadership of the US Navy.

A rare exception occurred in 1982, when Admiral Sir Henry Leech, the First Sea Lord and Chief of Naval Staff (the direct counterpart of the US Chief of Naval Operations) marched from the Ministry of Defense across Whitehall to 10 Downing Street via the Cabinet Office and directly approached the prime minister, Margaret Thatcher, without any prior approval from the secretary of state for defense. He simply told her that the Royal Navy and Royal Marines were standing by and were capable of retaking the Falkland Islands after the Argentinian invasion. Somewhat astounded, she immediately rose to the occasion and gave Admiral Leech an answer to his implied request in the affirmative. Admiral Leech had the full support of the Chief of the Defense Staff, Admiral Sir Terence Lewin. Admiral Leech knew that unless he made his mark directly with the prime minister there could be delay, vacillation and, in the worst case, compromise in Whitehall's highly bureaucratized decision-making process.

Other keystones of the countries' systems of government—and reflections of their democratic and common-law traditions—are their respective legal systems. The judiciaries of the two countries are appointed very differently. In the United States, federal judges and members of the Supreme Court are nominated by the president for confirmation by the Senate Judiciary Committee before a full vote in the Senate. There is therefore a definite political flavor to the judiciary at the federal level. In the United Kingdom there is more judicial independence; the barrister profession, whose members reside in the four Inns of Court, provides members of the higher judiciary via a professional and increasingly transparent process of selection by independent bodies of professionals. Judicial appointment recommendations are followed by confirmation by the Lord Chancellor after nomination to the Crown. Judicial independence in the United Kingdom has been a cornerstone of the separation of politics and political parties from judicial interference.

The above sets the stage for the fundamental changes that occurred in both countries in their post–World War II defense establishments. What follows has had significant influence not just on critical issues of strategy but also on defense and intelligence activity at every level and, therefore, on how the United States and the United Kingdom have conducted their national security programs and operations and, ultimately, made decisions to go to war.

The US National Security Act of 1947 had a profound effect on the US Navy. The Navy had been a separate department of government, established by act of Congress in 1798. The 1947 act and equally important the amendment to that act in 1949 created the US national defense establishment. The offices of secretary of defense and deputy secretary of defense were created,

with the Secretary of the Navy subordinate to the former. The 1947 act also
created the US Air Force, separating it from the US Army. The first secretary of defense, James Forrestal, had been Secretary of the Navy prior to the
act, and he had opposed the changes. Since 1947 the Office of the Secretary
of Defense has multiplied in size many times, with a large number of political appointees. In 1986 the Goldwater-Nichols Defense Reorganization Act
strengthened the statutory framework created by the 1947 and 1949 acts. Joint
service for aspiring general and flag officers effectively became mandatory.
However, the office of the Secretary of the Navy, the Chief of Naval Operations, and the Commandant of the Marine Corps remained intact, and their
staffs remained unimpaired. The US Navy assigned from 1947 onward officers within the Office of the Secretary of Defense and the Office of the Chairman of the Joint Chiefs of Staff to provide centralized support, advice, and
direction to the secretary and his various staffs. The secretary of defense sits on
the National Security Council, unlike the Secretary of the Navy. Until 1949
the Secretary of the Navy was a member of the president's cabinet but after the
changes became third in the secretary-of-defense succession, highlighting the
historical position of the Secretary of the Navy. In modern times but before
our period begins in 1960, there were many outstanding secretaries—Frank
Knox (1940–44) and James Forrestal (1944–47) took the US Navy through
the challenging years of World War II and to final victory.

*Fleet Admiral Chester W. Nimitz, C-in-C, US Pacific Fleet and of Pacific Ocean
Areas, at a Navy Department press conference in March 1945, with Secretary of the
Navy James Forrestal and Rear Admiral Forrest Sherman*   US NAVY

The US National Security Act of 1947 also created the Central Intelligence Agency (CIA) and the National Security Council. The director of Central Intelligence (DCI) was head of both the CIA and the US intelligence community until April 21, 2005, when the DCI lost his community-head role to the new position of director of National Intelligence (DNI) and his staff. The DNI also replaced the DCI as the principal intelligence adviser to the president. The DNI also became a member of the National Security Council. The CIA director continues to manage all aspects of the work of the CIA and to be responsible for the clandestine operations of the agency through the National Clandestine Service, which replaced the former Directorate of Operations.

All of the above changes persisted through our period and may be characterized as centralization, additional organizational structure and manpower, and a lengthening and deepening of the chain of command at all levels, whether operational, acquisition, political-military affairs, or personnel.

Secretary of the Navy Frank Knox, making a tour of US Navy bases and personnel abroad, visits the Royal Navy Scapa Flow stronghold. Mr. Knox's visit was followed shortly by the announcement that an aircraft carrier and other units of the US fleet would participate in a US-UK attack on Nazi bases in Norway. US NAVY

The goals for these changes and outcomes will be addressed shortly. The US Navy that emerged from World War II as a distinct and independent government department, with its politically appointed leader a member of the cabinet, went through significant change. By 1960 the US Navy had worked extremely hard and diligently to comply with and be a team player within the ever-growing Pentagon bureaucracy that stemmed from the changes of 1947 and 1949—an Office of the Secretary of Defense and a large staff that supported the chairman of the Joint Chiefs of Staff. The Navy sought to maintain its distinctive identity and to represent the strategic significance of maritime power. The Marine Corps in the Korea conflict added further distinction to its extraordinary battle honors and the Commandant of the Marine Corps, together with the Chief of Naval Operations, committed himself to making the relationship with the Joint Chiefs of Staff work as intended. However, the US Navy of 1960, as a national-security entity, had lost the preeminent position that it enjoyed at the end of World War II. Centralization and jointness had subsumed the Navy created by Congress in 1798. How well this has all worked in our fifty-five-year period bears close scrutiny and analysis, not for criticism's sake and certainly not to hark back to past glories in some arcane nostalgic way, but to analyze what the impact has been, how well it has all worked, and what the future may bring.

Before we address these issues, let us turn to developments in the United Kingdom, so that a side-by-side comparison and analysis can be made. The UK Ministry of Defense as we know it today was not formed until 1964. Its creation was based on a perception that there was a requirement for greater cooperation and coordination between the three British armed services—the Royal Navy, the British Army, and the Royal Air Force. The Royal Navy has always been regarded in the United Kingdom as the senior service and referred to as such. The Royal Marines are part of the Royal Navy, and the Commandant of the Royal Marines enjoys the same status and prestige as the Commandant of the US Marine Corps. However, the Royal Marines have always been a fraction of the size of the US Marine Corps and therefore have not enjoyed the level of national recognition rightfully enjoyed by the Marine Corps in the United States. A Chiefs of Staff Committee had been formed much earlier, in 1923, though the idea of a unified ministry had been rejected by Prime Minister David Lloyd George in 1921. In 1936 a cabinet-level position of minister for the coordination of defense was created to provide oversight for rearmament in light of growing Nazi aggression. When Winston Churchill became prime minister in 1940 he created the office of minister of defense, in order to coordinate defense matters more effectively and to have direct control over the Chiefs of Staff Committee. It is important to note that Churchill had been First Lord of the Admiralty (the civilian political head of the Royal Navy, equivalent to the US Secretary of the Navy) from 1911 to 1915 and from 1939 to 1940 (the famous "Winston is back" period after war was declared in September 1939) before he became prime minister. It is equally important that the position of First Lord of the Admiralty was created in 1628, the Earl of Portland being the first incumbent. The list of First Lords of the Admiralty reads like a litany of hugely distinguished Britons; the last two incumbents, Lord Carrington (serving 1959–63) and the Earl of Jellicoe (1963–64) very much representative of their illustrious predecessors.

Winston Churchill assumed the joint role of prime minister and minister of defense for the duration of World War II. In 1946 the government of Clement Attlee (the Labor Party won the 1945 general election) introduced into the House of Commons and passed the 1946 Ministry of Defense Act. Prior to this the First Lord of the Admiralty had been a member of the cabinet. The new minister of defense supplanted the First Lord, the secretary of state for war (political head of the army), and the secretary of state for air (the political head of the Royal Air Force) in the British cabinet. Between 1946 and 1964 there was a hybrid organization in the United Kingdom, with five separate departments of state running defense: the Admiralty, the War Office (army), the Air Ministry (Royal Air Force), the Ministry of Aviation, and the nascent Ministry of Defense. In 1964 a monumental change occurred in the United Kingdom—the above departments were all merged in a single Ministry of Defense, and the historically powerful position of First Lord of the Admiralty was abolished. One final event occurred in 1971, when the Ministry of Aviation Supply became part of the Ministry of Defense. The first secretary of state for defense was Peter Thorneycroft, who was short-lived in office, from April 1964 to October 1964, in the Conservative government of Sir Alec Douglas-Home. In the new Labor government of Harold Wilson the position was occupied by Denis Healey, from October 1964 to June 1970, a very significant period. He was followed by Lord Carrington in the Conservative government of Edward Heath from June 1970 to January 1974. The ten-year period from 1964 to 1974 witnessed the full solidification of British defense policy under a single minister and a very large bureaucracy. We will examine the impact on the former Admiralty structure and personnel shortly.

The civilian bureaucracy grew exponentially. The permanent secretary (the most senior civil servant) at the Ministry of Defense became very powerful, as did the civil service assistant secretaries, all of whom were expected to be apolitical. The growth of the Ministry of Defense civil service added costs that had not existed at the height of World War II.

The former Chiefs of Staff Committee became immersed in the Central Defense Staff (CDS), and the incumbent Chief of the Defense Staff was made the professional head of all British armed forces, and the senior uniformed military adviser to the secretary of state for defense and the prime minister. The First Sea Lord and Chief of Naval Staff in the United Kingdom retained his position and title as the military head of the Royal Navy, but his political lead—the First Lord of the Admiralty, a cabinet member—was gone.

The Chief of the Defense Staff therefore became an increasingly important figure in British defense. There followed a pattern of succession whereby the first incumbent, Marshal of the Royal Air Force Sir William Dickson (1959), was followed by Admiral of the Fleet the Earl Mountbatten of Burma (1959–65), who was followed by Field Marshal Sir Richard Hull (1965–67). The trend for many years was to follow the succession of Royal Air Force, Royal Navy, and British Army until 1977, when an airman, Marshal of the Royal Air Force Sir Neil Cameron, broke the pattern. Since September 1979 the Royal Navy has had only three Chiefs of the Defense Staff: Admiral of the Fleet Sir Terence Lewin (served 1979–82), Admiral of the Fleet Sir John Fieldhouse (1985–88), and Admiral Sir Michael Boyce (2001–3). The Royal Air Force has had the same number of Chiefs of the Defense Staff (three), and the army has had seven. The latter number indicates significantly what happened in British defense between October 1982 when Field Marshal Sir Edwin Bramall succeeded Admiral of the Fleet Sir Terence Lewin and 2015, with General Sir Nick Houghton becoming Chief of the Defense Staff in July 2013. The British Army had seven Chiefs of the Defense Staff to the combined Royal Navy and Royal Air Force six.

Before we examine and analyze the implications of these organizational changes and then compare and contrast the US and Royal Navies' places in the new order of things, let us look at the changes that occurred in the respective intelligence organizations in the United States and the United Kingdom. The key reason to do so is that intelligence has played a vital role in the development and operations of both navies during our period. The historical antecedents in World War II set the stage for why and how intelligence sharing between the two countries developed during the Cold War and in the twenty-six years since 1990. The dialogue between hard technical and scientific intelligence and the development of foreign navies' capabilities is not just axiomatic—it is at the heart of why both navies developed very specific capabilities, force structures, deployment strategies, bases, and logistics to meet the emergence of various threats to national security interests. How US and British naval intelligence fitted into the wider tapestry of both countries' other intelligence departments and agencies is as important for both navies as are the other organizational changes that occurred.

The World War II intelligence organizations of both countries were lean and mean. Growth occurred in the United States after the emergence of the Soviet Union and its Warsaw Pact allies. In the United Kingdom, the crown jewels during the war were the brilliant minds at the code-breaking center at Bletchley Park. In the United States their counterparts were in the Office of Naval Intelligence. The hugely significant roles of both entities have been extensively documented. Signals intelligence (SIGINT) and the vital code breaking associated with reading the enemy's traffic were central to the Allies' victories. The work of the OSS (the Office of Strategic Services) in the United States and the SIS (Secret Intelligence Service, or MI6) and SOE (Special Operations Executive) in the United Kingdom was geared to human intelligence (HUMINT). It was geared also to clandestine operations to thwart the enemy in multiple ways on the ground in highly sensitive covert operations, often linked to collaboration with the various European and Asian resistance organizations and groups. The leaders of these wartime organizations, such as Harry Hinsley, R. V. Jones and J. C. Masterman, influenced the various reorganizations after 1945. They trained the postwar recruits in the United States and United Kingdom in the various intelligence arts and sciences, so that by 1960 both countries had very capable cadres, mixtures of those with wartime experience and the new generation. The older generation was there to guide the new. Personnel recruited in the 1960s have now largely retired, with a few exceptions. Your author is one of the survivors from the 1960s—mentored by stalwarts like Sir Harry Hinsley and Vice Admiral Sir Ned Denning. Hinsley was at Bletchley Park working Enigma for predominantly naval operations, and Denning was in the Royal Navy's famous Room 40, at the heart of operational intelligence.

Post–World War II, the United States and the United Kingdom followed largely parallel tracks in terms of developing the organizational, skill, and experience bases inherited from World War II. This was generally so until the recent, post-9/11, period. Neither country went the centralization route, with the exception of the creation of the Defense Intelligence Agency in the United States and the Defense Intelligence Staff in the United Kingdom. This observation is very important for what follows.

The various departments and agencies were kept separate based on functionality—primarily SIGINT, HUMINT, counterespionage, and later space-based intelligence systems and operations. These functionalities corresponded to the National Security Agency (NSA) and the Government Communications Headquarters (GCHQ—the lineal successor to Bletchley Park), to the CIA and SIS, to the Federal Bureau of Investigation's counterespionage department, and the Security Service (or MI5). Later the unique National Reconnaissance Office (NRO) would be established in the United States as the only truly unacknowledged (until relatively recently) intelligence organization in the United States; the existence of the NRO was classified for many years. Within the above organizational milieu lay the naval intelligence organizations of both navies, headed by a director of naval intelligence. There were distinctive parallels in both navies, and the cooperation between both entities was never closer during the fifty-five years of our period; that closeness was perhaps equaled by the extraordinarily strong relationship between GCHQ and NSA, within which resided very important naval elements. Throughout this whole period the working relations between British and US naval intelligence and between GCHQ and NSA have been simply outstanding. The connections at the personal level, the cooperation developed and the abiding friendships made by successive staffs, meant that both navies were probably better served than any other single department of state in either of the two countries. The latter testifies to the bedrock created by their World War II predecessors.

The only main organizational difference between US and British naval intelligence was that the British did not recruit and train specialist intelligence officers. The British selected their intelligence officers from what the Royal Navy calls the "General List," the equivalent of career "unrestricted line" officers in the US Navy. The British argued that their naval intelligence officers should have a wide naval background before being recruited to intelligence and should in due course return to the regular Royal Navy. The US Navy by contrast had during our period specific separate personnel structures and career paths for designated intelligence and cryptographic officers. The same applied to Royal Navy ratings and US Navy enlisted personnel; the Royal Navy chose from the broad manpower base, while the US Navy had specialists trained within designated personnel codes. The US Navy considered the value of deeply trained and experienced personnel to be greater than did the British system, where intelligence officers were in post for shorter periods than in the US Navy. The Royal Navy believed that a too-institutionalized intelligence personnel structure would possibly encourage a too-ingrained view of intelligence issues and a personnel structure separate from the mainline navy, with the danger that what happened "behind the green door" would be the preserve of just a few. The Royal Navy liked its intelligence officers to be grounded in experience at sea. The US Navy ensured sea experience by creating a wide range of seagoing intelligence billets in key locations, such as fleet flagships and major units. Whatever the pros and cons of the two systems, both navies cooperated to a degree above and beyond any other known US–UK relationship, fortified by the special navy-related operations at NSA and GCHQ.

The US and UK naval intelligence organizations faced similar challenges in the creation of centralized defense intelligence agencies: the Defense Intelligence Agency (DIA) in the United States and the Defense Intelligence Staff (DIS) in the United Kingdom. The Office of Naval Intelligence (ONI) and the US Navy's DNI survived integration and remained totally separate, reporting to the Secretary of the Navy and the Chief of Naval Operations. In the case of the Royal Navy the British director of naval intelligence and his staff were subsumed under the DIS, who had his own organizational hierarchy and chain of command to a Deputy Chief of the Defense Staff for Intelligence (DCDS [I]) under the Central Defense Staff controlled by the CDS. This was a significant change in naval intelligence that the United States never experienced. Much to the chagrin of many in the United Kingdom, the position of director of naval intelligence was replaced by a lower grade post of Commodore (Intelligence), a one-star position. During World War II Vice Admiral John Godfrey was a three-star officer with immediate access to Winston Churchill, the prime minister. As a result of these centralizing changes, which occurred in parallel with the overall defense organization changes described earlier, the Royal Navy's intelligence arm found itself part of a highly bureaucratized central staff, with civil servants occupying many of the key posts. The one value of the latter was that the civilian staffs maintained continuity while the officer corps turned over.

Where the World War II special relationship endured most, after the above centralization processes had been put in place and the new hierarchies established, was in the very closely held, highly secretive operations conducted by and under the umbrellas of both countries' navies and their naval intelligence organizations. Because of the very nature of these operations, both navies were able to preserve their separation from the new central organizations, with access to the political leadership that no other service or intelligence agencies enjoyed. Furthermore, both navies were entwined in these operations. Such operations often required special, highly classified presidential executive orders or, in the case of the United Kingdom, orders signed by the prime minister. Everything and everyone in between was out of this loop. One very important element drove this requirement: the US Navy and the Royal Navy were forward deployed during the whole of this period, and globally. They were present where no other assets or intelligence entities could go. Even after space-based systems became significant, only naval assets could perform certain real-time intelligence functions based on persistent presence. There continues to this day a major requirement for forward-deployed naval intelligence assets; we will explore and analyze it later. Security and need-to-know are the guardian angels of these operations.

Let us return to the overall picture of post–World War II centralization, what this meant, and how it impacted both navies. We should also address absolutely core questions of whether the vast changes that occurred were indeed necessary: Were there better ways to do things? Would both navies be in better or worse shape today without them? Are the national security interests of both countries, individually and collectively, well served by the organizational changes since 1960? Now that you can appreciate the changes that occurred with the new organizations, let us form an analytical framework for looking at these questions.

The Western democracies have based their national-security policies on clearly identifiable values and strategic considerations. Primary among them has been the need to protect citizens from invasion and threats that challenge their core geographic and political integrity and identities: the right to live in peace and harmony; the right to make choices via cherished democratic institutions; and the right to exist as an independent nation, free from oppression or threat. Deep-rooted historical, cultural, ethnic, linguistic, and economic factors bond such nations. The strategic requirements that arise from the efforts of each and every nation to maintain its national identity and self-determination vary across time and geographic space. These factors have determined, for example, the reactions by the United States and the United Kingdom to a changing balance of power, whereby the status quo of free, well-established, independent states has been threatened.

A central generic lesson of the first half of the twentieth century may be summarized as the need to anticipate and prepare for defense when imminent threats indicate that the world is changing in ways that cause deep concern for future security. The clearest and best example of this is the rise of the Nazi Party and the German elections of 1933, leading to Germany's ever-increasing belligerence from 1936 to the outbreak of World War II in September 1939. Unpreparedness may lead to a perception of actual weakness and embolden an aggressor to challenge the status quo. The latter in today's environment may not be classical territorial violations, with invasion the worst-case scenario, but economic and resource challenges, acquisition of monopolistic trade in key raw materials, or the exploitation of cyberspace, water, and energy-source rights. The ultimate expression of this primary strategic requirement is national survival.

Second, nations have developed, mainly but not totally since the nineteenth century, the need to ally themselves for self-protection with other nations. Conversely, nations with belligerent and often expansionist intent have allied with nations where they perceived opportunities for gain. The Nazi-Soviet Pact, the Nazi-Japanese-Italian Axis, and the later denouncement of the Nazi-Soviet Pact by Germany are good twentieth-century examples of realpolitik played out by adversary nations who perceived gain in making and breaking alliances.

Third, the leading twentieth-century democratic powers, the United States and the United Kingdom, have led in the exaltation of self-determination and, in the case of the United Kingdom, decolonization and the right of self-government. President Woodrow Wilson was the father of the post–World War I League of Nations, and both nations were at the heart of the founding of the United Nations organization and the North Atlantic Treaty Organization (NATO). The former was conceived to foster international cooperation and allay future wars, the latter to preserve peace in ways that built on the lessons learned from the failure of the League of Nations to maintain international order. NATO's strength lay in its military cohesion, organization, and military capabilities, which aimed to deter, not threaten.

The cultural underpinnings of the United States and the United Kingdom and the need to show strength by clear military capability, national resolve, and cooperation in well-organized alliance structures point to a clearly definable thread that runs through American and British strategic thinking. It is that preparedness for a changing threat environment is paramount. The United States and the United Kingdom have found that the tools of international-security diplomacy and the use of power in the pursuit of peaceful outcomes constitute a very mixed bag. The former includes diplomatic pressure and multinational applications of economic sanctions, isolation, and restrictions on the flow of goods, materials, and capital. Where they have failed, the use of force has tended to be the tool of last resort, whether in the shape of blockade, mining, increased levels of war preparedness, or, in the worst case, open and declared war.

In certain cases the United States and the United Kingdom have been constrained in the use of these tools, because the overall strategic situation and balance of power were not in their favor. The Soviet invasion of Hungary,

Czechoslovakia, and Afghanistan showed how a combination of circumstances can render the United States, the United Kingdom, and their allies impotent—an unhealthy state of affairs. The sphere of influence of the Soviet Union in all three cases was such that NATO could not react in any meaningful way, only protest. There is a deep and abiding lesson in those three points, not least that military power as an instrument of foreign and overall national-security policy has limits. Understanding those limits is crucial.

Let us now return to the issue of US and UK centralization and the impact on both countries' navies. World War II was undoubtedly the greatest conflict fought in human history. What is quite astounding about it is that neither the United States nor the United Kingdom fundamentally changed its fundamental defense organization during the conflict. There was tighter control and enforced cooperation, but none of that was opposed, let alone resisted, by any of the military services. World War II was complex for the British and Americans at every level—particularly the quite amazing necessity to build in short order a massive industrially based war machine and to innovate technologically on extraordinarily short time lines. But one thing is very clear: the system worked. Nothing is perfect, but the US and UK World War II defense organizations performed brilliantly. Changes were made on the fly; bureaucratic inertia went out the window, and those who stood in the way of change or defied direct orders were soon removed. Any form of incompetence or inability to perform was rectified.

The question therefore arises, why change now? Furthermore, why did change, from individual service centricity to centralization, take place? None of the US and UK military services during or after World War II can be accused of not being team players—at the worst, of playing service politics in pursuit of self-serving goals. Nothing could be farther from the truth. The political leadership and the service chiefs and their staffs agreed on grand strategy and then allocated service resources required to execute it. Interservice rivalry was a matter not of deeply fought-over divisions of the resource pie but of rivalry to perform, to excel, indeed to show worthiness in all regards—a hugely healthy state of affairs. The US Navy and the Royal Navy were never in bitter contentious battles with the other services over resources and who would do what to execute the grand strategy. During the Battle of the Bulge, General George Patton's Third Army was never so pleased as when it saw the US Army Air Forces appear to provide air-to-ground support once the weather was clear enough, and on countless occasions surface naval forces heralded overhead Liberators or Short Sunderlands to attack surfaced U-boats. Interservice rivalry was about combined mutual effectiveness, not internecine competition.

World War II proved three axioms about defense organizations: they have to be relevant, they have to be efficient, and they have to be effective. What emerged from World War II was a desire for greater integration and top-level control, because centralization would lead to greater efficiency and less rivalry and inefficiency. What happened in reality, however, was that a massive bureaucracy with a significant political overlay was placed on top of the existing structure. Both countries' defense infrastructures grew. Once the basic political changes took place, underpinned by legislative action, the Office of the Secretary of Defense and the chiefs of staff structure in the United States and, later, the Ministry of Defense and the Central Defense Staff in the United Kingdom all grew exponentially. These changes incurred massive costs. The key question, again, is: Was it all worthwhile if what both countries had during World War II, aside from some lessons learned, worked well?

Several prominent post–World War II figures were centralists. In the United Kingdom the greatest advocate on integration was, perhaps surprisingly, Admiral of the Fleet the Lord Louis Mountbatten. He personally oversaw the creation of the Central Defense Staff. How could this be? Admiral Mountbatten genuinely believed that greater efficiency could be achieved by centralization. He believed firmly in interservice cooperation, not rivalry. He had been Chief of Combined Operations from 1941 to 1943 as his first major flag-officer appointment, and there he had been an advocate of joint operations. In the Far East he saw the great value of interservice cooperation as Supreme Allied Commander South East Asia from 1943 to 1946.

Lord Louis Mountbatten (June 25, 1900–August 27, 1979) was unique in all regards: a second cousin once removed to Queen Elizabeth and an uncle of Prince Philip, Duke of Edinburgh, husband of Queen Elizabeth. His family pedigree was impeccable: he was the youngest child and second son of Prince Louis of Battenberg and Princess Victoria of Hesse. He entered the Royal Naval College at Osborne in May 1913. In 1914 his father became First Sea Lord and Chief of Naval Staff. A very sad blight on the Battenberg family was the removal of Prince Louis from office because of anti-German feelings in the United Kingdom (the family's name had to be changed to Mountbatten because of its deep German relationships). The young Mountbatten overcame this heritage to achieve the highest military offices, as First Sea Lord and Chief of Naval Staff from April 1955 to July 1959 and as the first Chief of the Defense Staff from 1959 to 1965, making him the longest-serving Chief of the Defense Staff. He and his father made Royal Navy history by both being First Sea Lord and Chief of Naval Staff.

Lord Mountbatten had, therefore, enormous influence. The 1950s witnessed the Korean War, intensification of the Cold War, the invasion of Hungary by the Soviet Union, and the growth of nuclear rivalry after the detonation of the first Soviet weapon in August 1949. Mountbatten unequivocally

Lord Mountbatten, visiting an American aircraft carrier as Supreme Commander, Allied Eastern Forces, chats with US Navy officers.   US NAVY

believed that the British services needed to be one, not just in not name but in actual organization. He began to work systematically with the governments of Harold Macmillan (January 1957–October 1963), Alec Douglas-Home (October 1963–October 1964), and Harold Wilson (October 1964–June 1970) to transform the organization of British defense. In effect, he dismantled the historic organization of the Royal Navy, in terms of its political-military structure. The direct representation in Parliament of the Royal Navy as a service by the First Lord of the Admiralty, a member of the cabinet, was now gone. This single fact had dramatic and long-term consequences to which either Lord Mountbatten was oblivious or did not consider important, assessing that change was necessary. The essence of this change can be summarized as follows.

The Royal Navy no longer, as noted, had separate and independent representation in Parliament and direct access at the cabinet level. The Admiralty as an organization of state was subsumed by the Ministry of Defense, although the Naval Staff, headed by the First Sea and Chief of Naval Staff, still existed in its prior form. The key directorates of Naval Plans, Operational Requirements, and Operations and Trade remained intact. These key Naval Staff directorates, along with the Controller of the Navy's staff (which headed acquisitions and procurement) and the chief of naval personnel had always been lean organizations, renowned for their hard work and efficiency and never bureaucratic or overmanned. The Directorate of Naval Intelligence had been similar. With the loss of direct political access and influence the Naval Staff now had to work through a Central Defense Staff structure. This structure had new and what many perceived as duplicative coordination staff functions, functions that in prior decades had been handled through the Chiefs of Staff Committee, a similarly lean organization that was now expanded within the Chief of the Defense Staff's organization.

The latter replicated at the joint-staff level the individual functions that in the case of the Royal Navy were embodied in the highly effective Naval Staff. The latter had a historic record of high performance through two world wars in the twentieth century. The four-star leaders in the Navy now found themselves bereft of direct political access and of a reporting chain to a Central Defense Staff in a unified Ministry of Defense. There was now a Chief of the Defense Staff hierarchy and Deputy and Deputy Assistant Chiefs of the Defense Staff for all the main defense functions: policy, plans, operations, intelligence, personnel, and acquisition (including research and development, R&D). There was therefore an enormous layer of added staff function, with attendant manpower and bureaucracy, placed on top of the former Admiralty structure, one that had functioned well not just for decades and both world wars but indeed for centuries. The culture shock was not inconsiderable. In addition, the Royal Navy suddenly found itself working with and through not just these new defense hierarchies but also with a growing and, over time, entrenched civil-service bureaucracy, adding process and cost to the business of running the Royal Navy.

The possible long-term organizational impact of these changes was not fully analyzed or understood in 1964 or in the years leading up to them. Centralization and jointness were considered good for their own sake, in the names of greater service cooperation, integration, and planning to meet the security challenges posed by the Cold War. The Royal Navy over the fifty-one years from 1964 to 2015 faced competition in this new environment, and not just for resources vis-à-vis the other two services. The Royal Navy no longer had direct political representation in the formulation of maritime strategy. This was transformational, because since Nelson's time the Royal Navy had regarded itself as the self-evident and nationally accepted embodiment of British grand strategy through sea power, typified most of all by maritime expeditionary warfare.

In the 1960s, following Prime Minister Harold Macmillan's famous "Winds of Change" speech, the United Kingdom began systematic and wholesale decolonization, particularly in Africa, Asia, and the West Indies. The Labor government of Harold Wilson and his minister of defense, Denis Healey, saw the independence movements in the last vestiges of empire, beginning with Indian independence, as a reason to draw back to Europe. "Withdrawal" became an operative word in UK defense parlance, particularly with regard to the Far East and the British Far East Fleet, based in Singapore and Hong Kong. Defense Minister Healey saw no need for a fleet of the size that the United Kingdom had maintained through the 1950s into the early 1960s. He did not articulate a maritime policy or indeed any strategy that melded the Royal Navy into the new global maritime Cold War environment, other than that the nation was to become North Atlantic focused. The United Kingdom systematically withdrew from its historic domain of the Mediterranean; the Commander-in-Chief Mediterranean Fleet became "Flag Officer Malta," until the Malta naval base was closed and the continuous presence of the Royal Navy in the Mediterranean finally ended. This pattern continued with the downgrading of the Far East bases to support facilities and the eventual lowering for the last time of the Commander Far East Fleet's flag in Singapore.

This process was driven not just by budgetary and foreign policy considerations but also by the structural changes in defense organization. The new defense organization had created a totally different political-military environment for decision making. The new Ministry of Defense had many conflicting priorities at a time of colonial retrenchment and withdrawal. Not least of these were the balancing of conventional forces against strategic nuclear defense and the perceived need to support NATO in Europe with ground forces through the British Army of the Rhine (BAOR), as UK forces in West Germany were termed. Alongside these often conflicting claims for resources lay other underlying problems. Not least was the growing rivalry between the Royal Navy and the Royal Air Force.

After the historic meeting between Prime Minister Macmillan and President John F. Kennedy in Bermuda in December 1962, the United States agreed to share its nuclear-submarine and strategic nuclear ballistic-missile technology with the United Kingdom. The Royal Navy would build both nuclear attack submarines (SSNs) and SSBNs—the latter becoming the core, and today the mainstay, of UK national strategic defense through nuclear deterrence. The Royal Air Force competed for resources to maintain its nuclear-capable "V-bomber" force of Vulcan, Victor, and Valiant aircraft, with nuclear-bomb capabilities similar to those of the US Air Force's B-52 aircraft of Strategic Air Command. These were resource-intensive requirements and capabilities. Denis Healy associated withdrawal from the former UK territories as akin to withdrawal from maritime presence and forward deployment. This fact confronted a Royal Navy that had been globally disposed. Healey saw in withdrawal major cost savings, a downsizing of the Royal Navy, a focus on European defense via the deployment of the British Army and Royal Air Force to Europe, and the concentration of the Royal Navy in northern European waters. The latter would contribute to the NATO challenge to the burgeoning Soviet Northern Fleet, which increasingly sought access through the Greenland-Iceland-UK (GIUK) gap to the Atlantic and the oceans beyond. The overall strategy was driven by available resources rather than by deep analysis of the United Kingdom's primary strategic goals, beyond the need for a national, independent strategic nuclear deterrent based on US support and technology. The Royal Air Force wanted to maintain roles in the air defense of the United Kingdom in addition to Europe, plus maintenance of its role of maritime patrol.

The Royal Navy found itself in an unenviable position when the decision to replace the major fleet aircraft carriers reached Denis Healey's desk. The Naval Staff now had not just to compete with the Royal Air Force but do so in a central staff environment focused on not only strategy but also cost saving. The least factor considered was UK vital national strategic interest, other than nuclear deterrence. The core concept of maritime expeditionary warfare was not addressed in a global context as an alternate to a European focus.

Secretary of State for Defense Denis Healey was an intellectual. He achieved first-class honors at Balliol College, Oxford, graduating in 1940. He was commissioned into the Royal Engineers in the British Army and served from 1940 to 1945 in the North African and Italian campaigns, distinguishing himself at Anzio, and leaving the Army as a major. However, from 1937 to 1940, while at Oxford, Denis Healey had been a member of the Communist Party, leaving after the Nazi invasion of France in 1940. After the war he joined the Labor Party and worked his way up through the party hierarchy. His intellectual commitment to defense thinking was demonstrated by his positions as a councilor at the Royal Institute of International Affairs, 1948–60, and at the International Institute for Strategic Studies, 1958–61. Healey became one of the key thinkers in the postwar Labor Party. He had declared views on aircraft carriers, thinking them far too vulnerable to torpedo attack from the new nuclear-powered attack submarines and characterizing them as floating slums for their sailors. His analyses went no further and did not explore how the new hunter-killer submarines would in the future protect the aircraft carrier battle groups. He chose to not recognize that the Royal Navy's surface force was being configured around antisubmarine warfare to protect the carriers and amphibious assault ships as well as merchant shipping, with new air-defense missile systems. The strategic value of mobile fixed-wing strike from the sea was not in Secretary of Defense Healey's strategic lexicon. The scene was set therefore for a major challenge to British naval aviation, the like of which the Royal Navy had never witnessed. The new political-military structure would not help the Royal Navy in the debate about the replacement-carrier program. It is rather striking, if speculative, to contrast the situation of Secretary Healey with his counterpart in the United States in the 1960s—probably no one who had been a member of the Communist Party, whatever their later change of heart, could ever have acceded to such a position there.

The fixed-wing aircraft carriers HMS *Victorious, Hermes, Eagle,* and *Ark Royal* had well-understood service lives. Two light carriers, HMS *Albion* and *Bulwark,* had been converted to helicopter-operating commando carriers for the Royal Marines. The Royal Navy lost the battle for a replacement fixed-wing carrier program, a setback that would culminate in the end of Royal Navy major fixed-wing aviation until approximately 2020. HMS *Ark Royal* was the last large carrier to leave service in 1979, her service stretched as far as possible by the Naval Staff. Her squadrons of F-4s, Buccaneers, and Gannets

HMS Ark Royal *seen in the late fifties, showing her appearance as completed by Cammell Laird, Birkenhead, in 1955. She served in the Mediterranean, east of Suez, and in home waters until 1979 and in the following year was sold for scrap.*
ROYAL NAVY

were then either transferred to the Royal Air Force or scrapped. The Naval Staff set about planning a short-term recovery from what many naval and independent strategic experts regarded as a monumental error of judgment by the Ministry of Defense and the Central Defense Staff, one that will have taken fifty years to correct. The strategic and tactical implications will be addressed in due course.

The process by which this CDS decision occurred was very typical of the Whitehall environment within which the Royal Navy now had to operate. Without direct representation at the cabinet or parliamentary levels, the Navy lost access to political influence and debate in ways that had been traditional. The new central staff and ministry functions placed the Naval Staff out of the mainstream, beyond its own immediate service functions. The First Sea Lord was no longer the primary player in a historic Admiralty but a service chief who was increasingly required both to champion his cause and be a team player in a Chief of Defense Staff structure. The First Sea Lord had to recognize not only that his voice was just one of four at the table (the three service chiefs plus the Chief of the Defense Staff) but also that his naval staff had to contend with a powerful civil service secretariat and a Central Defense Staff, only a third of the members of which were Navy at best, often on a rotational basis among the three services. None of this was conducive to formulating or articulating maritime strategy or to convincing government of the need for a primary strategy based on the well-founded historical role of the Royal Navy as the guardian of the United Kingdom's security. The Royal Navy's ability to compete for the primary place was diminished.

The new Central Defense Staff became characterized as a process-driven organization in which intense highly bureaucratic committee work, balancing of conflicting interests and constant attempts to meet each service's require-ments and funding requests by compromise, became the order of the day. In this process the core and vitally important functions of debating, decid-ing, and agreeing on grand strategy based on vital national security interests were often lost. The UK Strategic Defense Reviews (SDRs) of the recent past decades have been described as emblematic.

As we move through this book readers should consider the impact of the above on the other key themes that we will address, in addition to the issue of strategic decision making, which we will review shortly. Meanwhile, let us return to the US Navy and address how the key changes that faced the Secre-tary of the Navy and the Chief of Naval Operations played out. We will then be in a position to compare and contrast the respective organizational changes between both navies.

The US Navy was most fortunate from 1960 onward in one critical regard when compared with the Royal Navy. The very nature of the politi-cal system and of the Constitution of the United States helped maintain the enduring influence of the Navy after the organizational changes described earlier. Two factors were paramount. First, the legislative and the executive in the United States are separate, and second, the position and role of the Secretary of the Navy remained intact and unchallenged, even though the secretary lost his seat in the cabinet in 1949 and the new secretary of defense was all-powerful, in a hierarchical sense. Seven secretaries, Franke, Connally, Korth, Fay, Nitze, Ignatius, and Chafee, from 1960 to 1972, still enjoyed autonomy to act in the best interests of the US Navy via well-established constitutional channels. The Chiefs of Naval Operations during this period—Admirals Burke, Anderson, McDonald, Moorer, and Zumwalt, from 1960 to 1974—never faced the dilemmas confronting the First Sea Lords and their staffs during the same period. Both the naval political and uniformed lead-erships had well defined and legally correct means to access the Congress at several levels and by multiple means. They had ways to represent not just their programmatic and funding interests but also core strategic issues that drive the annual defense budgets.

The open forum of public unclassified hearings served US Navy interests well. The personal strengths of successive Chiefs of Naval Operations shone through in open questioning in the House Committee on Armed Services (HASC) and the Senate Committee on Armed Services (SASC), as well as in the classified hearings, to which the public and press were not admitted. Key strategic issues were aired in public—hotly debated, often with rigor, candor, and good humor but sometime also with aggressive and well-placed direct questions by members and senators, who had been well briefed by extremely competent and knowledgeable committee and personal staffs. The chairman and ranking members of these committees were hugely powerful. The US Navy therefore had constant opportunities to state its case for resources, in thoroughly staffed congressional presentations. The staff of the Chief of Naval Operations has its own congressional liaison staff, which can legitimately interface with congressional committees and influence the defense debate and make the case for programs, manpower, ships, submarines, aircraft, weapons, and key Operations and Maintenance (O&M) funding.

Another element in this process is that of industrial-naval relationships, with the contractors who seek naval business at every level of production and service. These contractors, their lobbyists, and the very representatives and senators in whose districts and states they reside and run their businesses, have closely interwoven relationships by which they pursue programs in which they have crucial employment and other interests. The corresponding Appropriations Committees of record on both sides of the Congress control the purse strings for naval funding—the HASC and the SASC may authorize, but only the Defense Appropriations Subcommittee of the House and Senate Appropriations Committees can legally appropriate funding. These committees are all-powerful, sounding at one level the bell of success for a program or, by ending appropriations, the death knell of a failed program. The constitutional ability of the US Navy to influence this process is well defined, well understood, and practiced with great expertise. Senior flag-officer success in part rests on an ability to perform on Capitol Hill. Three- and four-star officers have their days on the Hill, often with the Secretary of the Navy sitting between the Chief of Naval Operations and the Commandant of the Marine Corps. The Royal Navy has no such privileged constitutional process to make its case in Parliament or to seek funding by direct influence.

Culture and relationships are factors that run deep, and often silently, in US Navy and congressional relationships. Many members of Congress have served in the US Navy, several with great distinction. In recent times, Sen. John McCain from Arizona and Sen. John Warner of Virginia are distinguished Navy veterans. There are countless others. Many members of Congress have served on both sides of the Potomac, in the Pentagon and on the Hill. As a result they not only understand the process but have predisposed loyalties and views on what is what and how things should be done. Their personal loyalties to the US Navy are ingrained, and they understand the Navy's strategic arguments. Their staffs fill in any gaps in technical knowledge and work with the uniformed Navy to obtain briefings and documentation from the staff of the Chief of Naval Operations. This is a healthy, dynamic, and ever-changing political-military dialogue between the executive and legislative branches of government. The system in the United Kingdom is very different indeed and does not serve the interests of the Royal Navy well in an era of defense cuts.

Nothing is perhaps more representative of the fundamental political-military differences between the environments in which the Royal Navy and the US Navy have to do business than in the very nature of their top political leadership and their leaders' constitutional positions. In the United States, several presidents have had prior experience in the Congress—they have seen the other side of government, and from a different perspective. President Franklin D. Roosevelt had been an Assistant Secretary of the US Navy earlier in his career, just as Prime Minister Churchill had twice been First Lord of the Admiralty. Several post–World War II presidents have been US Navy veterans; Kennedy, Johnson, Nixon, Ford, Carter, and G. H. W. Bush were all distinguished examples. Several were highly decorated, with extraordinarily commendable war records. They all understood the Navy: how it works, what the Navy does and why, and the strategic significance of sea power. By contrast, only one British prime minister since World War II has served in the Royal Navy: Prime Minister James Callaghan (1976–79), who served in World War II from 1942 to the war's end. His father had been a Royal Navy chief petty officer. Prime Minister Callaghan joined the Royal Naval Volunteer Reserve (RNVR) as an able seaman, completing the war as a lieutenant, RNVR, with very creditable service. However, the UK top leadership has enjoyed nothing like the deep personal knowledge and experience of the listed US presidents, several of whom experienced intense combat operations. This factor makes a significant difference when the US commander-in-chief faces difficult decisions and choices—that is, they know the face of battle and the consequences of their decisions. Moreover, regarding the equally critical aspect of budgetary allocations and priorities, a former Navy president was likely to understand and respect what the service was asking for and why. In the spring of 1982, Admirals Lewin and Leech had to provide Prime Minister Thatcher overnight a naval primer following the Argentinian invasion of the Falkland Islands. She had zero prior knowledge; most fortunately, however, she was a very quick study and under the most expert guidance of these two fine World War II veterans grasped the plans they laid before her. Twenty years earlier, in 1962, at the time of the Cuban Missile Crisis, President John Kennedy needed no such instruction in the use of naval power to thwart Soviet intentions and operations.

Let us now analyze and appraise the strategic significance of these changes to both navies. The changes in both countries were quite monumental with respect to the status quo of World War II. Two things become clear from the above review. First, the US Navy came out of them with a consistent and enduring ability to make its case directly to the Congress and argue for the resources required. The Royal Navy, by contrast, became politically constrained and found itself in the position of a second cousin, once removed—a member of the family but with no real direct standing with, or access to, the family leadership. One key observation needs to be made before we get into more detail. It is that inherent in the system in which the US Navy operates, constituting its backbone, are the US Constitution and the very culture and modus operandi of government that enables the Navy to work through bureaucratic and organizational change. The Royal Navy enjoys no such bountiful privileges. The changes described above stymied a service that had been used not just to being the senior service but to operating in an environment and ways where its case could be both constantly heard and understood. Centralization, jointness, and political concentration of power in a highly civilianized bureaucracy and process-oriented Ministry of Defense and Central Defense Staff rung the death knell of a tradition-bound Royal Navy that had enjoyed centuries of political access.

The 1960s witnessed strategic challenges. The United States faced in 1962 its greatest challenge since World War II and the Korean War—the Cuban Missile Crisis. It was followed in 1963 by the assassination of President Kennedy and the escalation of the Vietnam War during the presidency of his successor, Lyndon Johnson. As a backdrop to these events, the Cold War intensified and US-Soviet rivalries played out across the globe, not least in the oceans of the world, where the US and Royal Navies faced the Soviet and Warsaw Pact navies on a daily basis. Allies and client states of both the United States and the Soviet Union became parts of this great game, which persisted until the collapse of the Soviet Union (or USSR). The June War of

1967 between Israel and the Arab nations of Egypt, Syria, and Jordan saw a crisis erupt that Secretary of State Dean Rusk regarded as more threatening than the Cuban Missile Crisis. By the end of the decade the European situation had deteriorated even further—the Central Front that separated Western Europe from the Warsaw Pact and NATO's FEBA (forward edge of the battle area) was a zone of heavy military presence, constant exercises, and readiness events. Within the NATO military structure, the Supreme Allied Commander Europe (SACEUR), always an American four-star general, was the guardian of retaliatory plans that relied on an underlying nuclear deterrence posture of "Mutual Assured Destruction" (MAD). All this created a military balance across the Iron Curtain that made no sense in terms of a conventional invasion of Western Europe: the avowed policy of NATO was to respond with nuclear weapons if the FEBA collapsed and the Red Army made inroads. The MAD doctrine was, therefore, well named. When the Soviets occupied Czechoslovakia in 1968, after intense protests by the Czech leader, Alexander Dubcek, it was transparently clear that NATO could make no response, given the military balance and overwhelming threat of escalation.

The one domain where the Soviet Union and the West could play out their intense competition for global influence and the contest between communism and democracy was at sea, and in countries ripe for economic and ideological penetration that had maritime access. With regard to the Soviet Union, this process of influence by the growing Soviet navy became characterized as "Soviet naval diplomacy." It was on the oceans of the world that the Cold War was truly fought.

NATO responded with the creation of a naval command structure centered on the headquarters of the Supreme Allied Commander Atlantic (SACLANT), in Norfolk, Virginia, always led by a US Navy four-star admiral. Within this structure the strength and power of the US Navy was critical, as embodied in the "numbered fleets": the Second Fleet in the Atlantic and the Sixth Fleet in the Mediterranean. The Third and Seventh Fleets, in the Pacific, were important as countervailing forces to Soviet naval power in that theater, but geography and other geopolitical factors inhibited the growth of the Soviet navy in the Pacific comparable to that of its Northern Fleet, based on the Kola Peninsula, and the Fifth Eskadra, based in the Black Sea. The growth and operational activities of the Northern Fleet and its associated Warsaw Pact allies, together with the roles and missions of the Baltic Fleet, based in Leningrad (St. Petersburg today), challenged NATO in a sea war that was as real as any conflict could be, short of open hostilities. This maritime conflict, which endured for the life of the Soviet Union, was undoubtedly, with the benefit of hindsight and analysis, strategically far more significant than the land situation in central Europe, because at sea the Soviets had real opportunities, outside a nuclear umbrella, to expand and to influence and undermine the West. It was the task of the US Navy and its allies to prevent this. The strategy to achieve all this was complex, challenging, evolving, and highly technical.

Before delving into how the above played out in the NATO context, let us review where the United Kingdom was in its military-political posture and the fundamental strategy that drives thinking and policy. The United Kingdom experienced a decade-long identity crisis in the 1960s as decolonization reached a peak and then subsided, under what was termed an "east of Suez" policy. The military strategy that supported this policy was based primarily on a naval strategy of forward presence and basing that aimed to support the United Kingdom's allies and British economic interests east of Suez by naval forces—surface, air, subsurface, and amphibious. The United Kingdom's confrontation with Indonesia in the 1960s in support of its former colony, Malaya (now Malaysia), was hugely significant—it demonstrated that naval and marine forces, together with special operations forces (the Special Air Service and the Royal Marines' Special Boat Section [SBS]) could contain in the jungles and rivers of Borneo (East Malaysia) inroads by Indonesian regular and paramilitary forces. The Royal Navy and the Royal Marines worked together in fighting a war reminiscent of operations of the British Fourteenth Army in the jungle war against Japan and of the post–World War II operations against communist insurgency in Malaya. The Borneo campaign was in retrospect an example of how to conduct a jungle war against insurgent forces. British textbooks on such campaigns have been written with first-hand experience in Kenya against the Mau Mau, on Cyprus against the Greek-Cypriot nationalist organization EOKA, and in the Middle East, in the region that today comprises the United Arab Emirates, Yemen and Aden, Muscat and Oman.

The planned withdrawal of the British Far East Fleet, the reduction and later closure of the major facilities at the Singapore and Hong Kong naval bases, signaled not just the demise of empire but a shift in strategic thinking. The latter was no longer maritime or global. The polices of the Wilson government and Defense Secretary Healey were Europe focused and equated to a "maritime withdrawal" without a broad and deep analysis of the implication of not being a global maritime power any longer. The United Kingdom was, in fairness, resource constrained, and after several economic crises and devaluations of the pound the nation was in no position to support three services in global deployments. Foreign policy based on decolonization indicated a withdrawal to Europe and a concentration on the Central Front, the North Atlantic sea lines of communication, and the creation and maintenance of an independent nuclear deterrent.

The political-military reorganization analyzed earlier played to a highly bureaucratized process-driven view of defense. Significantly absent in the 1960s Ministry of Defense were the words "grand strategy." The case for a maritime strategy based on understood and extraordinarily well documented and analyzed concepts of maritime power were lost in a turmoil of NATO and nuclear jargon that produced a huge bureaucratic compromise. This was nowhere more evident than in the annual defense budget exercise, where the pie was cut to satisfy the needs of the three services within an environment driven by a Europe-centric view, not a global maritime view.

Psychology was as important, perhaps, as the economic realities that faced the United Kingdom in the 1960s. In retrospect, what happened was the balancing of an oversimplified equation: withdrawal from empire equals withdrawal from global maritime presence. Within this equation lay the seeds of decades-long strategic discontinuity in the United Kingdom. The United Kingdom in essence forgot its heritage as a maritime power, a heritage based not on colonization, but, very simply, on trade. The United Kingdom has always been since the time of the first explorations a maritime trading nation. In order to survive the United Kingdom must not just trade but to use the sea to do business. The daily prayer in many British schools for "Those who go down to the sea in ships and do their business in Great Waters" was not a patriotic curiosity. It was a real and abiding reflection on the basic economic fact that Britain depended on the sea to survive, first as an agricultural and later as an industrial nation.

Furthermore, the Royal Navy had not just been the protector of these trading, and indeed survival, interests, but the main military instrument for British foreign policy, through forward presence and operations to support political-economic interests. The United Kingdom's involvement in major land campaigns had historically been with "citizen armies," not large, regular, and permanently maintained ones. The latter was true of Henry V's army at Agincourt, that of John Churchill, later Duke of Marlborough, at the battle of Blenheim, and that of Sir Arthur Wellesley, later Duke of Wellington, in the Peninsular War during the Napoleonic era. It was just as true of General Bernard Montgomery's Eighth Army at El Alamain and General William Slim's Fourteenth Army at Kohima. All were citizen armies recruited and trained for the duration of conflict by a much smaller cadre of peacetime professionals. The Royal Navy was different—it was a large and permanent body of highly trained and experienced professional officers and men, sailors in the widest sense. When Denis Healey made the monumental decision not to replace the Royal Navy carrier fleet he was, in essence, disavowing centuries of well-conceived and well-executed British maritime strategy. It was indeed ironic that in the 1960s, while distinguished academics like Professor Bryan Ranft were teaching maritime strategy and naval history at the Royal Naval College Greenwich and in the war and staff colleges, the central staffs of the Ministry of Defense were systematically disestablishing centuries of successful exercise of both.

By contrast, the US Navy went in a diametrically opposed direction in the 1960s, in spite of the political-military organizational changes. The Cuban Missile Crisis in 1962 showed how a president who had served in the Navy during World War II could use naval power to avert a national crisis. The blockade of Soviet naval delivery of a panoply of nuclear missile capabilities into Cuba was one of diplomacy underscored by heavy-duty naval force—the power and strength of the US Navy to stop Soviet operations at sea in their tracks. Without the perception and physical reality of that power, backed by the avowed intent of the president to use it if need be, the outcome would undoubtedly have been very different. Furthermore, President Kennedy was able to offset the somewhat frightening countervailing recommendations of such members of his military staff as General Curtis LeMay of the Air Force by the use of naval power. As a naval man, Kennedy kept his hands firmly on the tiller; without the power of the US fleet he might not have been able to bring Premier Nikita Khrushchev to the negotiating table or keep at bay the extreme hawks within his own military establishment. The use of nuclear weapons in 1962 by the United States may seem in retrospect not just outrageous but somewhat unbelievable; however, the fact is that it was an option, one that had advocates, who pointed to certain circumstances moving out of control against US interests. President Kennedy remained cool, calm, and collected, in spite of intense pressure and used his Navy with great skill.

The Cuban Missile Crisis encapsulated US naval strategy in the 1960s. Resources were never a serious issue. The Navy received what it wanted for its well-documented requirements in support of its well-articulated maritime strategy. This book will later immerse readers in the more detailed aspects of the implementation of US naval strategy in the 1960s and beyond and of the role the changing face of the Royal Navy played in the emerging North Atlantic Cold War campaign. In addition to actual operations, and certainly US Navy combat operations in the Vietnam War and those of the Royal

A US Navy helicopter observes a Soviet submarine during Cuban quarantine operations.   US NAVY

Navy in East Malaysia, there were some aspects that were not given analytical prominence at the time but have significance for contemporary events and certainly future naval operations.

One such consideration comprised basing and base facilities. The Royal Navy had historically enjoyed a chain of naval bases and other related facilities, such as wireless stations and, in the days of steam, coaling stations. Their names reel off the tongue without effort—Hong Kong, Singapore, Gan in the Maldive Islands, Trincomalee in Ceylon (Sri Lanka), Masirah near the entrance to the Persian Gulf, Aden, Bahrain, Diego Garcia, Mombasa, Mauritius, Simonstown, Gibraltar, Malta, Bermuda, bases on Canada's eastern seaboard, a whole group of West Indies facilities, and the Falkland Islands (Port Stanley) in the South Atlantic. This was an impressive logistics chain, one that spanned the globe and involved reciprocity with Australia and New Zealand for port access. Without fixed bases and refueling, victualing, and maintenance facilities a navy faces serious problems unless it uses nuclear power and has a replenishment-at-sea capability that can be sustained in a transoceanic environment without recourse to land bases. Crews need rest and recreation, and port visits have always played a major role in diplomatic and trade relations. Access to port facilities on a guaranteed and regular basis is a must for a global navy.

Such facilities, or lack thereof, dramatically affect transit time, time on station, rearming, and crew morale. These are critical factors. Even a nuclear-powered attack submarine en route from Pearl Harbor to the South China Sea has to spend a long time in transit, and although its nuclear reactor will provide nonstop fuel, electricity, and fresh air and water, the crew's stamina is a major factor, as are such considerations as rearming in the event of hostilities, and routine and emergency maintenance. When the United Kingdom withdrew primarily to the North Atlantic, with occasional forays to other parts, sadly, it disengaged from its historical bases without due diligence as to what the future might hold. Decolonization and independence for countries where these bases existed did not necessarily preclude future usage, but once the knots were cut it would become increasingly difficult to reengage and proportionately important for a major ally, such as the United States, to engage in lieu.

Fortunately, time and international realignments have favored the United States. Outside the NATO theater the US Navy has established good relations in places such as Singapore and Bahrain, taking up the slack from the Royal Navy. The United Kingdom wisely granted to the United States base rights on Diego Garcia, a pivotal Indian Ocean location. Because Naples in Italy and Rota in Spain remain available the British closure of Malta has not affected US operations in the Mediterranean; though there were early fears that potential belligerents might seek access, none of their attempts have amounted to date to anything significant. Base relations become really important in the forging of navy alliances on a basis of mutual cooperation. This was never more true than during the Cold War, with northern European and Mediterranean port visits. Today the burgeoning relations in Asia between the US Navy and the Royal Malaysian Navy and with those of Singapore, Indonesia, the Philippines, Vietnam, Thailand, South Korea, and Japan all speak to one fact—that underpinning joint operations and exercises are port visits and the facilities that go with port visits. These make up the cement in the building blocks of naval cooperation in Asia today.

Rearming, refueling, and victualing at sea are major seamanship skills—they are acquired by practice and require the best technology to meet the needs of challenging and dangerous conditions. The US and Royal Navies are past masters of these skills. Both navies developed substantial fleet-replenishment capabilities—indeed, constituting a navy within a navy without which the fighting forces would not be able to function. Even nuclear-powered aircraft carriers need to replenish aviation fuel, rearm with munitions, and resupply. These tasks should be borne in mind in the chapters

ahead. Without the "fleet train," as the British dubbed the Royal Fleet Auxiliary (its replenishment ships) and its American counterpart, the US and Royal
Navies could not have achieved entire success in the Cold War. Conversely,
the Soviet Union was at an enormous disadvantage because of its slowness in
developing and mastering at-sea replenishment. The great work of the American Marvin Miller (1923–2009) at the US Naval Station, Port Hueneme,
California, in the development of advanced underway-replenishment systems
and technologies was never equaled by the Soviet navy.

Strategic technology exchange and intelligence cooperation and sharing
between the US Navy and the Royal Navy became third and fourth critical
dimensions in the 1960s. We will look at these dimensions in more detail in
later chapters. Suffice to say here that the impact of both in the 1960s did,
at the most important levels of daily operations and long-term acquisitions,
save the Royal Navy from a slippery slope of retrenchment after the policy of
withdrawal started to bite.

The Nassau Agreement, as a treaty negotiated by President Kennedy
and Prime Minister Macmillan and signed December 22, 1962, provided the
United Kingdom with the Polaris ballistic-missile capability, using British
warheads, and the US Navy with a long-term lease arrangement for a submarine base at Holy Loch in Scotland. The meeting in the Bahamas also meant
the end of the US AGM-48 Skybolt nuclear missile program, a system that
the Royal Air Force would acquire as a result of an earlier agreement between
Macmillan and President Dwight D. Eisenhower. The Royal Air Force maintained a tactical nuclear capability with its V-bomber force and later with the
Tornado aircraft. However, the Royal Navy was now the lead service for the
independent deterrent. This was in spite of earlier misgivings by such senior
Americans as Robert McNamara and Dean Acheson, who had questioned
the wisdom of the United States enabling the United Kingdom to have a
viable deterrent. They pointed to the failures of the UK Blue Steel standoff
missile system and Blue Streak intermediate-range ballistic missile, as well as
to technical difficulties with the AGM-48 Skybolt system, which the United
Kingdom planned to purchase.

As the Cold War heated up, the two navies became closer and closer in
collecting, analyzing, and sharing intelligence and providing information for
not just operational use but also, equally critically, the task of staying ahead
of the technological curve and ensuring that the acquisition process received
the very latest high-level threat inputs. The intelligence staffs of both navies
created in the 1960s a bedrock of highly classified cooperation at all levels of

the intelligence space. Nowhere was this more evident than in the underwater domain.

Intelligence sharing went hand in glove with technology exchange. The Royal Navy was the recipient of enormous largesse by the US government and especially the nuclear navy created by Admiral Hyman B. Rickover: nuclear submarine technology, which augured the beginning of the longest US-UK industrial relationship, that between the Electric Boat Division of General Dynamics at Groton, Connecticut, and Vickers Shipbuilding and Engineering (later acquired by British Aerospace) at Barrow-in-Furness. Underscoring this exchange was the extremely sensitive trading of acoustic intelligence (ACINT) and other special intelligence (SI). We will address this in detail later; the point here is that the impact on both navies' defense postures, and indeed on the nations' prime strategic posture at the national level, was such that the two services would march in step not just for the duration of the Cold War but also for the quarter-century after the Berlin Wall was torn down.

In spite of all the changes in both countries' defense organizations and all the turmoil of the UK withdrawal from east of Suez, the US Navy and the Royal Navy remained at the end of the 1960s tightly bound. This was a unique institutional relationship within two separate institutions, indeed constituting a state within two states, built not just on agreements and high-level security arrangements but equally on personal relationships, trust, and the abiding connectivity brought by at-sea operations, by facing a common threat on a daily basis. No such relationship has ever been enjoyed by other US and UK institutions or within the much wider context of the North Atlantic Treaty Organization or other major international agreements, treaties, and alignments that the two countries have.

Limited War in the Nuclear Era
Impact on the US Navy and the Royal Navy

There have been countless studies since World War II on nuclear warfare theory—the fine 1959 book by the man dubbed the "American Clausewitz," Bernard Brodie, *Strategy in the Missile Age,* comes immediately to mind, as does the work of Philip Winsor at the London School of Economics and Political Science and, more latterly, the work of Franklin C. Miller in the United States. There is indeed a whole separate lexicon associated with how the opposing nations of NATO and the Soviet Union developed nuclear-warfare theory, deterrence postures, and indeed the very plans for executing nuclear warfare at various levels of escalation. Brodie was the father of the West's understanding of the critical value of second-strike capabilities in nuclear deterrence theory. Brodie's thinking impacted significantly the nuclear capabilities and postures of the US Navy and the Soviet navy. Brodie, for instance, made the singular observation that "thus far the chief purpose of our military establishment has been to win wars. From now on its chief purpose must be to prevent them. It can have almost no other useful purpose."

The ending of the Cold War would seem prima facie to have ended that era. However, logic and common sense say otherwise, since the key nations that were the nuclear powers between 1945 and, technically, August 29, 1949, in the case of the Soviet Union (the day the USSR detonated its first nuclear device) are still in existence and have nuclear arsenals. In spite of the various nuclear arms-limitations agreements, the threat of nuclear war is still there. Other nations may acquire nuclear weapons in due course. The ongoing diplomacy to constrain Iran from becoming a nuclear-weapons nation exemplifies the position of the Western nuclear-weapons "have" nations to prevent the "have not" nations from acquiring these weapons of mass destruction (WMD). From our seventy years of international relations in the nuclear age (1945–2015) one factor is self-evidently clear, that all conventional warfare is by definition limited warfare if conducted by one or more of the nuclear-weapons-owning nations.

As we proceed to look at the US Navy and the Royal Navy in the fifty-five years from 1960, one key factor has to be assimilated. It is simple and perhaps obvious at one level, but still necessary to articulate: that both navies became nuclear-powered navies and both navies became the guardians of their nation's independent nuclear deterrents. These sea-based systems were on board submarines, and though the US Navy built and still builds nuclear-powered aircraft carriers (CVNs) and had nuclear-powered cruisers (CGNs) in the early part of our period, the submarine became the primary platform in nuclear deterrence strategy. The CVNs were nuclear-weapon capable, as were the Buccaneer aircraft of the Royal Navy's Fleet Air Arm, and both navies had other nuclear weapons: the nuclear depth bomb, for example. However, it is the submarine that is the mainstay and workhorse of the deterrent forces, with manned bombers and land-based missile systems (in the case only of the United States today) filling support roles. The first leg of the US triad is still today the ballistic-missile-firing *Ohio*-class nuclear-powered ballistic-missile submarines, and in the United Kingdom the *Vanguard*-class SSBNs have the same role as just a single leg. This basic fact is to be coupled to one other crucial fact, that nuclear-powered attack submarines have a service life of approximately thirty years–plus (the new US *Virginia*-class SSN has an infinite unrefueled life; its reactor never requiring refueling during the hull life of the submarine) and are stealthy, covert, and persistently present in the oceans and littorals of the world. It is clear that the nuclear submarine has a very special place in what follows.

All warfare is therefore limited unless the absolutely inconceivable but by definition always possible event of a nuclear exchange between major-state adversaries occurs or a third party (terrorist) or surrogate nation uses a nuclear device. The umbrella of nuclear protection for the West has been in position since the advent of nuclear deterrence theory. Tactical nuclear weapons, whatever posture changes their advent has brought, and whatever their yield, remain incontrovertibly weapons of mass destruction. The wars, conflicts, campaigns, counterinsurgencies, counterterrorist operations, and a plethora of other naval operations (such as the "Cod War" and the Beira Patrol in the case of the Royal Navy, operations in Central America in the case of the US Navy, and relief and humanitarian assistance, counterpiracy, counterdrugs, counter-weapons and -human trafficking in the case of both navies) of this period are overshadowed by the immensity and cost of both waging the Cold War at sea and the sustainment of the undersea nuclear deterrent posture. At

USS Ohio *(SSBN 726)*   U.S. Naval Institute Photo Archive

The Royal Navy's HMS Vanguard *(S28)*   UK Ministry of Defense

one level the intensity and complexity of continuous forward-deployed operations against the Soviet Union and the Warsaw Pact and the maintenance of the submarine-launched ballistic-missile (SLBM) deterrent can never again be matched.

The fact that the Cold War never developed into a hot war is a lasting tribute to both navies and their leaderships. When we examine several of the other major conflicts that occurred both during and after the Cold War it is critical to recall that neither navy ever yielded once in any dimension that was militarily and politically significant to the opposition. It behooves us to recall what was achieved both strategically and tactically, because of its significance for the contemporary challenges of an emergent China and a reemergent Russia. The one common denominator throughout is, simply, the sea, and it is the sea that likely holds the keys to the security of the post-2015 world.

Both navies worked hand in glove to keep the West safe under the nuclear umbrella by one critical strategic tool—ensuring the security of the Western European base by maintaining the sea lines of communication (SLOCs), not just in the Atlantic but globally, wherever the Warsaw Pact challenged the West. Securing the sea lines of communication is a fundamental strategic goal. It is a simple concept, written with simple words, yet within these words are enshrined one of the most important concepts for today and tomorrow—that the free flow of trade and people underpins the global economy. It is not merely a question of moving divisions of troops by sea from one place to another without hindrance in order to execute a land campaign. Without sea control there is no free movement, and without access to such key resources as food, minerals, manufactured products, energy sources, and sea-based products (like fish, oil, and gas), there is no serious global economic life. Who controls the sea, controls the global economic flow and all the oceans' resources. To upset that economic balance by means of war is to attack the very freedom that has sustained twentieth- and twenty-first-century economic life. The global, forward-deployed disposition of naval forces to maintain the balance of power at sea in order to sustain peace and prosperity is at the very heart of naval strategy. In the early part of the last century this was termed "the defense of trade." Nothing has changed. For examples, keeping oil flowing from the Persian Gulf, maintaining the integrity of the critical straits through the Indonesian archipelago and the Malacca Straits, and preventing the seizure of seabed resources by illegal occupation of island chains are no different from protecting the flow of goods and raw materials during the golden age of the first Industrial Revolution. The impacts of the second Industrial Revolution of the global, networked economy and the attendant issues of energy and critical raw-material acquisition, supply, and flow are already upon us. We will later look at more complex and sophisticated aspects of this fundamental point.

During our period there was only one overt act of military aggression using a submarine: the attack and sinking by the Royal Navy submarine HMS *Conqueror* of the Argentinian navy cruiser *General Belgrano* during the Falklands campaign of 1982. There were many covert acts of aggression, but this was the only true overt attack and sinking since 1945, and this raises many questions. But in this one event in the South Atlantic are many answers. Nuclear-powered attack submarines and nuclear-powered guided-missile-firing submarines are prodigious instruments of naval power—to be challenged only by those who believe that they have comparable capabilities or alternative means. It is not a simple question of David challenging Goliath but one involving a complex set of issues regarding generations of extraordinary technical and operational development and the creation of special cadres of nuclear submariners on both sides of the Atlantic, cadres fortified by many common bonds, total cooperation, and highly classified security and intelligence agreements. To create a rival club takes enormous energy, funding, and expertise. The Soviet Union made that challenge, and today China and Russia are desperate to rival the US-UK submarine special club. The strategic notion that who controls the underwater domain controls the oceans of the world, and therefore the largest segment by far of the global-network economy, is neither fanciful nor exaggerated. To fly slowly at low altitude over the Malacca Straits off Singapore on a clear day and simply observe the extraordinary volume of global maritime traffic is not just an exercise in counting ships but testament to the vibrancy of the global economy and to the fact that most of it depends on the sea.

Measures, countermeasures, counter-countermeasures, and so on are well-understood technological and operational requirements, of which intelligence and acquisition are prime drivers. Anticipating the enemy's or potential adversary's next technological development and getting ahead by finding the most cost-effective counter are buried deeply in the psyches and industrial processes of all military professionals and industry in the United States and United Kingdom. This is well understood and underscored by a huge acquisition bureaucracy. This process is at its best in the submarine communities of the US Navy and the Royal Navy. Perhaps it is no exaggeration to claim that this is the most sophisticated process on planet Earth: *Virginia*-class and *Astute*-class nuclear-powered attack submarines are the most technologically advanced engineering bodies ever designed and built, perhaps more so than space systems. The United States and the United Kingdom did not arrive in this dominant position by accident; this level of capability is a jewel in the strategic crowns of both countries.

The 1960s witnessed the beginning of a massive ship- and submarine-building enterprise by the Soviet Union. The Cuban Missile Crisis and the later US exploitation of the sea in that decade for carrier-based air strikes into Vietnam, the mining of Vietnamese waters, restriction of the movements of illicit weapons by sea, and the use of small-boat riverine forces all influenced the Soviet Union to build a blue-water navy. The Politburo and military leadership understood that if the Soviet Union was to expand its influence via surrogates and alliances beyond the geographic bounds of the USSR and the Warsaw Pact, then it would have to possess a navy that could support those national interests and be a countervailing force to the power of the US Navy and its NATO allies. The plans for a global maritime posture were laid in Moscow, and the Soviet Union began the challenge to US naval power and the support of its strongest naval ally, the Royal Navy. The Soviet Union created on the Kola Peninsula on the Barents Sea and in Leningrad in the Baltic a naval shipbuilding infrastructure that over the next thirty years would witness the greatest Russian shipbuilding program since the days of Peter the Great.

The Admiralty Yard in Leningrad and the other major Russian shipyards came to be supported by a plethora of research-and-development institutes that aimed to acquire technical expertise that would challenge the capabilities of the United States and United Kingdom. A critical element in this huge attempt to catch up in almost all naval technological and operational domains was intelligence gathering—espionage by the main Soviet agencies and the networks that they managed through Warsaw Pact affiliates. Nowhere was the intelligence Cold War more intense than in the naval race. As we have seen, the Central Front of Europe was a pivotal geopolitical arena, but the oceans were where the real confrontations would take place as the Soviets used the sea for hitherto unobtainable access to areas where it perceived national interests.

The boundaries of postwar Europe were drawn and the spheres of influence defined, as witnessed by the 1968 Soviet occupation of Czechoslovakia. The situation at sea was volatile, boundaries were totally ambiguous, and the freedom of the seas an opportunity for Soviet exploitation. That freedom would be undermined by the strategic nuclear imperative for submarine-based first and second strike and by a new concept of second-strike "withholding," in which ballistic-missile-firing submarines stationed under ice would aim to hold the West to ransom. From this latter strategy grew a whole new Arctic submarine regime. The oceans of the world would now

Los Angeles–*class attack submarine USS* Greeneville *(SSN 772) with the Advanced SEAL Delivery System (ASDS). ASDS is operated by a crew of two and can carry eight SEAL-team members. The vessel is connected to the host ship via a watertight hatch and has a sophisticated sonar and a hyperbaric recompression chamber.*   US NAVY

include the Arctic—an unprecedented development in the history not just of naval warfare but of grand strategy. The US and Royal Navies would rise to meet this challenge.

Intelligence became the key. Let us examine that statement. The Soviet Union had two key intelligence agencies, the KGB and the GRU. The KGB (Komitet Gosudarstvennoy Bezopasnosti, or Committee for State Security) functioned from 1954 to 1991, with headquarters in the infamous Lubyanka Building in Moscow. Its most notorious and longest-serving chairman was Yury Vladimirovich Andropov, from January 1967 to May 1982. The KGB was dissolved after the failed coup against Mikhail Gorbachev's government in 1991 and was split into the Foreign Security Service, the FSS (FSB, in the Russian acronym), and the Foreign Intelligence Service, FIS (or SVR), within the new Russian Federation. The second and by far the larger Soviet and now Russian intelligence agency was and is the GRU, the Foreign Military Intelligence Directorate of the General Staff. In 1997 the GRU was estimated to be six times larger than the SVR. It had at that time approximately 25,000 special forces troops, or Spetsnaz, to use the Russian term. In addition to its HUMINT operations the GRU managed (and still does) huge SIGINT and IMINT (imagery intelligence). Its capabilities and operations far exceeded the primarily clandestine HUMINT operations of the KGB, and today those of the SVR. From late 1967 until 1995 Soviet intelligence controlled a highly significant naval spy ring in the United States headed by Chief Warrant Officer John Anthony Walker. During those eighteen years the Walker spy ring gave away some, though by no means all, of the US Navy's secrets, an episode that we will address later. Fortunately, Walker did not have access to many key US and UK intelligence capabilities and operations, a tribute to "need to know" and compartmentation policies and procedures.

At the heart of all this lay the underwater domain. Submarine design and construction have to suit the environment in which submarines operate. The key to success is quieting, the ability to be acoustically stealthy, so that the opposition is unable to hear one's submarine, while the other side's is detected and its acoustic profile collected and stored for future identification, an acoustic fingerprint that will identify that particular submarine. The difficulties of designing such a quiet, stealthy platform, one that is nuclear powered, can run silently and deeply, can accelerate from slow to high speed in short order, and can change depth without being detected are nontrivial. Submarine safety, necessary nuclear safeguards, and weapons-launch quieting are critical. Crew habitability and sustainability are crucial operational factors; they mean producing enough fresh water and air and carrying enough healthy food to sustain the crew in long, two-month patrols underwater. Optimal ergonomics and use of space are required. Submariners like to listen and not transmit, to avoid detection. They need the very best communications technology to ensure that national command authorities can bring them at any time to communications depth in order to receive messages much longer than is possible at greater depths via extremely low frequency (ELF) transmissions.

A submarine is only as good as the weapons it launches and the targets that it can destroy, however capable the platform. The United Kingdom and the United States have produced and systematically improved during our period one generation after another of highly capable acoustic torpedoes, their design and technology based on understanding of the environment in which submarines operate. Knowledge of the complexity of the ocean, particularly changes in its acoustic characteristics from location to location, permits exploitation of complex signal-processing algorithms for long-range detection of threat submarines or surface ships in often inhospitable ocean conditions. Oceanographic data and knowledge of how various acoustic sensors perform

in varying ocean conditions predicate how to use a submarine's sensors optimally. The 1960s saw the final demise of active acoustic transmissions as a
means of detection (the transmission itself yielding one's own position) and
a transition to passive detection, using knowledge of the sound-velocity profiles of different acoustic emissions from threat platforms and differentiating
a Soviet submarine from a whale or ambient noise. The United States has
invested tens of billions of dollars in both submarine quieting technology
to preserve stealth and acoustic signal processing. Parallel to this investment
the United States spent billions on oceanographic research to understand the
noise characteristics of the oceans and how to best exploit them. For example,
knowledge of deep sound channels and convergence zones allows US and UK
submarines working together to position themselves the better to hear discrete
threat submarine "tonals" at significant ranges.

This accumulated knowledge and experience amounted in due course
to an immense technical and operational advantage vis-à-vis the Soviet navy,
and today the Chinese navy. This vast knowledge embodied in multibillion-
dollar platforms and in the ocean science that underlay them was a major
target for Soviet intelligence. The Soviet Union knew the one vital weakness
of its submarines in the 1960s: they were noisy and could be easily detected
by US and UK submarines. What they did not know was how this detection
was achieved. The key was the science behind narrow-band signal processing,
which could pick a signal from a vast background noise and match it to a piece
of equipment in a particular threat submarine, identified by hull number,
home base, and other vital profile information. The United States and the
United Kingdom enjoyed, very simply, a massive operational advantage. It
was the goal of the Soviet Union to narrow that gap.

As part of the counter-countermeasures philosophy mentioned earlier,
the United States and the United Kingdom constantly anticipated and stayed
ahead of the game. One classic example of this was the Sound Surveillance
System, or SOSUS, a network that was laid on ocean floors where Soviet
submarines regularly transited. It enabled the United States and the United
Kingdom to know the location of Soviet submarines without costly and
time-consuming individual searches. Submarines, surface ships, and aircraft
could be vectored to the projected location of a Soviet submarine detected
by SOSUS. The network's cost was prodigious, but it worked extremely
well. Another example was the deployment of special surface ships that
towed extremely long passive acoustic arrays that collected acoustic intelligence. Together with other collectors (submarines, surface ships, aircraft
sonobuoys, and other fixed ocean-based sensors), they created a vast ACINT

data base. There were the keys to the kingdom, the ability to track an individual submarine by its unique ACINT profile—a capability of the US and UK Navies only.

A quiet, well-handled submarine can go where no other platforms can and listen to everything, across the electromagnetic (EM) spectrum. This includes collecting SIGINT across the radio frequency (RF) spectrum; collecting ELINT across the radar, infrared, multispectral, and laser spectra; measure and signature intelligence (MASINT) multispectral techniques for crucial measurement of other discrete parts of the spectrum associated, for example, with nuclear effluent and effects and materials from other highly sensitive events; telemetry collection from missile shoots; and underwater device laying and disruption, cable cutting and interception, and watching, listening to, filming, and recording all manner of threat activities.

The submarine in our fifty-five-year period was therefore the most effective of all US and UK platforms. It had in addition one other extremely valuable operational capability, a fourth weapon, supplementing torpedoes, missiles, and "soft kill" EM capabilities. These are special operations forces. SEAL (Sea, Air, and Land) teams, and, in the case of the United Kingdom, elements of the Special Boat Section of the Royal Marines and the Special Air Service (SAS) are launched and retrieved stealthily from US and UK submarines. A whole panoply of technological advances were made in our period to enhance the capabilities of special operations forces to inflict disproportionate damage on the enemy. SEAL delivery systems and other manned and unmanned underwater systems have enabled the United States and the United Kingdom to stay ahead in the covert and clandestine use of these and other unacknowledged operatives hosted by US and UK submarine crews on special missions.

In the constant cat-and-mouse contest of the Cold War, the United States and the United Kingdom stayed ahead, and we will examine why shortly. However, the Soviet Union sought, and today the Russians and Chinese still seek, to break into the most sensitive secrets associated with the design, building, operation, and maintenance of both nations' nuclear submarines. Guarding those secrets remains a national counterintelligence priority, one not helped by the arrival of the Internet and cyber operations.

In the first part of the Cold War the Soviets were partially disabled, unknowingly so. They did not know what they did not know until the Walker spy ring complemented other espionage. They simply wanted to know how the United States and the United Kingdom did it all: the technology, the design, operational modes, and communications. Most of all, they wanted to know just how quiet the US and UK submarines were. What were they really up against? The Soviets became creative at the operational level.

New words entered the NATO lexicon; fresh abbreviations and acronyms were added regularly. One such acronym was AGI, Auxiliary General Intelligence (collector), a bland description of Soviet and other Warsaw Pact surface ships that were intelligence collectors disguised as civilian merchant ships. The Soviet Ocean Surveillance System (SOSS, for short) had many components; AGIs were crucial ones. These otherwise innocuous vessels gave themselves away by the antennas they sprouted over their superstructures— SIGINT and ELINT systems that were well known in NATO handbooks. Occasionally a unique system would appear, and it became the job of the technical intelligence-collection systems and the analysts at GCHQ, NSA, UK Technical Intelligence (Navy), and the US Naval Intelligence Center to figure out what it was. The Soviets positioned their AGIs in locations well known to and well surveilled by US and UK systems.

For example, the NATO-designated "Malin Head" AGI was stationed off Malin Head with the clear and explicit goal of collecting intelligence from the UK submarine base at Faslane and the nearby US strategic-missile-submarine tender and submarine support activity in Holy Loch. US and UK submarines followed similar routes from their bases down the Firth of Clyde to the outer channels between the Scottish islands and then the North and Norwegian Seas and the eastern Atlantic. US and UK submarines were on the surface for a considerable part of the transit for safety and navigational reasons before they could dive and leave their protective escorts, which included antisubmarine helicopters.

As the 1970s progressed the Soviets became more adventurous and clever. They coordinated data from the AGI with other SOSS sources and methods and espionage data to intercept a deploying SSBN heading for the deep ocean to begin a two-month strategic deterrent patrol. The patrol areas became increasingly distant from the Soviet Union as the range of the missiles increased from that of the original Polaris through Poseidon to the Trident D-5 and everything in between. From a Soviet perspective, intercepting, destabilizing, and potentially causing a mission abort of a UK or US strategic patrol would send a message to both countries' leaderships that their primary strategic deterrent was not invincible. From a US Navy and Royal Navy perspective, ensuring that this did not happen was paramount, so a range of technical, operational, and intelligence ploys evolved to counter such assets as the Malin Head AGI. Along similar lines, the Soviets and their Warsaw Pact allies developed the simple tactic of following US and Royal Navy surface ships of all descriptions, from US nuclear-powered aircraft carrier battle groups to frigate squadrons and supply ships and oilers.

Where the latter went the shadowers hoped to find the fleet, and they were correct. From a Soviet Northern Fleet, Baltic, or Black Sea Fleet perspective, following a fleet tanker to its rendezvous point with a major formation could lead to significant SIGINT and ELINT collection opportunities. NATO's EMCON (emission control) would obviate the latter, and Soviet listeners would be left only with listening to VHF (very high frequency) communications between combatants and supply vessels. NATO named these Soviet followers "tattletales." There was more to them, however. As its capabilities improved through the 1970s and right up to the demise of the USSR, the Soviet navy developed a strategic and tactical plan that involved striking first against major US and NATO naval formations. This required significant coordination, timing of deployments and arrival on station, secure low-probability-of-intercept (LPI) communications, and weapons that the planners in Moscow assessed would do the job—that is, deliver a massed surprise and decapitating strike. The tattletale was only one of the assets involved. Others included surface, subsurface, and air assets of several types, and, increasingly, space-based systems for tracking and targeting. Breaking into, compromising, and rendering ineffective this part of the Soviet Ocean Surveillance System was a crucial task, one that the US Navy and Royal Navy, along with their intelligence communities, addressed in full.

There was, however, an additional Soviet component, one that was extremely flexible, deceptive, and at times difficult to locate and track. This comprised the noncommercial use of Soviet and other Warsaw Pact merchant fleets, plus the even more challenging flag-of-convenience surrogates used clandestinely by the KGB and GRU for a variety of intelligence operations. This added component was nontrivial. The KGB and the GRU recognized that they could place merchant vessels in places that a Soviet or Warsaw Pact naval vessel could never go, into the very ports and hearts of the European NATO navies, including the Royal Navy, and into certain US ports that the US government had opened to Soviet- and Warsaw Pact–flag carriers. In the case of surrogate flag-of-convenience vessels there was little NATO governments could do legally and overtly under the various maritime agreements together with the law of the sea. (It should be noted at this point and for future reference that the United States is, unlike the United Kingdom, not a signatory to the United Nations Convention on the Law of the Sea [UNCLOS] or to the United Nations convention establishing and maintaining the International Criminal Courts [ICC] at The Hague in the Netherlands.)

The KGB and the GRU selected merchant vessels that ostensibly belonged to well established trading organizations and equipped them with often very capable intelligence collection systems, including sonar and the latest SIGINT and ELINT devices. Photographic collection was easy. A merchant ship visiting Greenock on the Clyde could listen to local communications while sending highly trained crew members ashore on collection missions. These individuals could travel by rental car to such sites such as the Royal Navy nuclear storage facility at Coulport or to the Holy Loch, where they could observe US nuclear submarines berthed. Deployment schedules could be collected, tug frequencies monitored, weapon movements noted, and perhaps most dangerous of all, some of those who went ashore did not return. UK port immigration and customs officials checked crews in and out but could never guarantee that the same persons arrived with the ship and sailed with it. The KGB and the GRU had an ideal way to insert agents and recover them, without the risks of airport and regular port transit, or indeed of clandestine insertion by other means, such as submarines. The KGB inserted agents regularly into and out of Europe in such ways, and the GRU inserted the far more dangerous long-term "sleepers," tasked to integrate with and live among local communities.

These sleepers were extremely highly trained personnel with perfect language skills, culture, and detailed local knowledge, acquired after multiple clandestine visits before final insertion for what in some cases was decades, often without the knowledge of their owners or operators. They were equipped with totally fictitious identities and documentation. The objectives for these GRU personnel, many of them Spetsnaz trained, was not classic espionage, recruiting and running agents, but rather acquiring detailed local intelligence. In the case of the Royal Navy, they were interested in the location of crucial strategic communications systems and likely routing, weapon storage facilities, strategic fuel-supply sites, and covert command-and-control facilities. Perhaps most worrisome of all was the task given to a select few to assassinate, in the event of a major confrontation between the West and the Soviet Union, the key leadership of the United Kingdom. In the 1980s Mrs. Margaret Thatcher was indeed at the very top of the target list.

At the operational level, these vessels had highly classified war orders to which only their political officers had access: mining in key ports and approaches, scuttling in crucial channels, and destroying with hidden weaponry military infrastructure, and even, where access was possible, attacking warships in harbor or in transit with heavily disguised surface-to-surface weapons. Other targets included logistics and infrastructure oil tanks, aviation fuel supplies, communications sites, and bridges.

The nuclear era did not prevent limited war. The 1960s were a decade of considerable challenge for both the US Navy and the Royal Navy. We will look at operations in due course, but before we do let us examine the technological challenges posed by the Soviet and Warsaw Pact threat and the ways in which the two competing systems, communism and capitalism, vied with one another in unprecedented ways to gain the military edge at all levels of naval warfare. The 1960s witnessed the Cuban Missile Crisis, the war in Vietnam, the Six Day War in the Middle East of June 1967, the United Kingdom's confrontation with Indonesia in support of its former colony, Malaysia, and the Soviet invasion of Czechoslovakia. They also saw the beginning of a space race and, most important of all, confrontation at sea on a scale and in ways not seen before in peacetime.

The Technology Race Is On

*The US and Royal Navies Face an Emerging Soviet Navy
That Seeks Technological Parity*

Before we examine the detail of the Soviet naval technological challenge, it is important to note that the Soviet navy was constrained by the inner workings of the USSR's system. This was most fortunate for the West. At the strategic level the Soviet navy had to fit into the overall war plans and staff structure of the General Staff. The Soviet navy had also to fit into General Staff doctrine, not vice versa, and this included technological improvements and force structure. There was therefore little or no give in the system for the Soviet navy to step outside this organizational straitjacket and be independently innovative. The US Navy and the Royal Navy enjoyed much more freedom to innovate and were not constrained inside political monoliths.

We knew from intelligence at the time and later, in retrospect, from post–Cold War assessments that the General Staff was pursuing a "conventional war" option, in which reduction of the risk of nuclear escalation was paramount. In essence they wanted an escalation bridge to make the world "safe for conventional war"—hence the Soviets' willingness to trade SS-20 missiles for Pershing II and ground-launched cruise missiles. They wanted to demonstrate in successive five-year plans that they could provide a tactical nuclear response to a tactical nuclear threat from NATO. What this meant for the Soviet navy doctrinally was a directive to be able to fight a conventional war with NATO—through the use of surprise and the early attrition of vital US naval forces and those of its principal naval allies, particularly the Royal Navy, while maintaining a secure strategic second-strike capability and the ability to strip away US and UK strategic capabilities by anti-SSBN operations. These points are fundamental for understanding what drove the Soviet naval-technology race with the West.

From an operations viewpoint, the above meant that Soviet naval offensive and defensive war plans called for attacks on forces likely to prevent the achievement of Soviet objectives on land or that presented any threat to the homeland. The latter aim would eventually produce rear-area defenses in areas such as the Arctic, the Barents Sea, the Sea of Japan, and the Sea of Okhotsk, in addition to forward-deployed operations. Northern Fleet submarine dispositions between the early 1960s and the middle to late 1980s reveal Soviet strategic thinking, technology status, orders of battle (OOBs), and fundamental capabilities. They also displayed locations of patrol stations and duration on station for five key domains: SSBN patrols; Norwegian Sea operations and pro-SSBN operations (to protect Soviet SSBNs); anti-SSBN operations (to destabilize and hold at risk US and UK SSBNs); anti-amphibious and anti-SLOC; and Mediterranean operations against the US Sixth Fleet and in support of client states.

For example, by 1985 the Soviet navy had within the Northern Fleet area of responsibility (AOR), which included the Mediterranean, the following OOB: Typhoon SSBNs (three); Delta I, II, and III SSBNs (twenty); Yankee I and II SSBNs (nine); a Hotel SSBN; SSGNs (twenty-three); SSGs (three); SSNs (thirty-nine); and nonnuclear attack submarines (SS, with thirty-six). The year 1985 was significant for US naval war planning, insofar as it had been selected ten years prior as the time to plan in detail a strategy for future naval warfare with the Soviet Union. (Your author produced the blueprint for US naval forces, with Captain John L. Underwood, USN.) Analysis of Soviet long-term operational goals showed four main scenarios for their naval forces: operations off the east and west coasts of the United States, Arctic operations (with defense in depth in the Norwegian and Barents Seas), operations against the US sea lines of communication at strategic points (for example, where the Soviet Oscar-class SSGN, with its twenty-four SS-N-19 antiship cruise missiles, could engage high-value targets), and sea-control operations (at key straits, for example).

From a technical perspective, by the early 1970s the Soviet navy (which had been the poor relation among the Soviet armed forces since the Cuban Missile Crisis) and its intelligence specialists had realized several key points. First, only a few acoustical "lines" would normally emanate from a well-handed quiet US and UK nuclear attack submarine, such as the new US *Los Angeles* and UK *Swiftsure* classes. These lines included blade-rate tonals, the noise associated with cavitation at higher speeds, and broadband hull-flow noise, especially at the after end of the hull with the onset of turbulent flow at higher speeds. (The United Kingdom invested later in water- and pump-jet technology to obviate cavitation; diving to greater depth had always been a tactical means to reduce cavitation-induced noise.) The Soviets made key research-and-development and design decisions to escape the necessity of what the West termed their "bastion strategy" and to protect their SSBNs in transit to these safe havens. Meanwhile, until they could learn and then implement the technologies necessary for building quieter submarines, they concentrated on domains that might offset their considerable acoustic disadvantage.

In the 1960s and into the 1970s the Soviet navy aimed for: high speed, for occasions when it was tactically necessary; deep diving, using double hulls for added strength; quietness at speeds below fifteen knots; high reserves of buoyancy; capable decoys and countermeasures; nuclear-tipped torpedoes; large weapon payloads and maximum numbers of torpedo tubes; and a mix of torpedoes (SS-N-15s and SS-N-16s, in their NATO designations). They worked diligently on the underwater endurance of their nonnuclear submarines, and this paid off much later in the Kilo and Tango diesel-electric submarines. The Soviet navy sought to mitigate its disadvantage in passive sonar by developing discrete, pseudorandom active sonars. The latter were never quite good enough, and until the Soviets figured out the physics and technology behind passive sonar signal processing they were, in essence, in the acoustic dark.

The other major step that the Soviets took to reduce their vulnerabilities was to send some of their SSBNs under the Arctic ice. This practice was well established by the 1980s, when the capable Typhoon-class SSBN joined the Delta III and Delta IV classes. The US and Royal Navies responded to this challenge, the United States in particular with a very capable under-ice program, including hardening of SSN hulls for under-ice operations, coming to periscope depth, and surfacing. By the mid-1980s all Soviet nuclear submarines had been configured for under-ice operations, and some diesel submarines could use their high battery capacity to operate along the fringe of the Marginal Ice Zone at the edge of the Arctic.

The early and later Soviet classes of both SSNs and nonnuclear hunter-killer submarines (SSKs) never matched their US and UK rivals. The Cold War–era Romeo-, Tango-, and Kilo-class SSKs were all, for their day, capable submarines, but they were never quite good enough. The case was similar with the Sierra- and Victor-class SSNs. The later Victor III SSNs were good submarines but had nothing like the finesse of the US and UK SSNs. Soviet improvements occurred with the 1980 launch of the Typhoon-class SSBN and the Oscar-class SSGN, followed later by the Akula, Mike, and Sierra classes of SSN. (We will discuss the intelligence implications of these launches and how the Soviets managed to catch up in the quieting business and what this meant for the last ten years of the Cold War.)

In parallel to their quietness quest the Soviet navy also aimed for much higher power-density ratios, with little or no attention to hotel facilities or habitability. The Soviet navy did not have to concern itself with manpower retention, like the US and Royal Navies, for which crew health and well-being were design considerations. As a result Soviet submarines had much larger weapon complements and more torpedo tubes: more volume was available to their designers.

Two quite outstanding achievements were liquid-metal reactors and titanium hulls. The latter required highly specialized welding techniques. The Soviets concentrated on compliant (i.e., minimum-drag) and anechoic hull coatings to reduce hull noise and drag, and they spent enormous resources on hydrodynamic hull-form research. The Soviet submarine classes that were introduced in the 1980s incorporated all these. The design bureaus and their research institutes, such as the Leningrad Institute of Hydromechanics, had exceptionally able and well qualified academicians. Once the Soviets bridged the computer and signal-processing gaps they began to put together what may be called the total package, including detection and analysis of low-frequency tonals.

The year 1980 was a turning point, and by the middle of the decade the United States and the United Kingdom had realized that by the mid-1990s the Soviets would have a submarine force as powerful, modern, and quiet as the early US "688" SSNs (that is, *Los Angeles*–class, so called after the hull number of the class's name-ship). In the middle to late 1980s it was assessed that because of the daunting Soviet build rate, and if the US Navy adhered to a hundred-boat submarine force, by the year 2000 the Soviet Union would achieve qualitative equality and a quantitative advantage of potentially three to one. Fortunately, the end of the Cold War and the disestablishment of the Soviet Union reversed this trend, and the West never faced this enormous challenge. Nevertheless, the Soviets had improved dramatically in quieting, propulsion, hull technology, diesel-electric technology, and nonacoustic signature reduction. It is of note at this point (before further discussion later) that the Soviets recognized that under-ice operations reduced the probabilities of detection across both the acoustic and nonacoustic spectra.

Before they bridged the critical noise and signal-processing gap the Soviets compensated with tactics, coupled to strategic deception and use of the SOSS for targeting. The one main vulnerability of the Soviet approach was a highly centralized command structure, with little flexibility for individual initiative and innovation; even lower-echelon flag-level commands did not take area responsibility or change central plans and orders. The Soviets opted for well-proven, rugged, and dependable communications, with heavy reliance on high-frequency (HF), very-low-frequency (VLF), and ELF communications. Later their satellite communications, towed antenna, and communications buoys followed Western systems. In submarine operations the Soviets placed high emphasis on redundancy, survivability, and security. Their submarine tactics relied heavily on patrolling near US and UK bases in order to make contact and commence trailing while allied submarines were on the surface or beginning their transits to the edge of the continental shelf, and then into deep water beyond the hundred-fathom curve (six hundred feet–plus). The approaches to the Clyde estuary were ideal for Victor III–class Soviet SSNs for such purposes, as were locations off the east-coast US submarine bases, the straits of San Juan de Fuca in the Pacific Northwest, and off such bases as Pearl Harbor, Hawaii, and San Diego, California.

The Soviets knew that US carrier (CV and CVN) battle groups would have SSNs for protection or sanitization from threat submarines—trailing these carriers from their home bases was therefore a practical way to make contact, because the probability of detection of a quiet, well-handled US or UK SSN or SSK in the deep ocean or littorals was minimal, if not non-existent. The Soviets would lay ambushes with one or more submarines in narrow barrier formations to interdict US and UK submarines returning to base—lying in wait at very low maneuvering speeds at critical navigational points, where Western submarines had to transit because of navigational factors or hazards. Incidents where the Soviets announced their presence with active-sonar transmissions to send a message of surprise and vulnerability were rare, but when they did occur they became subjects of intense analysis in the operational and intelligence communities of both the US and Royal Navies. We will discuss the joint US-UK submarine-security program later, but suffice here to say that one of the major operational issues for both navies was ensuring the secure transit of both countries' national strategic-deterrent SSBNs from the departure phase to the transit phase on the surface and then to the initial dive and transit phase, to the deep recesses of the oceans, where they would remain undetectable for the typical two months of their deterrent patrols.

The two countries worked in harmony, sharing operations concepts, tactics, techniques, and procedures to ensure the uninhibited egress and ingress of these vital national assets. The process was continuous, with information shared round the clock when the situation demanded; at annual submarine-security meetings a full year's operations were reported on so that plans could be agreed and laid for the future. The combination of the operational experiences of navies' submarine forces at these annual gatherings was a unique and critical reflection of the US-UK sharing of information at the very highest security levels. These events were supported year in year out by both intelligence communities. However, in certain domains both navies maintained extraordinarily strict "need to know," so that even the highest levels of American and British intelligence did not have access. However, the sources and methods that underlay these events and scenarios were generated solely with these two specialist communities—the submarine forces of the United States and the United Kingdom—and it was kept that way, with political control and oversight only at the presidential and prime-ministerial levels.

The Soviet navy had, for the long duration of the Cold War, a constant problem of how to detect at long range, localize, and then target with a reliable fire-control solution, US, UK, and NATO naval assets. The latter included carrier battle groups, amphibious assault groups, and other formations such as cruiser, destroyer, and frigate echelons. The Soviet Union was aware of its acoustic disadvantage with respect to US and UK submarines and sought every means to narrow it. Given the large number of NATO surface units, culminating in the US six-hundred-ship era of the 1980s, the Soviets faced a daunting problem to use their assets, supported by the SOSS, to locate, track, and target Western naval forces. What they could not achieve in antisubmarine warfare (ASW), particularly the submarine-on-submarine variety, they attempted to ameliorate in the antisurface mode. What they endeavored to achieve was the aggregation of their various intelligence and reconnaissance assets in order to provide close to real-time information on the disposition of major US and NATO forces.

Their tactic was to time attacks so as to achieve saturation of targets with air-to-surface and surface-to-surface missiles and torpedo and cruise-missile attacks from submarines. The centralization process raised serious coordination and timing issues, particularly for aircraft departing Soviet bases; these were easily located and tracked by NATO air forces and the carrier aircraft of the frontline US fleets—the Seventh in the Pacific, the Sixth in the Mediterranean, and the Second in the Atlantic. In addition to the various US naval intelligence centers around the globe and the central facility at Suitland, Maryland (the lineal antecedent to the current National Maritime Intelligence Center), the carrier battle groups had self-contained, highly competent intelligence staffs that plotted all Soviet movements. The Soviet tattletale was there to provide positional data back to fleet headquarters; the United States and the United Kingdom would have an SSN ready with a torpedo firing solution on the tattletale. It was the same with Soviet submarines trailing major NATO naval forces: a US or British submarine (often both) would be tracking the Soviet submarine's every turn. The nuclear-powered US cruisers of the 1960s and 1970s would keep station at high speed to provide additional air defense, with ASW support from destroyer and frigate escorts.

The Soviets had therefore to rely on one simple tactic—surprise. This was not going to be easy to achieve, given the close monitoring of almost every facet of Soviet and Warsaw Pact activities around the clock by US and British intelligence. Indicators and warnings (I&W, as they were termed) were a paramount function of the multiple agencies checking on Soviet intentions and military movements. A coordinated, surprise attack on the West and its naval forces was almost impossible for the Soviets to contemplate seriously, let alone achieve without the prospect of serious escalation. However, in the nonglobal confrontation/checkmate scenarios of the Cold War in which lower-level Soviet goals and aspirations played out gave concern for a potential conflict at sea, one that could be kept under the nuclear threshold and in which Soviet tactics might have some credibility. To this end the Soviets worked extremely hard and diligently, constantly trying to catch up with the US and UK Navies' technological superiority, and in some domains the Soviet navy did move ahead, or at least along positive, alternative lines, of the British and Americans. But the Soviets did not know what they did not know. Let us examine this observation.

As noted, the Soviets pursued double-hull designs for their submarines. They were concerned with survivability through reserve buoyancy than increased drag and loss of speed. The technical leadership at the design bureaus assessed that the double hull would cause most weapons to detonate away from the pressure hull, thereby reducing the impact of an explosion. Soviet hydrodynamicists believed that extra ballast tanks in the standoff area would allow a damaged submarine to remain neutrally buoyant and maintain trim. Also, a double-hull design permits framing stiffeners to be external to the pressure hull, instead of internal as in single-hull construction. This leads to space saving within the pressure hull and relaxes the requirement to smooth these frames. Air tanks could be moved to between the hulls, freeing additional internal volume for other uses. Weapons and hard auxiliaries, such as heat exchangers, could also be placed external to the pressure hull; by removing the hard auxiliaries, fuel, and auxiliary from the inner hull, internal volume could be increased by more than 10 percent. In addition, a large number of weapons, such as torpedoes, which weighed typically about one and one half tons, could be housed between the hulls with only a modest effect on the submarine's displacement.

The Soviets pursued several innovative programs for drag reduction and hull-form improvement, constantly revising their thoughts on length-to-beam ratio. Design bureaus staffs were extremely capable and considered the many key factors of power density, hull-material strength-to-weight ratio, collapse depth, propulsion efficiency, and the all-important coefficient of drag. The Soviets put enormous intellectual and financial energy into drag-reduction and coatings programs, all of which were as impressive as the work of such drag specialists as Bushnell and Ffowcs-Williams in the West. The Soviets recognized from the 1960s onward the direct relationship between drag reduction and flow noise and therefore detectability. On the nonnuclear-propulsion side of the house the Soviets crept ahead in fuel-cell and closed-cycle-engine development while the US Navy over time became an all-nuclear-submarine navy. The water, or pump-jet, propulsion system that the Royal Navy developed for the *Trafalgar*-class SSN was of both great interest and some concern for the Soviet research institutes. Had the British stolen a serious march on technology? This issue bedeviled the Soviet designers right through until the end of the Cold War, and indeed their successors thereafter.

In submarine towed-array and fixed-wing- and helicopter-launched sonobuoy technology the West stayed ahead for the duration. The Soviets never bridged the gap in discrete narrow-band signal processing. However, since the ending of the Cold War, with the resurgence of the Russian and the rise of the Chinese submarine navies one factor has clearly militated against this advantage—the difficulty of designing and building submarines that can operate very quietly in extremely challenging environmental conditions, atypical of Cold War open-ocean ASW. A quiet, well-handled Kilo-class Russian submarine presents a challenge in shallow waters with dense merchant traffic and severe background noise.

The domain where the Soviet navy placed massive investment was one where they believed they could seize the technical, and ultimately the tactical, advantage. In fact, they hoped for the ultimate prize: the ability to destabilize US and UK submarine forces and thus Western strategic deterrents. This domain was the new area of nonacoustic antisubmarine warfare. We shall address this issue in detail as a separate subject, because this arena involved US and UK intelligence in a contest that has yet to play out fully. From the 1970s until the present this subject received most significant covert attention in the United States and the United Kingdom. In due course the issue of nonacoustic ASW became an acknowledged fact when the US Congress openly addressed it in public committee hearings. Representative Les Aspin, the chairman of the House Armed Services Committee and future secretary of defense in the first Clinton administration, posed questions associated with potential Soviet capabilities in nonacoustic ASW. He may have done so from concern to stimulate public awareness of a possible serious threat or as a result of the perceived unwillingness of the intelligence community to be transparent with Congress on this matter. The book is by no means closed on nonacoustic ASW; it continues to require close attention with respect to the Russian and Chinese navies.

The Soviets were most innovative, from both an operational and technical viewpoint, in two environmental domains. The first was that of Arctic under-ice submarine operations—launching submarine ballistic missiles from leads, polynyas (areas of unfrozen sea within the ice pack), or through thin ice, or from the surface inside Soviet waters, often as far away from their targets as the Kamchatka Peninsula. Communications were always a problem for the Soviets under the ice—trying to receive the Soviet equivalent of the US-UK out-of-area HF broadcast or an ELF or VLF transmission and communicating at periscope depth in a lead in satellite ultra- and super-high-frequency (UHF and SHF) communications bands. Despite the many technical challenges and operational risks the Soviet navy threw down the gauntlet to the US and Royal Navies—in essence, come and find us if you can. From an SSBN-security point of view, hiding in the most inhospitable and environmentally challenging areas made absolute sense. The Soviets put considerable resources into understanding and exploiting sound propagation under the Arctic ice. The United States did the same, and to this day it enjoys a huge tactical advantage over any threat under the Arctic ice. The United States invested the same level of commitment and intellectual horsepower that had earlier driven its acoustic programs, such as SOSUS. For example, US knowledge of sound propagation under the Arctic ice is, simply, prodigious. This does not make operations less challenging or risky, but it does mean that the United States has great understanding of what it takes to fight an underwater battle in the Arctic. The Royal Navy has benefited enormously from this US knowledge base.

The second domain was in shallow water, typically less than one hundred fathoms. Shallow water is an acoustically challenging environment, easier to hide and be masked by ambient noise than in the deep ocean. Shipping lanes converge there; shallow water was therefore an ideal location for attacks on merchant shipping or reinforcements for the Central Front if NATO faced a conventional attack. Although perhaps unlikely in retrospect, there was no assurance of that until the demise of the Soviet Union and the disestablishment of the whole Warsaw Pact edifice. The Soviets learned the tactical techniques for submarine masking under merchant ships and to use the environment to hide. To this end, as the Soviet Union reached the end of its political life the Soviet navy initiated advanced technology programs in several major areas. These programs foundered during the immediate post–Cold War period but have been reinvigorated; the original 1980s advances have been continued under Vladimir Putin's leadership. The Soviets at first, and now the Russians alone, sought and are seeking a series of technological goals: increased submarine speed without increased volume; increased overall stealth (acoustic and nonacoustic signatures), also without increased volume; reduction in hydrodynamic noise flow; reduction in vortex shedding from various parts of the hull; much-increased efficiency of the main propulsor with quieter operation; increased endurance; and increased weapon load.

Having looked back at what the Soviet navy tried to accomplish between 1960 and 1980 (when the Typhoon SSBN and the Oscar SSGN were launched, followed by capable SSNs such as the Akula class), the key question is: What

Three nuclear-powered submarines rendezvous and surface together at the geographic North Pole for the first time. The historic event occurred May 6, 1986, during Arctic Ocean operations. The mission of the submarines was to collect scientific data and test readiness under Arctic conditions without logistics support. The three attack submarines were USS Ray *(SSN 653),* USS Hawkbill *(SSN 666), and USS* Archerfish *(SSN 678). They remained surfaced for several hours to allow crew members to explore the ice.* US NAVY were its guiding principles, technologically? What drove the massive R&D organization and vast industrial base that produced such a large order of battle in so little time? The answer is that their fundamental philosophy was producing reliable platforms and weapons that might not be the best but they were good enough. The "good enough" was matched by a simple but extremely important Soviet concept: numbers count. How many submarines, in particular, could be deployed at any one time versus how many of the opposition? Admiral S. G. Gorshkov, the service's commander-in-chief in these years, realized that if his navy could not be qualitatively superior to the US and Royal Navies, while he was catching up he would build a numerically superior navy based on the critical notion that one platform can be in only one place at a time. Even the most capable *Los Angeles*– or *Trafalgar*-class SSN is not ubiquitous. The planners in Moscow conceived a force level such that even if attrition was very high indeed, enough would survive to block the reinforcement of Europe.

Soviet naval strategy at the industrial-base level was about quantity and the use of any advantages to maximum effect. The results included weapons such as the SS-N-19 (NATO designation) antiship cruise missile. By the same token, the United States in particular would have to respond with costly countermeasures. The Soviets would ultimately fail in this technology race because the United States had the resources and intellectual base to rise to every challenge in advance. Nowhere is this more evident than in the US Aegis system, still the most capable missile-defense system on the planet and a testament to American technical ingenuity and, indeed, intellectual brilliance, sustained by an industrial base that has never failed to respond.

It is perhaps appropriate to end this chapter with the observation, however self-evident, that Western capitalism defeated Soviet communism at several levels. The Soviet political system cramped innovation; direct control from the center in Moscow and unbridled oversight were compounded by a security system that watched everything and everyone. This was not a national organizational structure that could foster individual and corporate experimentation and risk taking. Investment by the state precluded the free flow of investment capital that was the cornerstone of Western capitalism. As a result the defense and intelligence industrial base in the Soviet Union did not enjoy the benefits of capitalist ingenuity, innovation, and competitive economics enjoyed by a democratic society. Soviet communism was outmatched.

It is salutary to observe that the Chinese are at the time of writing pursuing a naval policy not dissimilar to that of the Soviet Union. However, the state-managed capitalism of contemporary China is very different indeed from the orthodox Marxism-Leninism that drove the Soviet navy's production machine. What requires close monitoring is whether the Chinese system of state capitalism in a one-party communist state can match Western qualitative performance. The answer remains to be seen, but we can state that complacency would be foolhardy. A key strategic factor will be how well the combined naval strengths of the United States and its allies, particularly in Asia, will be able to counter and indeed surpass a growing Chinese navy, both quantitatively as well as qualitatively.

The 1960s

The Soviet Navy Challenges the US Sixth Fleet and the Royal Navy

This will be the first time that we address in some detail actual operations involving the US Navy, the Royal Navy, and the Soviet Union and its Warsaw Pact allies. We have touched on the impact of the Cuban Missile Crisis and the Vietnam War on how the Soviet Union reacted to US naval strength. Nowhere in the 1960s after the crisis of 1962 passed did the growing confrontation at sea witness more daily contact and events than in the Mediterranean. Several core strategic factors require clarification. The Middle East was a growing hotbed of East–West rivalry, not so much in the Persian Gulf, with its vital oil fields and traffic through the Straits of Hormuz, as in the eastern Mediterranean. There friction was growing between Israel on one side and with Egypt and Syria (known jointly until 1961 as the United Arab Republic [UAR], a name Egypt still used) on the other, with Jordan (led by King Hussain) playing a waiting game with its Arab neighbors. This was a political tinderbox, and the Soviet Union had clear and unequivocal alignments with both Egypt and Syria, the latter in particular.

The Soviet navy was constrained by the Montreux Convention, which regulated when and how it was to give notice of transits of ships and submarines from its Black Sea base into the Mediterranean via the Bosporus and Dardanelles. This fact placed the Soviet navy in the unenviable position of having to augment its Mediterranean presence with units from the Northern Fleet, based on the Kola Peninsula, requiring a long transit through NATO-patrolled waters in the GIUK gap to the entrance of the Mediterranean off Gibraltar, a British naval base, and close to Rota in Spain, where the US Navy maintained a base. The Royal Navy had its historical Mediterranean Fleet headquarters at Malta, with its deepwater harbor of Valetta, strategically placed in the eastern Mediterranean. In addition, NATO had naval facilities at the Italian base at Naples, and there were other naval aviation and air force bases in several locations, including Cyprus (at Akrotiri) and Sigonella (in Sicily). US submarines enjoyed facilities at La Madelena in Sardinia. The Soviet navy was therefore at a serious disadvantage.

The Soviet navy nevertheless played a critical role in the events that led up to Middle East confrontation and eventually the June War (also known as the Six-Day War) of 1967. This episode marked a significant shift in how the Soviet navy was integrated with the USSR's overall non–Western European political-military strategy, plans, policies, and operations. More specifically, the June War marks a turning point in Soviet deployments to the Mediterranean. The USSR doubled its force during the crisis, and force levels continued to rise thereafter. Furthermore, as a direct result of the war the Russians were able to gain access to both Alexandria and Port Said, which had hitherto been denied them. Such was the rate of Soviet increase that by the October War in 1973 the US Sixth Fleet was to be outnumbered by Soviet units. Unlike in 1967, by 1973 the Soviets were able to deploy amphibious ships in large numbers and to use anticarrier tactics. Although in 1967 Soviet activity was still marginal compared with its later efforts, the 1967 war is important, because it saw the Soviets attempting to use naval power in ways that would have been impossible a decade earlier.

An essential precondition for successful maritime crisis management is the ability to respond quickly to the situation and to act not only in light of one's own best interest but also of the opposition's infrastructure and the extent to which it matches the situation at sea. This is particularly pertinent in fast-moving, real-time situations such as the Six-Day War, where quick, effective response became the essence of success. It became even more relevant after the 1967 war, with the upheaval of the naval status quo in the Mediterranean and the resulting need for tactical and command-and-control advantages that would enable the West to maintain some advantage in crisis situations. At the same time, speed of response became increasingly a major variable in the calculations of both sides when taking risks that could end in escalation and thus required special attention.

Let us first look at Soviet objectives. The acquisition of Egyptian bases can be seen as fulfilling both naval needs and political goals in an area where US interests could be countered. To ascribe a master plan to the Soviets clearly is unsupportable, given the complexity of the Middle East in 1967; they could not, any more than the Western powers, claim the causal control that must be the core of any successful grand design. Beneath the Soviets' pragmatic and opportunist approach was their defense doctrine of the late 1960s. The need for warm-water bases for launching counterstrikes against US SSBNs and carrier forces was as critical as the need to gain influence in the Third World, and both might have been fulfilled by a Soviet policy to promote Arab interests against the West. Besides its strategic position, the Soviets were also acutely aware of the significance of Middle East oil to the West.

The chronology of Soviet visits and arms deals with Egypt reveals just how little the Arabs had been prepared to make concessions to the Soviets. The regime of President Gamal Abdel Nasser was aware that a Soviet presence and patronage would not necessarily be any more equitable or domestically palatable than the British one had been. At the same time, Egypt needed Russian equipment and expertise. In the event, Arab defeat would in fact force Nasser into a measure of temporary dependency. Even after the large arms deal of June 1963 (two submarines, two destroyers, and over thirty Osa and Komar fast patrol boats, a very significant increase in capability), Egypt had still declined to allow the USSR use of naval facilities. The last major Soviet arms deal with Egypt before the Six-Day War was in August 1965, and there was only one Soviet port visit to Port Said between a March 1966 visit of five ships from the Black Sea Fleet and the war. (The visit of ten Sixth Fleet destroyers to Port Said in September 1966 may have been a deliberate counterstroke to the Soviets'.)

Given the Soviets' lack of success in making inroads in Egypt, their vocal and diplomatic support was disproportionately large. Russia regularly claimed that it would support the Arabs if attacked, but it denied charges of wishing to start a major military conflict. Ambassador Dimitri Pozhidaev is alleged to have given excessive encouragement to Nasser in his war aims. Information provided by the Russians that the Israelis were planning a preemptive strike and a false report, in the face of United Nations (UN) observers' disclaimers, that they were massing on the Syrian border indicates a desire by the Russians to provoke Nasser. This may be ascribing too much influence to the Russians, however, since the Arabs had very much charted their own course in the weeks before the war. This is borne out by the Russians' disapproval of the Arab closure of the Gulf of Aqaba, despite their propaganda about American fleet reactions. All Nasser probably expected from the Black Sea Fleet was the neutralization of the Sixth Fleet. However, that was a nontrivial expectation.

Western intelligence sources expected the Arabs to lose a war with Israel. The Russians' own assessments could not have widely differed. In this equation, Nasser's view of the Russian role is significant. To maintain credibility, Russia would need careful reinforcement plans, but this need was contrary to the mainstream of Soviet-Arab relations prior to the war. If the Soviets were to give assistance it was much more likely to be on an ad hoc basis, as a direct response to military events. The last thing the Soviets desired was the

Russian navy Komar-class patrol boat   U.S. NAVAL INSTITUTE PHOTO ARCHIVE

liquidation of Israel. This they knew to be highly unlikely, and moreover something that the United States would not tolerate. At the same time, they had to keep face with the Arabs and show a measure of support. All this made the method and speed of a Russian buildup paramount, and in certain contexts intervention would risk a general war with the United States.

What were the US objectives? The factors shaping US policy have been examined by multiple scholars. Their analyses have focused on the Americans' problem of Mideast intervention concurrent with the Vietnam War, on the interaction of public opinion with decision making in the White House, on the economic interests of the United States in the Mideast and Washington's desire to remain on good terms with Arab countries such as Saudi Arabia, Kuwait, and Libya as much as to be Israel's protector, so as to prevent polarization.

The United States had good reasons for avoiding a second involvement, irrespective of domestic pressures, not least because its reinforcement capability was reduced. Amphibious capability in the Mediterranean had been much reduced because of Vietnam; only a battalion of two thousand Marines was currently on station in the Mediterranean. Despite this, the Joint Chiefs of Staff (JCS) saw no immediate problem, since the Atlantic Fleet, currently containing an attack carrier and an ASW carrier, could be dispatched immediately. Within two weeks, four carrier task forces and a marine brigade could be sent to the Mideast. Furthermore, as Secretary of Defense McNamara said, the opponents of the United States could not meet several commitments at once either.

More relevant, however, was that Israel expected the United States to neutralize the Soviet Black Sea Fleet in the Mediterranean and to redeem the guarantee that the United States had already given to maintain the sovereignty of the state of Israel. Aside from Jewish influence within the United States, President Lyndon Johnson was committed to that tenet, as indeed were most Americans. The real problem was how best to demonstrate US support without intimidating the Arabs and at the same time containing the Russians, all with the whole US and British intelligence community firmly predicting an overwhelming Israeli victory. In fact, restraining the Israelis became one of President Johnson's major problems.

When on May 22, 1967, President Nasser closed the Gulf of Aqaba, Israel's southern outlet to the sea, at the north end of the Red Sea, he created a thorny problem for the United States. It was not only a violation of international law, a most dangerous precedent, but a casus belli in the eyes of Israel and a test of the solidarity of the UN. In the event this was to be the only area during the crisis where hostilities at sea could have occurred. A premature move could have upset the balance and yet not have directly affected the land battle.

The UN's rejection of a multinational maritime force and the speed of the events themselves saved the situation. This was fortunate for the United Kingdom which was still militarily overextended and also economically vulnerable. The United Kingdom was loath to take a leading role in lifting the blockade of the Gulf of Aqaba, because of an Arab threat to cut off UK oil. Despite this, the United Kingdom was still a factor which the Russians had to consider, since it could still deploy, on paper, three carriers, two commando carriers, and two assault ships with attendant escorts, although the British, like the Americans and the Soviets, had the normal availability problems. For the moment, Britain wanted to appear to be taking no side at all. Nevertheless, although it had not been as demonstrative as the United States in supporting Israel, the United Kingdom would not stand by and see Israel go under.

A question remains as to the extent to which either US or multinational intervention in the blockade could have prevented the war. If such a move had been successful, Israel would have lost its main casus belli and might have legitimately been castigated as the aggressor had it gone to war anyway. The issue of responsibility was made partly moot by the events of the weeks preceding the war, with aggressive acts from both sides and a request for the removal of the UN peacekeeping force from the armistice line between the UAR and Israel. All this pointed to intent on both sides; the lifting of the blockade would probably not have altered matters but merely exacerbated relations between the relieving states and Arab nations.

Throughout 1967 the mean daily Soviet presence of warships in the Mediterranean was ten major and minor surface units and intelligence-collection ships (see table 4-1). Of this total there were usually four or five large units, light cruisers, and guided-missile destroyers. The minor units consisted of light destroyers and a mixture of frigate-sized and light escort vessels. On some days during 1967 there were only two (occasionally three) missile-armed ships in the Mediterranean and at most two intelligence-gatherers. The total mean daily deployment of Soviet vessels of all types, including support ships and various categories of oceanographic ships, was only eighteen. During the June 1967 crisis the total number of Soviet ships of all types (warships and support vessels) in the Mediterranean at any one time was only twenty-seven.

On May 22, 1967, the day that President Nasser began his blockade in the Straits of Tiran, at the mouth of the Gulf of Aqaba, the Soviets notified Turkey that they intended to send ten warships through the Golden Horn (at Istanbul); they did so in accordance with the Montreux Convention, which stipulated eight days' notice. The Soviet transit began on May 30, and the first groups consisted of support vessels. No further requests were made during the crisis period. The Soviets soon made it clear that they did not intend to support the United States in raising the blockade, so the movement could not be construed as a preparation for this. Although the ten warships would double the Soviet naval contingent, they would not challenge the numerical superiority of the Sixth Fleet, let alone the strength that would be amassed if the Royal Navy joined. Of the total Soviet force deployed in early June, however, six were missile firing and could potentially pose a tangible threat to the two US carrier groups.

What is significant is what the Russians did *not* send into the Mediterranean. Although their new deployment was a major departure from past patterns, they could have made a much greater show of force. Their Black Sea order of battle in June showed a force of fifty-three units, and there was always the possibility of reinforcement from the Northern and Baltic Fleets, particularly of subsurface units (see the chronology below).

The Soviets had ample time in which to implement a policy that later was to become commonplace, "contingency scheduling"—that is, alerting the Turks to naval moves yet retaining the option not to deploy. Such a policy enabled them to deploy a larger-than-normal force in a crisis. The Soviets either had not realized the potential of such a policy in May 1967 or were not convinced of the value of a dramatic surge of naval power. The latter is much more likely. It is possible that the Soviets fully realized that in the last resort any naval intervention was foolhardy. They had neither the tactical air nor the amphibious capability.

What then was the purpose of the initial Soviet response? The additional units may have been deployed in response to the move of the two US strike carriers (*Saratoga* and *America*) into the Sea of Crete area on May 29. This is an unlikely explanation. The Sea of Crete could be regarded as a normal holding position of the Sixth Fleet for such a situation, and a move there could not be construed as a departure from the normal operating pattern or a declaration of intent. The Soviet reinforcement can also be seen as a gesture of support for Nasser, as an augmentation of the normal shadowing effort or to field sufficient force to complicate US decision making without posing more than a short-term threat in the event of confrontation. The avoidance of confrontation was clearly paramount in Moscow's thinking.

What has to be considered therefore is what the Soviets assessed as the most likely mode of American intervention and how it could best be countered. The role of the eighteen-unit Soviet naval force assumes less importance in this context, except that by increasing the number of shadowing vessels the Soviets were able to track American movements—and, incidentally, confirm to the Soviet high command that US carrier aircraft were not supporting Israeli land actions, despite public Soviet and Arab claims to the contrary. The Soviets, then, would align themselves with the Arabs, derive great propaganda benefit from doing so, and probably enjoy considerable tangible gain from an Arab defeat. In this context, the Soviet deployment makes sense and the role of the Sixth Fleet as a transmitter of national intentions toward the Soviets assumes more significance.

The Soviet navy conducted shadowing. At no time did the Soviets become aggressive in the way that they had been in the Sea of Japan on May 11, 1967, when a US destroyer had been harassed and eventually bumped by a Soviet ship. They kept track of all major US Navy and Royal Navy movements and did so in full view of the international press, there being many reporters on board the US carriers. The two carrier groups that had arrived in the eastern Mediterranean and taken station, one to the northeast of Crete and the other to the southwest, were shadowed throughout. On June 3 Reuters told the world that a Soviet destroyer had joined the two minesweepers that had arrived off Malta three days earlier and were observing exercises between the British carrier *Victorious* and four of her frigate escorts. *Victorious* had left the Suez Canal on May 22, en route to the United Kingdom from the Far East. The British government kept her in Malta to await developments.

On June 3 the Turks reported that three Soviet frigates and two auxiliaries (part of the Soviet ten-ship force) had transited the Bosporus. The following day the world learned from the newspapers that a guided-missile destroyer

The aircraft carrier USS America *(CVA 66)* US NAVY

had relieved the destroyer tailing the USS *America*. The *Saratoga* was being tailed by a Soviet intelligence trawler, an AGI. The world was kept informed of the Western fleet's movements. In 1956 during the Suez crisis, the world had known that the US Sixth Fleet had left its normal operating areas, but the fleet had then closed in on Suez without anyone knowing where it was. However, in 1967 the Russians were able to observe every move and report it. As the crisis developed, it was in the best interest of the United States that this should be so.

During the buildup to the June War the USS *Intrepid* was transiting the Mediterranean en route to Vietnam. She was deliberately routed well to the south of the main task forces and directed to wait off Libya for permission to pass through the Suez Canal. The Americans in this way deliberately gave an unmistakable sign to the Soviets that they were holding back and not augmenting the Sixth Fleet. It was made clear to the Soviets that *Intrepid* remained under the command of Commander-in-Chief US Naval Forces Europe (CINCUSNAVEUR), as a unit transiting to another theater normally would, and not of Commander Sixth Fleet—a clear message that *Intrepid* was not joining the Sixth Fleet. On May 31 *Intrepid* entered the canal and then headed east. She had been trailed by the Soviets throughout.

While the Soviet ships shadowed major US units, others exercised between Sicily and the Ionian Sea. On June 4, the one cruiser that the Soviets

USS Saratoga *(CVA 60)*   US NAVY

had deployed to the Mediterranean was sighted with ten other ships at anchor a hundred miles northwest of Crete. In other words, shortly before President Nasser was to suffer military humiliation the small Soviet force was largely inactive but for the tattletales. There were no signs of a tacit blockade of the Israeli coast or serious intervention with the Sixth Fleet. It was not until June 8 that the Soviets offered USS *America* any harassment. If the Soviets were going to intervene, it was not going to be from the sea.

In this context, the permission of the president of Yugoslavia, Josip Broz Tito, for Soviet overflights assumes far more significance. Tito's aim was solely pro-Arab. Tito interpreted the Israeli attack as an American-inspired move to cause Nasser's downfall. He was not pro-Soviet. His consistency of policy is shown by the fact that he later advised Nasser to reconsider seriously the wisdom of allowing the Russians into Egypt.

Initial US naval moves were precautionary and limited, designed to indicate a "wait and see" posture to the Soviets; these moves were made known internationally. All routine visits and leave continued; the US Marines in Naples left for Malta on May 25, arriving on the 29th, and normal leave was promptly given. The movement of the USS *Intrepid* has already been mentioned. Despite the Soviets' somewhat ominous rejection of France's plan for a four-power conference to try to settle the crisis, the Sixth Fleet remained passive. The whole striking force of the Sixth Fleet, except for the two-thousand-strong Marine battalion, cruising the Sea of Crete, was in a good position for a quick move toward the two-hundred-mile zone off the eastern Mediterranean coast. This was about twenty minutes' flying time for a US Navy F-4 Phantom to main Arab targets. There was a US naval force east of Suez patrolling the Gulf, Arabian Sea, and Red Sea area. A destroyer was sent south from the Sixth Fleet at the end of May. Normally a ship from this detachment would have gone north, but as a precaution this was not done, leaving three destroyers in the area and a command ship. This happened on June 2, at the same time that US ASW forces were moving from the North Atlantic into the Mediterranean.

What were the options for the use of the Sixth Fleet? Until the Arab closure of the Gulf of Aqaba, the Sixth Fleet remained in a wait-and-see posture. The geographic position that the White House told the fleet to hold was a natural one, given all the factors discussed above. However, there were options that the president could have exercised. He could have kept his force well to the West, increasing air reconnaissance. In fact, air reconnaissance operations were shifted eastward from Rota in Spain to Sigonella, Sicily, and Souda in Crete and were accelerated without difficulty. It is unlikely that Israel would have been less belligerent after its initial successes if it were indicated that the US guarantee was not inviolable. At the same time, US absence from the immediate area would not have jeopardized Israeli integrity, since a reversal of its military fortunes therefore requiring US intervention on Israel's behalf was most unlikely.

However, the Arab nations and the Soviets might have been impressed by a US clear indication that Washington was not going along with an Israeli attack on the scale that had ensued after the first strikes. Not only would the Arab nations be less critical of US policy after the loss of the war and propaganda opportunities, but the Soviets (and indirectly the Yugoslavs) could not have made capital of the so-called US commitment to Israeli policy. The effect after the war could have been considerable and the US position might not have been eroded as much as it was. Had the war gone badly for the Israelis, a sudden surge of US naval power from the Balearics to eastern Cyprus would surely have impressed everyone and sent a clear signal, perhaps far clearer than the steady-state deployment during the buildup. A small force could have been left in the eastern Mediterranean with the ostensible role of evacuating American citizens if the need arose, although most evacuation plans centered on airlifts. On June 10 the Greek ship *Karena* left Alexandria with American evacuees, escorted by two destroyers from Sixth Fleet.

An alternative option, and one at the opposite end of the spectrum from the western position, would have been the Greek islands. This, however, would have reduced the ability of the president to send clear signals to the Soviets of his intentions and would have led to doubts in the Soviet mind as to the true purpose of the fleet. If this had been associated with evasive tactics and US harassment of Soviet tattletales, tension could have been increased, not decreased.

What was the nature of US/Soviet exchanges? Given the American firepower available, the Soviets appeared to have become onlookers. The early hotline discussions between Moscow and Washington revealed a wait-and-see approach on the Soviets' part as well. The Soviets' rejection of the US plan for a cease-fire and their prevarications in the UN indicate several possible scenarios. Israeli successes, although great, may not have seemed totally conclusive to the Russians. They may have expected an Arab counterattack. The quality of their intelligence may have been poor, especially when the Arabs themselves became confused and disorganized. The Soviets may well have wished the Arab nations to be at the brink of disaster, to open the way for the Soviet patronage. When the Israelis began their attack on the Golan Heights at 0600 on June 9, the Soviet premier, Aleksey Kosygin, in Moscow became more alarmed. Although he knew that the United States was not assisting the Israelis and that the Sixth Fleet was passive, he now wanted Washington to put pressure on the Israelis. Kosygin had certainly miscalculated in his assessment of the ability of the United States to influence Israel.

In Moscow and Washington it seemed clear that Damascus might fall. After a strongly worded note to the Israelis, Kosygin warned Washington of the possibility of Soviet intervention. At this point President Johnson ordered the Sixth Fleet toward the Syrian coast. On the face of it, the Russians now faced the possibility of massive US and Israeli air attacks if they attempted a paratrooper drop or gave air-to-ground support, with all the consequences should this start a general war. But what was the true significance of the movement of the Sixth Fleet toward the Syrian coast? The above is too simple. An alternative interpretation is that it was a gesture, that no tangible political gain stemmed from it even in terms of "signaling." The Russians probably realized this too and so were not at all concerned that their naval presence was so inferior, the reason being that they saw the crisis in different terms.

The Soviets knew, as indeed did the United States, that the Americans' creation in 1967 of an infrastructure with Israel to facilitate military intervention in the event of a crisis was highly dangerous diplomatically. It was also counter to general US policy. The need for "all situation" contingency planning could not support it. If the UAR and USSR had exposed it, not only the United States would have been weakened but also Israel. It may also have tied the United States to Israel in an unacceptable way; the Soviets knew that the Israelis would go it alone and that the state of US-Israeli relations did not permit this sort of cooperation. In Soviet eyes this point may have reduced the role of the Sixth Fleet, and it goes some way to explaining the relative inactivity of the Soviet units. The Sixth Fleet's position in the eastern Mediterranean may have been counterproductive in the light of the aftermath of the war.

In Soviet eyes, any force, in order to be credible, must have the capacity to adjust to changing tactical situations. From the command-and-control center in Moscow, how credible did Sixth Fleet intervention appear, and how effective would it be? It must be remembered that the United States had always stressed that it would intervene only to save Israel from invasion. Contingency planning in any fast-moving situation is difficult. Such planning tends to be on a twenty-four-hour basis and would have been completely ad hoc, unlike today, when the United States and United Kingdom can react in much shorter time frames. The Israelis have always been well prepared for military eventualities, and their air force's centralized command system would facilitate Sixth Fleet air coordination. Sixth Fleet's real problems may have arisen from its own system. The Seventh Fleet had learned in Vietnam that in a complex politico-military environment the president and the secretary of defense take virtual command of coordinating air strikes in the initial stages. The JCS would be transmitting White House orders for the rules of engagement, target and weapon selection, and the timing and frequency of attack.

At the same time, US-Israeli coordination would have to embrace quickly such factors as intelligence, target selection, search and rescue (SAR) for Sixth Fleet aircraft, frequencies, code words, call-signs, identification-friend-or-foe (IFF) and air-traffic-control liaison, electronic warfare (EW) coordination, and the use of fueling facilities and airfields. The United States might insist upon having forward ground controllers. Although the US Navy had considerable experience of this sort of coordination in Vietnam and there were several officers with this background on the staff of the Sixth Fleet's commander, Vice Admiral William Martin, the real problem when launching this sort of operation is not technical but political. The instant creation of a barrier to protect the attack carriers (CVAs, as known then) against all eventualities would pose a major problem to the fleet staff. The Soviets could see these dangers as well as the Americans and would be as wary of intervention as anyone.

There were significant wider implications as well. If the Soviets had sent a token force into Syria in the event of the bombardment of Damascus by Israel, it is unlikely that the president of the United States would intervene to support a client who was now going beyond the bounds of acceptable gain. This consideration lessens the significance of the Sixth Fleet in Soviet eyes but heightens that of a clear understanding between superpowers of each other's positions and the extent to which they would support their clients. On the other hand, the extent to which the Soviets would have tried to restrain the Arab nations is speculative. They would most certainly not welcome the prospect of the United States being forced into intervention to help a beleaguered Israel. The "rules of the game" proposed by the distinguished American analyst of the USSR James McConnell most certainly apply in this context. The late Secretary of State Dean Rusk told the author in 1977 that the president and he had assumed that the Soviets would use airborne forces for intervention had the Israelis not desisted in their thrust toward Damascus. Damascus was the line that the Soviets could not allow the Israelis to cross, and Washington was well aware of it. Pressure from the United States on Israel to accept a cease-fire was exerted very much with this in mind, as well as concern about Israel's true intentions.

As far as is known, the Soviets never placed any of their airborne forces on alert. Helmut Sonnenfeldt, a National Security Council adviser at the time, confirmed with the author in 1977 that Kosygin's threats were real enough but that it was unlikely that the Soviets would have intervened directly. They were more likely to have increased pressure by announcing such an alert if the Israelis had not stopped. It is a point of conjecture as to what the United States would have done in the event of Soviet intervention to deter a further Israeli advance. Dean Rusk suggested in our conversation that Sixth Fleet aircraft would most likely have been sent to Israeli airfields, but he could not envisage them being used beyond that. He confirmed that there were no contingency plans and certainly no joint US-Israeli plans. The United States was steering a most difficult course and in the event was to suffer considerable Arab invective in the aftermath for in fact having kept as neutral as was feasible. However, it is the long term that is important, and the benefits of a consistent policy were reaped, despite Soviet propaganda, when Soviet-Egyptian relations reached their nadir in July 1972.

The Israeli-Syrian peace saved the situation, and the Sixth Fleet turned westward. The Israelis had achieved their aim, and the Syrians wanted peace.

The Soviets had been faced with a major decision, and although the peace preempted any real threat, the presence of the Sixth Fleet in a potentially hostile position had been a factor, one that they could not ignore. At the same time, Kosygin's threat to President Johnson that the Soviets would intervene had had to be backed up by some tangible sign of capability.

What may we conclude from the above analysis? The size of the Soviet commitment had been in keeping with the state of Arab–Soviet relations. It had reflected Soviet interest and support, but the capability and deployment pattern showed that Moscow had had no intention of using sea power other than for tracking purposes. A much larger force could have been deployed, but this again would not necessarily have achieved the desired results but merely antagonized the United States. The presence of the Sixth Fleet had been a major obstacle to any form of Soviet intervention from the sea, either directly or in some way meant to deter the Israelis (e.g., a threat of a blockade).

The superpowers became acutely involved once the Israelis made gains disproportionate in Soviet eyes and that seemed counterproductive to Washington as well. The preponderance of US naval power may have become less significant to the Soviets in the context of Israeli military success. The Soviets had an alternative contingency available in the form of air supply. This was not affected by the naval configuration. As a result the Soviets were able to give tangible support to the Arab nations and thus maintain credibility. At the same time, they were able to claim that they had neutralized the Sixth Fleet. Whatever the naval realities, it was Egyptian perception of Soviet assistance that counted.

The Sixth Fleet did have a clear diplomatic role, as a fast and effective transmitter of signals. Aside from "hotline" calls, nothing else gave more tangible expression to American intentions. The Soviets, again, could have deployed a much larger naval force, and it remains a point of conjecture how much that would have assisted the peace negotiations and therefore the furtherance of Arab interests.

The Soviets were concerned with one key domain: their national self-interest. The details of their later aid programs and deployments are well documented and analyzed in several studies. They achieved their primary aims—use of Egyptian ports and considerable influence through reequipping and retraining the defeated Arab armies. Soviet-built Tu-16 Badger aircraft with Egyptian markings but flown by Soviet crews began maritime reconnaissance of the Sixth Fleet. One month after the war was concluded, two Soviet naval groups entered Port Said and Alexandria. The Russians claimed that they were there to prevent aggression. This not only was a gesture to the regime but acted as a deterrent to further Israeli strikes, inasmuch as damage to Russian ships could act as a casus belli for intervention.

Whatever the nature and extent of Soviet propaganda during the crisis, the Kremlin was able to assess the extent of the US commitment partly from the posture of the Sixth Fleet. The Soviets knew that the United States had not encouraged the Israelis to attack. If the United States had maintained a lower profile with the Sixth Fleet and awaited initial military results before formulating reactions to the Israeli position, the postwar position of the United States in the Arab world might have been more favorable. Only hindsight allows this sort of speculation.

Where did the United Kingdom and the Royal Navy fit into all this? Despite the strong British presence in the Gulf of Aden (a force headed by the carrier HMS *Hermes*), the British government played a waiting game, because of the ramifications of any Arab oil boycott. Lifting the blockade of the Gulf of Aqaba would have made the Israeli strike less justifiable but would not necessarily have prevented it. The Israeli postwar position would have been the same, and Anglo-US intervention would have been seen as another pro-Israeli posture. However, the United Kingdom had significant naval assets in the region as a whole, and the Soviet Union was very much aware of it. In the very worst case, the Royal Navy would have augmented US naval and Marine capabilities.

It has been said that a superpower may forego support to a client if the latter engages in excesses that produce greater risk of general confrontation than the marginal gains they achieve, and similarly that a major threat to the client's vital interests can justify intervention. In the June War of 1967 the US Sixth Fleet could not become directly involved on either count. However, as has been argued earlier, a lower profile for the Sixth Fleet might have produced a better postwar diplomatic position for the United States. The Royal Navy kept a much lower profile, for the political reasons mentioned above.

The extent to which a major fleet can augment political goals is not always directly proportional to its apparent military capability. A fleet may be militarily effective but if deployed inappropriately may defeat the very object of the exercise. This may be true of the use of the Sixth Fleet during the 1967 war. Evacuation of US citizens could have been achieved by other means with a limited naval effort in the eastern Mediterranean. The availability of airpower to support other US interests, such as the USS *Liberty* after the attack on that ship (we will address this attack later), has to be weighed against the benefit of not deploying forward. Incidents such as that involving the USS *Liberty* further increase risks of escalation. In that case US carrier aircraft were launched to go to its rescue. The timely message from Tel Aviv expressing Israel's "abject apologies" for the attack may have forestalled an unfortunate clash of US and Egyptian forces.

If forward deployment in a crisis situation is to have credibility in strict military terms, the opposing superpower or adversary must perceive one's ability to intervene in time and within other constraints. In 1967 the ability of the US Sixth Fleet and the Royal Navy to intervene was limited. Forward deployment in a hostile diplomatic environment without the infrastructure to conduct tangible military intervention within necessary time scales can therefore be counterproductive. The Soviets' logistical capabilities and their ability to establish a military infrastructure in client states may have been as significant, or more, than the outward demonstration of naval deployment. Political intention and, in the event, military capability should be assessed with these background factors as much in mind as straightforward naval considerations when reviewing the Soviet ability to use naval power during the Cold War for diplomatic purposes. However, by the same token, the very presence of significant naval and marine forces poses a hugely countervailing factor for any adversary to consider if the situation escalates out of control. The deterrent aspect is self-evident. This theme is one that we will explore and examine as we move through our time frame.

The compressed time scale of the events leading to the 1967 war and of the war itself may have militated against a more flexible deployment policy for the Sixth Fleet. The need to be within quick flying time from the Israeli and Egyptian coasts must have seemed compelling. Holding back was more difficult than sailing the fleet eastward. However, if the fleet had been withheld in the west and a sudden surge later found necessary because the situation deteriorated, the Soviets would have done little to oppose it. It is unlikely that the Soviets would have construed this surge as unduly provocative. Hotline calls would have confirmed its necessity.

Later crises subsequently revealed the different ways in which Washington could use the US Sixth Fleet. The response required in 1973 was surely different from that required in 1967. What the 1967 war demonstrated was that the Sixth Fleet could be used as a flexible instrument of diplomacy. The events of 1967 also demonstrated that forward deployment is not always most advantageous and that non–forward deployment does not necessarily weaken the role of the fleet or undermine its raison d'être. The US Navy learned that by varying the operating patterns of the Sixth Fleet it could signal the Soviet Union its intentions. Key to all this was one, very simple but overriding factor: continuous operational presence in a region with at-sea support, basing, and a sustaining logistics chain. The US Navy has never forgotten this critical factor. The need to be able to complement this capability with surge forces in a timely manner was also a lesson that was never forgotten; it has impacted readiness preparation in the continental United States.

Table 4-1 lays out the Soviet Black Sea Fleet deployments of its surface ships into the Mediterranean. Submarines are not covered. To this day, neither the US Navy nor the Royal Navy discloses its knowledge of the positional data or movements of Soviet or other threat submarines. The chronology provides a detailed breakdown of the main political and naval events of the 1967 June War.

Let us now address one of the most sensitive aspects of the 1967 June War, the attack by Israel on the US Navy spy ship USS *Liberty,* the most highly decorated ship in the service's history for a single action. Thirty-four members of the crew were killed in action. The commanding officer, Commander (later Captain) William McGonagle, was awarded the Medal of Honor, and his crew was awarded two Navy Crosses, eleven Silver Stars, twenty bronze stars, and 205 Purple Hearts, thirty-four posthumously. In addition USS *Liberty* was awarded a Presidential Unit Citation, with all crewmen receiving the

TABLE 4-1 Black Sea Fleet Deployment of Surface Ships to the Mediterranean

TYPE	MEAN DAILY 1967 DEPLOYMENT	MAY 1967 MINIMUM	MAY 1967 MAXIMUM	JUNE 1967 MINIMUM	JUNE 1967 MAXIMUM
Major Combatants					
Missile-Armed	2.4	0	2	1	6
(SAM)	1.5	0	2	1	4
(SSM)	1.0	0	0	0	2
Nonmissile Cruiser/Destroyer	2.0	0	–	2	4
Escort	2.2	3	6	2	6
Total Major Combatants	6.6	3	8	5	16
Minor Combatants	1.4	0	3	2	3
Intelligence (AGI)	1.8	1	2	1	3
Amphibious	1.3	0	0	0	3
Auxiliary	5.4	2	6	5	8
Other*	1.4	0	0	0	0
Total	17.9	6	19	13	33

* Other includes base development and scientific ships.

Combat Action Ribbon and the National Defense Ribbon—an extraordinary and unique record of their valor in fighting and saving their ship.

It is not the intention in the analysis that follows to enter into some aspects of the controversy that remains over Israeli actions and intentions. The issues have been discussed in multiple books and journal articles, and they have been the subject of several documentaries around the globe. The attack on *Liberty* gained the attention of several highly reputable media outlets, such as the BBC. Readers may consult any of these sources for what occurred in the eastern Mediterranean on June 8, 1967, and form their own opinions on what may have happened. However, readers are encouraged to consult one online source, namely, the usslibertydocumentcenter.org, which contains a collection of unique documents relating to the attack on the *Liberty*. This collection is the result of the decades of work by a late former Chief of Naval Operations and chairman of the Joint Chiefs of Staff, Admiral Thomas Moorer, and several other luminaries dedicated to ensuring that as much material as possible regarding the attack was available to the public. Admiral Moorer's colleagues included US Marine Corps four-star general Ray Davis, who won the Medal of Honor at the Chosin Reservoir in Korea; Rear Admiral Merlin Staring, who was the Judge Advocate of the Navy during the tenure of Sen. John Warner of Virginia as Secretary of the Navy; Ambassador James Akins, a former ambassador to Saudi Arabia; and Rear Admiral Clarence "Mark" Hill, a distinguished naval aviator and carrier battle group commander. This document center is rich in both factual and interpretive material.

Your author was involved in the mid-1970s with assembling and analyzing for the US Navy what happened on that fateful day during the height of the June War. We examined data at an all-source level; some of the key material has still not been released and may not be for many years. However, the documentary evidence available is substantial and authoritative. The evidence of the US secretary of state at the time, Dean Rusk, and of the director of the Central Intelligence Agency, Richard Helms, in 1967 is compelling and perhaps decisive if analyzed alongside data in the document center.

It is the intent here to confine the discussion to the nature of operations of a US Navy spy ship, how such a ship fitted into the overall intelligence tapestry in the 1960s, and how the US Navy and the Royal Navy worked together. We have seen already how the Soviet AGIs, together with the clandestinely used Soviet and Warsaw Pact merchant fleets, fitted into the overall Soviet Ocean Surveillance System. The US Navy went one step farther, in terms of both technical sophistication and exploitation, by building highly capable spy ships. The USS *Liberty*'s hull number was AGTR 5, denoting an innocuous

Main Political and Naval Events during the June War 1967

NAVAL

APRIL 24
1 Riga-class Soviet destroyer escort in the Mediterranean (April 24–June 24).

MAY 11
2 Soviet Mirka II PECs arrive off Gibraltar from the north. They remain in the Mediterranean until June 22.

MAY 10
Soviet anticarrier exercises begin in the eastern Atlantic, lasting to May 27.

MAY 12
1 Soviet Kirov-class cruiser in the Mediterranean until June 25. Soviet Kashin-class DLG in the Mediterranean until June 23. 1 Soviet Riga-class DE in the Mediterranean until June 16.

MAY 10/11
US destroyer bumped in the Sea of Japan by a Soviet warship.

MAY 20
1 Soviet Kotlin-class DD in the Mediterranean until July 16.

APR 24 25 26 27 28 29 30 MAY 1 2 3 4 5 6 7 8 9 10 11 12 13 14 15 16 17 18 19 20

POLITICAL

APRIL–MAY Israeli villages shelled from Syria. Israeli air raids against Syrian positions.

MAY 8
Major Syrian terrorist action inside Israel.

MAY 16
State of emergency declared in Egypt.

MAY 14
UAR parliamentary delegation leaves the USSR having been given a warning of a possible Israeli strike. Egyptian armor and infantry move into Sinai.

MAY 18
On request from Cairo the UN withdraws from the armistice line between Israel and the UAR. IDF and IAF reserves are mobilized.

CINCEUR: Commander-in-Chief US European Command   DE: destroyer escort   DD: destroyer   DDG: guided-missile destroyer   DDGS: antiship-missile destroyer   DLG: guided-missile frigate ("destroyer leader")   HQ: headquarters   IAF: Israel Air Force   IDF: Israel Defense Force   LSD: dock landing ship   LSM: medium landing ship   LST: tank landing ship   OPLAN: Operation Plan   PEC: patrol escort   USAREUR: US Army in Europe   Z: "Zulu" (Greenwich) time

MAY 22
The British carrier HMS *Victorious* leaves the Suez Canal for Malta. The USSR notifies Turkey of its intent to transit 10 warships through the straits (8 days' notice required).

MAY 23
USS *Saratoga* and *America* are ordered toward the eastern Mediterranean.

MAY 25
US Navy delays plans to send the USS *Intrepid* through the Suez en route to Vietnam. The British carrier HMS *Hermes* is ordered to return to the Red Sea area from her passage to the Far East. The US amphibious task force leaves Naples for Malta.

MAY 29
USS *Saratoga* and *America* rendezvous in the Sea of Crete, with the fleet commander, Vice Admiral William Martin, flying his flag in the cruiser USS *Little Rock*, accompanied by cruiser *Galveston* and 10 destroyers.

MAY 30
1 Soviet submarine tender in the Mediterranean until June 8. An AGI begins tailing the *Saratoga* and breaks off on June 7.

MAY 31
USS *Intrepid* is ordered through the Suez Canal to the Gulf of Aqaba. Other US units remain in the Sea of Crete. Soviet submarine tender arrives in the Mediterranean and remains until October 3.

MAY 21 22 23 24 25 26 27 28 29 30 31 »»

MAY 21
Israel and Egypt announced the calling up of reserves.

MAY 25
Israeli foreign minister arrives in Washington, D.C. UAR doubles its forces in Sinai. US suggests a multinational maritime force to keep open the Gulf of Aqaba; this fails.

MAY 30
Turkey says that it will not allow US bases in Turkey to be used against the Arabs. Egypt and Jordan enter a defense pact.

MAY 23
President Johnson's speech calling for restraint.

Main Political and Naval Events
during the June War 1967 (continued)

NAVAL

JUNE 1
USS *America* is tailed by a Soviet destroyer 50 miles south of Crete.

JUNE 3
1 Soviet Kildin-class DDGS in the Mediterranean until August 31, 1 Soviet Kashin-class DLG in the Mediterranean until September 13, 1 modified Soviet Kotlin-class DD in the Mediterranean until August 13. Two Soviet auxiliaries also transit from the Black Sea.

JUNE 2
USS *Liberty* sails from Rota, Spain, for the Mideast. A Soviet destroyer joins 2 mine-sweepers off Malta tailing the British carrier *Victorious* and 4 frigate escorts. The destroyer USS *Dyess* joins 2 US destroyers and a command ship in the Red Sea. US ASW forces move from the North Atlantic into the Mediterranean. Six frigates and a minesweeper squadron have joined the *Hermes* near Aden.

JUNE 4
1 Soviet Krupny-class DDGS in the Mediterranean until August 31. A Soviet GMD relieves the destroyer tailing *America*. The Sixth Fleet is ordered to operate NW of a line from 36° 28' N, 30° E and the coast of Libya at 23° E. A Soviet cruiser and 10 other ships are sighted at anchor 100 miles NW of Crete.

JUNE ① ② ③ ④

POLITICAL

CINCEUR: Commander-in Chief US European Command   DE: destroyer escort   DD: destroyer   DDG: guided-missile destroyer
DDGS: antiship-missile destroyer   DLG: guided-missile frigate ("destroyer leader")   HQ: headquarters   IAF: Israel Air Force
IDF: Israel Defense Force   LSD: dock landing ship   LSM: medium landing ship   LST: tank landing ship   OPLAN: Operation Plan
PEC: patrol escort   USAREUR: US Army in Europe   Z: "Zulu" (Greenwich) time

JUNE 5
2 Soviet W-class submarines sighted at the Kithera anchorage. USS *America* 50 miles SE of Crete (370 miles east of Port Said and 540 miles from Haifa). *Saratoga* is 110 miles NW of *America* on the northern side of Crete. Both carriers steam approximately 800 miles per day. Both carriers are at readiness State 3. The LSD USS *Shadwell* sails from Souda Bay to rejoin the amphibious task force at Malta.

JUNE 6
1100 local, *America* 100 miles east of Crete and steaming eastward at 20 knots. This is Admiral Martin's decision, not the White House's.

JUNE 8
Soviet airlift to the UAR, Syria, Algeria, and Iraq begins. Soviet harassment of USS *America* occurs. 1200Z, USS *Liberty* is attacked by Israeli forces. Carrier aircraft are launched to protect her. The amphibious task force leaves Malta.

JUNE 7
1200 local, USS *America* steaming westward 60 miles SE of Crete. USSR announces the indefinite postponement of a visit by a Kashin-class guided-missile ship to Portsmouth, England. An AGI leaves the Black Sea to supplement the Mediterranean AGI force.

JUNE ⑤ ⑥ ⑦ ⑧ >>>

JUNE 5
At 0600 war begins with Israeli air strikes. 0730, King Hussein summons all heads of missions and claims that US carriers have been used in a preemptive strike. 1300Z, HQ USAREUR and 7th Army Operations Center stand by to implement OPLAN T-3 AE 215.

JUNE 6
UN Security Council unanimously adopts a resolution for an immediate cease-fire.

JUNE 7
CINCEUR message of 1200Z states, "The activities of Soviet military forces do not indicate preparations for direct military participation. Soviet and East European ground and air force training appear to be routine." US ambassador in Amman signals Washington to push for a cease-fire, because Hussein regime may fall. Jordan stops fighting at midnight, but Israelis continue to attack Jordanian West Bank.

Main Political and Naval Events
during the June War 1967 (continued)

NAVAL

JUNE 9
USS *America* and the cruiser *Little Rock* sailing to the rescue of USS *Liberty*. 1230Z, the rendezvous occurs.

JUNE 30
2 Polnocny-class LSMs deploy from the Black Sea. 2 Alligator LSTs deploy east of Cyprus.

JUNE 10
President Johnson orders the Sixth Fleet eastward; later the fleet reverses course. Kotlin 514 breaks off surveillance of USS *Saratoga* at midday. The US amphibious task force discontinues passage eastward.

JULY 2
Soviet units visit Port Said and Alexandria.

MAY 4, 1968
First Soviet reconnaissance flight against a US CVA in the Mediterranean by Egypt-based Soviet aircraft.

JUNE 12–22
NATO ASW exercise Go Ahead in the Atlantic.

JUNE 14
Soviet combatants east of Cyprus.

JUNE 9 10 11 12 13 14 15 16 17 18 19 20 21 22 23 24 25 26 27 28 29 30 JULY 1 2 ... MAY 4, 1968

POLITICAL

JUNE 9
0600, the Israelis attack the Golan Heights.

JUNE 10
USSR delivers an ultimatum to Israel. The war ends.

JUNE 15
Libya asks the US and Britain to remove bases.

CINCEUR: Commander-in Chief US European Command   DE: destroyer escort   DD: destroyer   DDG: guided-missile destroyer   DDGS: antiship-missile destroyer   DLG: guided-missile frigate ("destroyer leader")   HQ: headquarters   IAF: Israel Air Force   IDF: Israel Defense Force   LSD: dock landing ship   LSM: medium landing ship   LST: tank landing ship   OPLAN: Operation Plan   PEC: patrol escort   USAREUR: US Army in Europe   Z: "Zulu" (Greenwich) time technical research ship, one that might be deployed for oceanographic and meteorological research or as an equipment test ship. Nothing, of course, was farther from the truth. The USS *Liberty* and her sister ships were highly equipped clandestine SIGINT and ELINT collectors, with state-of-the-art collection and communications systems. In addition, they were staffed with the best of the best from the US Navy cryptographic community, including linguistic experts as well as code breakers. These ships belonged to the special Naval Security Group, not the National Security Agency per se. They came therefore under US Navy command and control, but typically by direction of the Joint Chiefs of Staff. In other words, they were national assets, not echelons of the Fort Meade, Maryland, and the "special" community.

USS *Liberty* did not collect intelligence in the way that a typical US Navy or Royal Navy warship might intercept communications or collect ELINT on a Warsaw Pact target of opportunity. Its team was highly sophisticated and was augmented as the situation demanded. For example, in June 1967 the cryptographic staff on board *Liberty* was augmented in Rota, Spain, with additional specialists, including Mr. Alan Blue, a civilian from the NSA. Special intelligence collection operations by clandestine and often covert assets are fundamentally different from routine naval operations. This point is a bedrock understanding of American and British naval and related intelligence operations. The USS *Liberty* incident is a good starting point.

Before addressing the detail of what occurred in the eastern Mediterranean in June 1967 we need to examine the wider context. In 1977 your author conducted special interviews with Dean Rusk and one of his key advisers, Helmut Sonnenfeldt. My initial focus was the use by the Soviet Union of its navy for political purposes. I was part of a US Navy team trying in the mid-1970s to understand fully the Soviets' modus operandi, their strategic goals, and the role that their growing naval power would play in pursuit of their national interests.

In this connection I asked, what had motivated Israel to perpetrate what appeared to have been an egregious act against the USS *Liberty*? What were the total circumstances, strategic and operational, that had led the Israeli leadership to make the fateful decision to attack and destroy a US eavesdropping ship operating in international waters at the end of the Six-Day War? These were important questions, and in 1977 the attack on *Liberty* was still very much a raw issue. The June war had witnessed Israel redefining its boundaries and asserting its military supremacy. I concluded in 1976–77 and still believe today that the strategic backdrop and US-Soviet relations hold the answers to these questions. Your author concluded that Israel's actions during

USS Liberty *(AGTR 5)*   US NAVY

the Six-Day War brought US–Soviet relations to a stressful peak not seen since the Cuban Missile Crisis.

We need to first recap a few salient facts. In May 1967 President Nasser of Egypt took several major aggressive acts against Israel at the same time that the Syrian government began to encourage the Palestinians to intensify guerilla operations against Israel. On June 5, 1967, Israel launched a stunning preemptive attack. By June 10, when a cease-fire was established, Israel had defeated Egypt, Jordan, and Syria, occupied the Sinai Peninsula and the West Bank of the Jordan River, and had taken the Golan Heights.

Why then would Israel attack the *Liberty* on June 8? The Soviet Union was a key player, not a mere presence in the shadows but a demonstrative protagonist. The Soviets were supporting the new Syrian regime with economic and military aid, while Palestinian guerillas were intensifying their operations against Israel from Syrian bases. At the same time, the Soviets increased their support for Nasser. In mid-May 1967 the Syrians warned the Soviets that the Israelis were going to invade Syria, occupy Damascus, and topple its Baathist regime. The Soviets were obstructionist, derailing international peace efforts.

It was at this point that USS *Liberty* and its brave crew was forward deployed. It was at the "pointy end of the spear"; in one sense, as an eavesdropping ship, she was the point itself. What did Washington want? The administration wanted to be inside the minds and see the intentions of all the main players, including Israel. The *Liberty* was on station to help unravel the plans, goals, and operations of the key players. The US president and secretary of state realized that Israel's war plan could spell disaster for US–Soviet relations should it produce an attack upon Syria, Moscow's client.

We will sidestep for a moment and then come back to the main theme. Where was the US Navy while all this was happening? The Soviets' Fifth Eskadra, although their Sixth Fleet equivalent, for want of a better comparison, was qualitatively and quantitatively weaker, despite augmentations via the Turkish Straits. The Soviets created what became known later as standard anticarrier task groups, for the effective shadowing of the *America* and *Saratoga* battle groups. The word "tattletale" entered the US Navy's lexicon at this time. The USSR made preparatory moves with its ground forces and, in particular, its airborne forces. Both the United States and the Soviet Union showed constraint at sea, despite incidents in the Sea of Japan on May 10 and May 11. It became very clear how Moscow intended to respond militarily.

Did the Soviet Union plan to intervene, and why? The first answer is "yes"; the "why" is that Israel intended to invade Syria and take Damascus. This single fact is the key. In response the Soviets planned to do two things: provide military resupply to Syria and intervene directly. The Soviets began operations on June 8, 1967, the day that the *Liberty* was attacked. Their plan was to drop paratroopers into Syria and place them between an advancing Israeli army and Damascus. How did the Soviet Union plan to execute retaliation? An-12 Cub aircraft, the standard Soviet paratroop and cargo transports, flew from fields in Hungary across Yugoslavia and then over the Adriatic and Mediterranean to Syria. The Soviet operational plans and actions were not spontaneous reactions to the Israeli advance. They were well planned in advance; Yugoslavia had granted overflight rights. The Soviets were poised to take on the Israelis. The threat to intervene was made emphatically when the Syrian forces collapsed as the Israelis stormed the Golan Heights on June 9, a collapse that left the road to Damascus virtually undefended. The Cold War balance was now becoming dangerously out of kilter. The hotline quickly became an extraordinary successful means of preventing a major conflict. By that channel Moscow made it clear: if the Israelis did not desist, the Soviet army would execute a massive airborne drop into Syria and confront the Israelis.

It was in March 1977 that I interviewed, as noted above, Dean Rusk and Helmut Sonnenfeldt. They made me privy to remarkable perspectives and data not previously released. Both men gave permission to publish their comments at the unclassified level. Rusk told me that he and President Johnson "had never assumed any other" than that the Soviets would use their airborne forces. I wrote the following about Dean Rusk: "His feeling at the time was one of despair if the Cease-Fire had not held and the Israelis not halted when they did." I asked Rusk what the United States would have done; he believed that the United States would have landed Sixth Fleet aircraft in Israel to deter the Soviets from invading it. He believed the latter highly likely once the Soviet airborne forces had overwhelmed the Israelis: they would retake the Golan Heights and invade Israel itself, a total disaster. President Johnson demanded that the Israelis end their advance into Syria and sent the two Sixth Fleet carrier battle groups nearer to the Syrian coast. The Israeli-Syrian cease-fire came not a moment too soon. As the Duke of Wellington said after the battle of Waterloo, "It was a very close run thing."

USS *Liberty* was in the middle and was finding out more than the Israelis would tolerate. In the heat of battle and crisis, nations can make disastrous mistakes. The Israelis made such an error of judgment. Moreover, their advance into Syria bought superpower confrontation dangerously close. The timing of the *Liberty* attack on June 8, 1967, was such that Washington knew that the Soviet Union was not responsible—the Americans had very good intelligence on the location of Soviet assets.

What were the dynamics of communications during this critical period? What might *Liberty* have been listening to? The United States was interested in everyone's communications: Soviet, Israeli, Syrian, Jordanian, Egyptian, and all their communications with their allies and friends, in particular those of their intelligence services. It was possible to learn a lot from Soviet communications, as much as if not more than from Israeli communications.

Secretary Rusk concluded that the Israelis wanted *Liberty* sunk without trace or survivors, no one to tell what had been done or by whom. The attack was conducted by intense airborne and torpedo boat strikes to minimize communications from *Liberty*. *Liberty*'s destruction would ensure that she could no longer collect vital intelligence, while potentially garnering US support for Israel through a false belief that an Arab country had been responsible. Perhaps it might even push the United States over the edge into supporting Israel's invasion of Syria and possible entry into the outskirts of Damascus, or at least leave Washington publicly neutral, while privately supporting Israel. However, a retaliatory strike by the United States against, for example, Egyptian airfields would have precipitated the very crisis that Dean Rusk sought to avert. If the Israelis had continued into Syria and the United States had attacked Egyptian airfields, one can only speculate on the Soviet reaction. The Israelis could have dragged the United States into a war without the Americans really knowing why. Secretary Rusk believed that Israel had no concern for the consequences of its actions for US–Soviet relations as long as Israel's security objectives were achieved. *Liberty*'s survival denied Israel any ability to exploit its loss and thus compelled President Johnson to urge constraint on Israel, which was also under intense pressure from Moscow. The brave crew of the *Liberty* ensured that their ship survived. They fought for their ship with all means at their disposal. Their courage and survival constitute the enduring hallmark and legacy of USS *Liberty*. These brave men, by fighting for their ship and not giving up, saved the United States from a potentially disastrous embroilment with the Soviet Union over Israel.

Let us now look in detail at the technical and operational events and issues. The relationship between the United States and Israel in 1967 bears no comparison with that of today—Israel was still a relatively new state in 1967, and both the Dwight D. Eisenhower and John F. Kennedy administrations had kept Israel at arm's length since its founding, wishing to be even-handed, both actually to be and appear to be an a honest broker between Israel and the Arab nations. US intelligence in the Middle East was not extensive. The British provided the United States with intelligence from GCHQ and the Secret Intelligence Service often more significant than the United States could garner itself.

The United Kingdom had very special sources and methods in the Middle East in the 1960s. At their heart was data relating to Moshe Dayan's decision to mount a heedless and headlong invasion of Syria, without the prior knowledge or approval of either the prime minister, Levi Eshkol, or the foreign minister, Abba Eban. This latter point is absolutely critical in what happened. The whole of British intelligence in the Middle East was in overdrive, and Washington was as much a customer as the prime minister and foreign secretary in London. The Israeli leaders were never informed until after the event of what Moshe Dayan had ordered. They were not personally culpable, but they were ultimately responsible; they apologized deeply and compensated the United States accordingly.

Secretary Rusk would vehemently state, against strong opposition from the US-based Israeli lobby, that the *Liberty* attack had been deliberate. Why would he do this? Dean Rusk was privy to all the intelligence, some key parts of which have not been disclosed to this day. Neither the British nor the

Americans ever release data that can be used to reconstruct sources, methods, locations of various sites, HUMINT sources, or tradecraft, and certainly not networks that still exist. For example, it was not until 1974 that the British disclosed that a capability called Enigma even existed, let alone its product and effect.

It is crucial to understand the command structure in Israel in 1967, the political-military interfaces, the personality issues, and the agendas that prevailed. Israeli communications, the nation's capabilities, weaknesses, and vulnerabilities, the identities of people in Israel and elsewhere in the Middle East who were either agents or confidants of foreign intelligence services all have to be addressed. Were former Russian Jews in Israel communicating with their Soviet handlers, and if so, might their communications have been intercepted? Key people on the ground in Israel most certainly knew of Moshe Dayan's intentions regarding Syria. Dayan was the wildcard, suddenly appearing as minister of defense. He became the short-lived man of the moment, so considered for several very good reasons and two very unfortunate ones

One other key point needs to be remembered: the USS *Liberty* was spying on Israel, directly and indirectly (via surrogate communications intercepts), and on all the other protagonists in the region. It was listening to the Soviet Union's communications with its clients, Egypt and particularly Syria (and indeed, the Soviet Union was listening to the Israelis). In 1967 and thereafter the United States, for self-evident reasons, did not wish the world to know that it possessed this seagoing intelligence-collection capability, far more capable than anything within the SOSS or anywhere else. So how important was *Liberty?* Very—it represented the ability to milk all the local Soviet communications and to translate and transmit them in very short time frames to decision makers. Secretary Rusk and President Johnson and Prime Minister Harold Wilson in London wanted to know from every source possible not only whether Israel was about to do something so rash that the Soviets would launch forces into Syria but if so when and how the Soviets might intervene. The extra personnel embarked on board *Liberty* while en route to the eastern Mediterranean were critical augmenters to extend the ship's capabilities for these purposes.

From an intelligence-gathering perspective, let us address the fundamental issue of causation, the "why," in context. Various apologists over the years have argued that the devastating air and torpedo boat attacks on the *Liberty* likely resulted from what the Israelis interpreted as naval gunfire, by presumably Egyptian destroyers, in the El Arish area; such apologists have argued that misidentification of the USS *Liberty* as an Egyptian destroyer or other such adversary led to a mistaken attack. Did smoke in the El Arish area really trigger this whole series of events? The documents that Admirals Moorer, Staring, and Hill collected with General Davis point to a striking and somewhat shocking alternative interpretation of events, as do the records of Secretary of State Rusk and CIA director Richard Helms.

There is a very old saying in the national security and intelligence business, "You don't know what you don't know." The absence of Hebrew translators on board USS *Liberty* never detracted from her onboard translation capabilities, because the languages needed were Arabic and Russian. Other sources and methods were monitoring Israeli activities and communications, and they did have immediate Hebrew translation capabilities. The Israelis had no idea what translators were on board *Liberty*. Commander David Lewis, the senior SIGINT officer on board *Liberty* and the Naval Security Group detachment's officer-in-charge, was interested in listening to the Soviets listening to the Israelis.

USS *Liberty* was intercepting Israeli plans and moves via a series of surrogate communications. The notion that *Liberty* had virtually zero capability for SIGINT collection, because of its geographic position and capabilities, raises a fundamental technical question: Would the US Joint Chiefs of Staff and the Naval Security Group dispatch *Liberty,* with the utmost secrecy and urgency, to a location where she would have no capability to collect intelligence? The additional notion that the Israelis essentially told the United States their battle plans, particularly regarding the attack on Syria, the Soviet Union's client, verges on the outrageous. The last thing that Moshe Dayan wanted was for the United States to meddle with his surprise strike on Syria, which it would oppose. As was stated earlier the Israeli prime minister and foreign minister were unaware of actions by Moshe Dayan. *Liberty* was right there, on the line, listening to everything that it could collect. *Liberty* needed all the Russian and Arabic specialists that could be mustered at short notice. NSA civilian specialist Allen Blue gave his life doing what the White House urgently required.

Let us address the claim that *Liberty* had no real SIGINT role because the United States already knew the Israeli game plan and that therefore the Israelis had no reason to attack her. In this view, the attack was a classic "blue-on-blue" incident in which Israeli pilots, with *Liberty* in their gun sights, could not tell what was what.

For several years Commander David Lewis and I have communicated about many aspects of the *Liberty*'s roles and missions. Commander Lewis has been dismayed by several writers' technical misrepresentations and lack of basic knowledge on this subject. He wrote to me very recently regarding the apparent near-obsession of some *Liberty*'s VHF and related line-of-sight (LOS) capabilities and how their limitations would have diminished *Liberty*'s ability to intercept in VHF frequencies. Commander Lewis has stressed to me that VHF was only a part of *Liberty*'s coverage and that VHF is not always LOS: "In 1956 in Germany I heard 5 watt Chicago taxicabs using VHF." There is a very clear implication here. USS *Liberty* was reading all the VHF traffic in the region until an Israeli torpedo destroyed Lewis' special compartments, killing everyone except Lewis, who was severely injured. He confirmed to me at the unclassified level that *Liberty* could listen to Tel Aviv with no problem. USS *Liberty* was not an NSA ship but a Service Squadron 8 asset and a "SIGINT activity," reporting directly to the commander of the Naval Security Group. The NSA had to make requests of *Liberty* via the JCS.

Commander Lewis also drew my attention to the CRITICOM network, established by Eisenhower. This was a sensitive-communications architecture by which a "CRITIC" message could go directly to Washington, closing all switches and bypassing all other emergency traffic; it had to be in the president's hands in no more than ten minutes after origination. He also emphasized another inaccuracy in the *Liberty* literature, the idea that secure voice was the only way to communicate securely in 1967 and for many years thereafter. He stressed that only a few have had access still to the most sensitive aspects of USS *Liberty*'s mission.

Israel planned a surprise attack. This fundamental fact is irrefutable. Both President Johnson and Secretary Rusk knew in due course what was transpiring inside Israel. Both were deeply concerned but also somewhat sympathetic to Eshkol and Eban, because of Dayan's transgressions. It is easy to see why the United States created a cover story and played down a whole panoply of Israeli errors of judgment: Israel had achieved an incredible military victory, with new possessions in Sinai, the West Bank, Gaza, and the Golan Heights; the Soviets had been restrained by Rusk's brilliant diplomacy from flying major forces into Syria to confront the Israeli army. The official unclassified US line was that the Israelis had made a regrettable mistake. Certainly the very top Israeli leadership at the time had no malice toward the United States, but this hides the inner truth of the lack of political control over the minister of defense during a most critical period. What if events had gone awry, if the Soviets had intervened and brought in the forces they had on immediate standby in Hungary? What if Moshe Dayan had not been brought to heel and had tried to send the Israeli army into Damascus? It would have been worse than the Cuban Missile Crisis.

This is how Dean Rusk explained to me his deep concerns and fretful days in June 1967. To his undying credit, Secretary Rusk was a man of such integrity that he would follow only his conscience, what he knew it to be true from all and every source of very special intelligence available. The attack on USS *Liberty* was deliberate.

It is speculative what David Ben Gurion would have done had he been the Israeli prime minister in 1967. Hindsight says that it is unlikely that Moshe Dayan would have been minister of defense. The late Captain Ward Boston Jr., Judge Advocate General Corps USN (Ret.), who had been involved directly in the initial *Liberty* investigation, swore a declaration/affidavit on January 8, 2004, that readers may wish to study. It makes extraordinary reading. His affidavit reflects the fine work of Admiral Moorer's distinguished team that for many years fought for the cause of USS *Liberty* and the revelation of the true story.

Let us now return to the wider issues of what happened to USS *Liberty*. In 1967 the United States and United Kingdom had undoubtedly the best intelligence capabilities in the world. Specifically, the two navies were uniquely capable and were forward deployed around the globe on a 24/7 basis. The Cuban Missile Crisis had emphasized to the United States the urgent need for satellite intelligence, surveillance, and reconnaissance (ISR). U-2 aircraft flights by the US Air Force (USAF) played a crucial role in determining ground truth inside Cuba. However, these flights were hugely risky for the pilots, who had to fly at low altitude and at speeds that enabled them to capture photographic intelligence. One USAF pilot died flying one of these missions over Cuba; President Kennedy took action that marks the beginning of the National Reconnaissance Office. It would be some time before the NRO could deliver the types of capabilities that President Kennedy demanded. Meanwhile, the community had to make do with existing capabilities.

One key fact endures until the present: satellites in the visual (imaging), SIGINT, ELINT, infrared, and multispectral parts of the EM spectrum and its myriad applications can only do so much. Satellites are hugely expensive to design, build, launch, and maintain in space, as is the attendant infrastructure. The processing and distribution costs alone are massive. There are even more significant downsides: satellites are limited in orbital paths (whether or not they are geostationary) and can collect only wherever they are and whenever they are over a given point. "Overhead," as it is colloquially termed in the intelligence community, is limited in time, space, and coverage. Satellites are not ubiquitous, and to build a constellation of them that would be is currently out of the question—maybe sometime this century this will be made possible by improvements in processing, bandwidth, and most of all, cost.

In a word, unless a satellite is overhead at the right place at the right time, it will not be able to collect imagery or ELINT or listen to communications. What does this mean for the USS *Liberty*? In contrast to a satellite, a spy ship can be stationed in a geographically appropriate location to listen and collect across the EM spectrum. A ship can stay there 24/7 and capture everything within its listening capabilities, including classified and encrypted traffic. Most of all, the spy ship can provide real-time, or near-real-time, intelligence. USS *Liberty* and other US and Royal Navy collectors that we will discuss in the next chapter were therefore critical components in the Middle East in 1967. As the crisis mounted *Liberty* was dispatched from her station off West Africa posthaste to the eastern Mediterranean via Rota, Spain, where, as we have seen, she embarked additional cryptographers and linguists. Her electronic fit remained the same, the most advanced array of antennas and processing and analysis systems of its day. She could do things that no other collection system, organization, or human being could in 1967. Her geographic location was paramount and was the point of her urgent dispatch to the eastern Mediterranean.

This is a most appropriate point to segue into how both the US Navy and the Royal Navy fitted into overall American and British intelligence throughout our period—a fascinating and exciting story that it bears considerable analysis and discussion. Our next chapter will explore the challenges and changes that occurred in US and UK intelligence from the 1960s through to today and the roles both navies played.

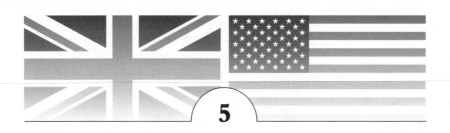

5

The US Navy and Royal Navy as Key Echelons of American and British Intelligence

The great British naval historian of the Royal Navy in World War II, Captain Stephen Roskill, once told your author that without the intelligence that the United States and United Kingdom possessed throughout World War II, the outcome of that war might have been entirely different. Plans, policies, and operations were critical, he said, but intelligence was simply golden. This assessment was reinforced by my personal mentor, Professor Sir Harry Hinsley, the official historian of British intelligence in World War II, writing five quite outstanding volumes that would be published by Her Majesty's Stationery Office. Hinsley had worked at Bletchley Park during World War II. At the time of his passing in 1998 he was regarded as one of the fathers of British intelligence.

I worked with him in the late 1960s in the basement of a British government facility adjacent to the Foreign Office near Parliament Square in London. My eyes were opened to the wealth of all-source, highly classified intelligence material from the 1930s through World War II and its aftermath. None of the material had been declassified. In 1974 the Cabinet Office designated Group Captain Frederick William Winterbottom, a retired Royal Air Force (RAF) officer who had worked at Bletchley Park during the war (he was then a wing commander), to publish a book that divulged the existence of Bletchley Park and the means by which the Ultra data had been obtained. Unfortunately, *The Ultra Secret* has many inaccuracies and was severely criticized for its errors of both fact and interpretation. Wing Commander Winterbottom was never involved in any of the operational and cryptologic aspects of Bletchley's work; he was one of the distributors of the highly classified Nazi SIGINT intercepts. In any case, the British government did not permit the release of the detailed product: the actual raw intelligence material or the analysis and reports that were produced. It also did not release documents on actions that were taken and their impact on plans, policies, and operations during World War II.

Official release and declassification of much, but by no means all, of the material happened much later, when Professor Hinsley was commissioned by the government, with the direct permission of the prime minister, to begin writing the official history *British Intelligence in the Second World War*. His volumes changed the interpretation of what happened before, during, and after World War II. Their impact on the understanding of naval operations was quite dramatic. Even more dramatic were revelations of the intensely close cooperation between the United States and the United Kingdom throughout the war pursuant to the various agreements between Winston Churchill and Franklin Roosevelt. These agreements constituted the beginning of the "special relationship," a simple phrase that underscores one critically important fact—that the Americans and the British shared vital intelligence at all levels and from all sources, in particular the golden products of US Magic and UK Enigma data sources.

Before we move ahead, it is vital to note that at that time the most significant links in this chain of cooperation and data exchange were the intelligence organizations of the US Navy and the Royal Navy. The management of Bletchley Park was largely in the hands of the Royal Navy, and the US Navy was lead for the Magic program. Both Churchill and Roosevelt had direct personal control and influence over how, when, and by whom material from these special sources should or should not be used or exploited. Neither leader, naturally, wanted the special sources ever to be compromised. They decreed that security-related and operational costs should not be factors. Also, on the operational side, they decreed that material was not to be exploited if the risk of revelation to the enemy was too high, even though this might involve serious losses. Short-term gain could not stand in the way of long-term benefits. The culture, tradition, and the security structure that underpinned their policies endured well after their passing and persists to this day. No British prime minister or US president has ever deliberately or inadvertently divulged substantive classified information about the nature of the still-continuing special relationship. It is essential to note that from 1960 to 2015 the overarching infrastructure laid down in World War II has expanded and matured, with naturally greater complexity. Of all the American and British intelligence organizations and departments of state, none have been so closely bound or shared such sensitive data as the US Navy and the Royal Navy.

Interestingly, the creator of the whole James Bond culture, the books and the movies, was in British naval intelligence during World War II. Ian

Fleming (May 28, 1908–August 12, 1964) was the personal assistant to the Director of Naval Intelligence, Vice Admiral John Godfrey, from August 1939 onward, with the code-word designation "17F," in the famous Room 40. Fleming later wrote that James Bond was "a compound of all the secret agents and commando types that I met during the war." He worked alongside MI6, the Political Warfare Executive, the SOE, the Joint Intelligence Committee (JIC) in the Cabinet Office, and members the prime minister's personal staff who were cleared into the various programs. From 1941 onward, after he and Admiral Godfrey visited Colonel "Wild Bill" Donovan in Washington, DC, Fleming had a direct working relationship with the forerunner to and later the actual US Office of Strategic Services. It is not surprising, therefore, that after the war Ian Fleming was able to put pen to paper with such authoritative skill. Fleming was a commander, Royal Naval Volunteer Reserve; James Bond was modeled on a Royal Navy commander.

What Ian Fleming and his many colleagues on both sides of the Atlantic initiated during World War II endured into the postwar period and beyond. Nothing has fundamentally changed, in spite of the ups and downs in other US-UK intelligence communities. The two navies have lived through the turmoil of political and international change without any of the differences that have occurred between the two nations. The United States, for instance, was very much against British and French actions during the Suez crisis of 1956, and the United Kingdom declined to join the United States in Vietnam even though a former British dominion, Australia, committed military forces. None of these differences affected the intelligence relationship of the nations' navies.

It is always important when looking at the investments that nations make in their intelligence services to ask: What is the true added value, whether to national security, national economic or political interests, or the maintenance of the international order? In the long run, does intelligence make a difference?

In 1978, I was privileged to provide a Royal Navy honor guard from HMS *Collingwood* for a special ceremony in Southampton to mark the anniversary of the commando/special forces raid of February 27–28, 1942, to capture key components of a Nazi radar station on the French coast at Bruneval. Operation Biting was stood up by the newly formed Directorate of Combined Operations, led by then Rear Admiral Louis Mountbatten. Knowledge of the Wurzburg radar's capabilities at Bruneval was regarded by the British technical intelligence community, led in this matter by the legendary R. V. Jones, Prime Minister Churchill's special programs lead, as absolutely vital. This radar was assessed to be used by the Nazis for detecting and track-ing RAF Bomber Command's raids into Germany and also for assisting the Luftwaffe in its attacks on the United Kingdom. In 1942 the RAF was suf-fering heavy losses in its nighttime raids over Germany; the US Eighth Air Force had not yet arrived in numbers in the United Kingdom to begin day-light raids with B-17 aircraft. There was urgency in defeating German capa-bilities to detect RAF bombers entering Germany. Combined Operations Headquarters (a War Office branch that coordinated raids onto the continent) determined that the optimal way to capture the key radar components and bring them to the United Kingdom was a nighttime parachute drop into the Bruneval area, followed by an attack on the radar site and then a naval evac-uation from the beach.

This was a daring raid, and it was 100 percent successful. In addition to bringing back the radar components the raiding force captured a Ger-man technician. British specialists were then able to design countermeasures against this and similar German radars. The raiding force was led by Major John Frost's C Company of the 2nd Battalion of the Parachute Regiment and a part of the British 1st Airborne Division. Major Frost was to follow his exploits at Bruneval with yet more such actions.

In the fall of 1944, now Lieutenant Colonel Frost was in command of the 2nd Battalion and led it after being dropped into the Low Countries to the famous Arnhem Bridge, as a key part of the ill-fated Operation Mar-ket Garden. This was conceived as a daring thrust to capture the key Rhine bridges. This would be a precursor to invading Germany by the northerly route that would take General Sir Bernard Montgomery's army to Berlin before the Soviet Red Army could occupy parts of eastern Germany and Berlin itself. The strategic concept was bold and imaginative but was fatally flawed, for reasons that we will address. Frost's battalion held the Arnhem Bridge, waiting for the arrival of nine thousand men from the British XXX Corps who never arrived. On September 17, 1944, Frost's men, 745 total and very lightly armed, with no armored support whatsoever, faced the wrath of a full German SS Panzer corps. In a quite extraordinary feat of arms and her-oism, Frost's men fought to the bitter end, a four-day battle that left only one hundred of his men. (In 1978 the Arnhem Bridge was named the John Frost Bridge. In the movie *A Bridge Too Far,* the British actor Anthony Hopkins plays Lieutenant Colonel Frost.)

To return to 1978: after Lord Mountbatten and now Major General Frost had inspected the guard and warmly complimented the officer of the guard, Royal Navy Special Duties Lieutenant Derek Rowland, on the fine turnout and performance of his men, I had the privilege to meet the attending distinguished dignitaries at a reception. After pleasantries and a discussion of the modern Royal Navy, General Frost and I entered into a detailed conversation on the intelligence successes of Bruneval and the total failure of intelligence in support of Operation Market Garden. What did General Frost think?

General Frost expounded. All-source intelligence had gone into the planning of the Bruneval raid—from SIGINT collection, Enigma data, and aerial photography to work by MI6's agents in France and reports from the French Resistance. Timing and the weather had been everything, and the role of the meteorologist had been paramount for the drop into the Bruneval area and for the Royal Navy's evacuation from the beach—wind, tide, wave height, moon status, and beach profile. The Navy needed precise data on the whereabouts of opposing German naval forces, and Frost and his men needed not just estimates but precise knowledge of the opposition that they would meet—force composition and locations down to the unit level, details of weapons, training status, combat experience, and likely state of readiness. Surprise and security were crucial. Intelligence did not fail them, and the mission was a huge success and a great morale booster for the British public in the dark days of 1942. The general stressed one overwhelmingly important factor, the need for reliable, secure, and redundant communications that would hold up in any weather condition and location. The number of radios counted, in case one radio failed or was damaged or the operator became a casualty or was captured. Multiple systems were required to ensure survivable communications.

What General Frost described to me was what today we call "situational awareness"—the ability to know in or near real time the overall picture regarding the enemy. In 1942 British intelligence gave Frost and his men the best situational awareness possible for the time, as well as the best communications available. Simple techniques work well. For instance, just one code word can summarize a total situation; many code words can cover a whole range of contingencies and events, so that reporting is kept to a minimum and the risk of interception and decryption kept limited. By contrast, Operation Market Garden was, to quote General Frost, an unmitigated disaster caused largely, but not wholly, by extremely poor intelligence planning and execution and the failure of the high command to accept the intelligence provided as ground truth. He said that underscoring this failure to appreciate the intelligence provided was a mind-set so fixated on the strategic plan that tactical detail and execution were assumed to follow automatically.

He was emphatic that the key failure lay in the assessment of the locations, movements, and strengths of potentially opposing German units, in particular heavy armor. These tanks proved to be the nemesis of the 2nd Battalion. Tell-tale signs of one key German panzer division were overlooked to the point of incompetence. Also, Frost stated, insufficient thought and planning had gone into a Plan B should the original operational plan begin to fall apart. There was no backup and nowhere to go for Frost's brave men. There was no relief on the way, because the British corps that was supposed to drive hard and fast to the key bridges soon faced threats and terrain problems that had not been anticipated. Communications became nonexistent because of radio failures. The general stressed that in the two-plus years since Bruneval the knowledge and operational templates developed by Combined Operations had not become doctrine and had certainly not influenced the mind-set of Operation Market Garden planners. Most of all, vital intelligence was ignored.

One of the simple but important lesson learned from this conversation was that as the years pass, technology tends to produce better solutions and operational experience can be built into the doctrine, tactics, techniques, and procedures of fighting forces. However, if there is no organizational or cultural willingness to make changes and implement lessons learned, the same mistakes can be made time and again in new and often totally different operational settings. Intelligence aims to diminish the risk of failure by providing total situational awareness and the best and most timely information flow that communications permit. There are fundamental checklists that can be derived from 1942, that were still valid in 1944 at Arnhem and continued to be valid throughout our fifty-five-year period. Checklists collect what needs to be known for planning and execution and why, at all levels, whether strategic or tactical. Checklists address likely threats, force levels and composition, deployments, basing, and logistics, together with tactical development, R&D, acquisition, and most of all, the intelligence that frames the choices, options, and decisions associated with the foregoing domains. In the end, what happens at sea is predicated on all the above. The relevance of the events in which I participated in Southampton is that they set the scene and provide a framework for looking at our period: what happened and why, where things are today, where they may go, or should go, in the future, and as asked earlier, what vital value added has intelligence provided.

Between 1960 and 2015 the US Navy and the Royal Navy remained closely knit in all matters of intelligence. At the operational level of intelligence the overall picture has been one of almost total harmony. That is a simple summation; let us look at the detail. The pressures of the Cold War not only demanded a constant evaluation of Soviet force levels, dispositions, capabilities, and operational patterns that showed their tactics, techniques, and procedures versus those of the NATO allies but imposed an ever-increasing need to stay ahead of the Soviet Union technologically. The latter imperative required not just maintaining a more capable industrial base and the R&D that was a precursor to innovation and keeping an edge but also preventing the opposition from stealing secrets by espionage and other means. It was a never-ending process of measure, countermeasure, and counter-countermeasure, an incessant burden on both governments to commit the right resources to sustain the lead that would ensure naval superiority in the very worst scenarios. At another level, the arms race also reflected British and American determination to uphold the values of the Western democratic and capitalist system and way of life. As a result, the United States shared its best technologies with the United Kingdom, and the United Kingdom was able to respond in ways that helped keep the balance even. Nowhere was this truer than in intelligence exchange.

We saw earlier how organizational change impacted the structures of defense intelligence in both countries. The Royal Navy was more affected by these changes than the US Navy. However, what did not change was a series of well-established and ever-developing joint US-UK programs. Whatever organizational changes occurred, the highly secret world of these navy-to-navy programs endured, and under their own direction and with special security and safeguards that prevented the new bureaucratic machinery from inhibiting them as it did other parts of defense intelligence. Access was severely limited, and need-to-know criteria rigorously applied. The programs had deeply buried lives of their own. The need to stay well ahead of the Soviet Union in the special relationship reached its climax in the period in the 1980s, before the beginning of the end of the Soviet Union and the Warsaw Pact. These were the Reagan-Thatcher years, eight solid years of President Ronald Reagan espousing a maritime strategy that was implemented by his young and hard-charging Secretary of the Navy, John Lehman, a US Naval Reserve commander and naval aviator, who was totally supported by Caspar Weinberger, the secretary of defense.

This was the era of the six-hundred-ship Navy and of head-on challenges to the Soviet navy and its allies—forward operations that took, for example, the US Second Fleet (ably assisted by the Royal Navy) to the doorstep of the Soviet Northern Fleet in such major NATO exercises as Northern Wedding. The US Navy recommissioned the *Iowa*-class battleships, extended the lives of older ships, began a major construction program, and increased the production of the *Nimitz*-class nuclear-powered aircraft carriers. Just as the United States was challenging the Soviet Union in space with the "Star Wars" initiative, the US Navy carried the flag forward with its British counterparts. Reagan and his advisers sought to challenge the Soviet Union's defense-industrial base to such a stressful level that it could not compete. Moscow would have either to yield or go bankrupt. Even within the stringent communist regime, in the end there were only so many resources that the Soviets could muster. The Soviet Union dissolved in the early 1990s.

The situation in the United Kingdom was not quite as rosy as that of the United States. Although the Royal Navy more than kept its part of the bargain at sea and in spite of the huge success of the Falklands campaign, the sad fact is that the Thatcher government had begun before the Argentine invasion the systematic reduction of the Royal Navy. This was an unhealthy turn of events, one that sent the wrong messages to Washington and confused the Reagan, and later the G. H. W. Bush, administrations. It is ironic that it was Margaret Thatcher's government that began the slow decline, one that only recently was reversed. The trend is now upward: the Royal Navy is projected to have 50 percent of the UK total defense budget by 2022, a huge turnaround. Let us first address the earlier period.

The components, agencies, and directorates of both US and British intelligence have been outlined earlier. It is critical to observe that the size of the British intelligence organization is minuscule compared to the United States, with the possible exception of GCHQ, which, though not comparable with NSA in size, does nonetheless more than hold its own with its cousin in Maryland. The HUMINT arm of British intelligence, the Secret Intelligence Service, is almost tiny compared to the Central Intelligence Agency or even its former Directorate of Operations, known today as the National Clandestine Service (NCS). Similarly, the British Security Service, or MI5, is tiny in comparison with the combined counterespionage and counterintelligence organizations in the United States, led by the Federal Bureau of Investigation (FBI) and overseas by the CIA and the defense intelligence and service intelligence agencies. As we shall observe, size does not always predict success in terms of quality of product.

British intelligence benefited enormously from its colonial or imperial past, predicated on geography. The residual relationships and facilities that endured for the United Kingdom after decolonization meant that there still existed locations from which the British could both operate and, in many cases, retain special clandestine and covert facilities. This applied not just to the SIGINT and ELINT domains but also to HUMINT. While the United States developed and expanded its space intelligence systems and capabilities, the United Kingdom quietly and unobtrusively expanded in areas that were uniquely suited to postcolonial Britain. There was mutual benefit all round: for the United Kingdom, US space-based intelligence; for the United States in return, quite extensive benefits from the United Kingdom's worldwide special communications networks and HUMINT from myriad MI6 sources and methods, many of which the United States has never been quite able to replicate. The United Kingdom was able to place at the disposal of the United States various key sites around the globe and also inside the United Kingdom. There are generations of Americans who look back to the Cold War and remember being posted to very sensitive facilities inside the United Kingdom, often in local communities not privy to what was going on behind secure fences.

What were the US Navy and the Royal Navy seeking? Both navies always aimed to be technically and operationally superior to the Soviet navy and its Warsaw Pact allies in scenarios that war planners envisaged; they meant never to be outclassed in any crucial domain and always to have enough strength that the Soviets could not achieve superiority by numbers alone. In 1977, as mentioned in chapter 3, I worked side by side with Captain John L. Underwood, USN, in creating blueprint scenarios, with force levels, capabilities, and likely dispositions, for a full-blown war at sea with the Soviet Union. This was "Sea War '85," a projection out to the mid-1980s to establish what capabilities and force levels the United States and its NATO allies should have in that time period. Critical to that study was excellent all-source intelligence that framed our thinking and permitted the many operational analysts and war gamers involved to play out this projected war at sea. In 1977 the six-hundred-ship Navy was not even a twinkle in the eye of anyone in the US Navy, let alone a smile on the face of anyone in the White House. However, Sea War '85 and other work set the stage for political change, recognition of the critical need for maritime superiority and how vitally it would contribute to keeping the Soviet Union in check. No one in 1977 could have foreseen the demise of the Soviet Union, but one thing was certain: that a powerful and well-led US Navy and its principal naval ally, the Royal Navy, could and would counteract any aggressive moves from the Soviet Union. In order to stay ahead, various key elements had to be identified, understood, and acted on.

The Soviet Union rapidly realized in the 1960s that a maritime war, and certainly one on a global scale, could be won or lost as a result of submarine warfare. The nuclear-powered attack submarine armed with highly capable torpedoes and antiship (and much later land-attack) cruise missiles, could, with its endurance, range, speed, stealth, covertness, and persistent presence, destroy not just vital merchant traffic but also high-value surface targets. These included aircraft carriers, cruisers, destroyers, frigates, and a wide range of amphibious and supply ships. In other words, it had the ability to destroy fleets, when disposed in sufficiently large numbers. Once the Soviet Union embarked on building a large, capable submarine force, US and British intelligence knew that the balance of effort and resources had to shift dramatically in that direction. What were the key requirements and the driving parameters?

It was not just about knowing where the threat was most of the time, being able to locate, track, and observe the Soviet navy close up and collect operational and technical intelligence. There was a constant and urgent need to know exactly what the baseline design and technical capabilities were of the Soviets' new classes of submarines. Their surface navy was much easier to observe, collect against, and then analyze with regard to technical parameters and capabilities than was their submarine navy. The United States and the United Kingdom needed to know on a 24/7 basis where Soviet submarine forces were, but they also had to know well in advance, in fact several years in advance, what the Soviet design bureaus were planning and what their shipyards would produce and when, in what numbers, and for what fleet dispositions. Breaking into the Soviets' hugely complex R&D, design, and production organization was a daunting proposition. At the heart of the initial challenge was acoustic intelligence.

Submarine-quieting technologies establish the noise levels of a submarine class and individual boats. Noise reduction, or quieting, is a quintessential design and production requirement. A noisy submarine will be detected, and then tracked, and, in the worst scenario, destroyed by a very quiet, well-handled opposing submarine. Noise is produced by machinery, the propulsor or propeller(s), and by various types of flow noise associated with the hull's movement through the water as a direct function of its design, shape, and surface. Even the most minor badly designed or housed equipment may be a fatal giveaway. A small pump or generator that is not on the right type of sound-suppressing mounting or that generates acoustic tonals at certain frequencies may in due course at sea be the nemesis of a well-armed and well-trained submarine. In short, the noise profile of a Soviet submarine class and of each boat in that class was like knowing the submarines' DNA. Most of all, noise profiles revealed submarines' critical vulnerabilities, acoustic emissions that would give away their presence and locations. Baselining each Soviet submarine class and predicting next-generation Soviet submarine class design and noise levels were not only essential but critical to success at sea for the Western alliance.

This challenge was compounded by the fact that the Soviets began to design and build multiple submarine classes in parallel, both nuclear- and nonnuclear-powered boats. This daunting proposition was further exacerbated by the large numbers of Soviet institutes where R&D was performed, the many design bureaus, and the complexity of what in the West is termed the "acquisition process." Furthermore, the submarine building yards were diverse and scattered, and the Soviets had quickly reacted to US overhead capabilities with large, fully covered halls that hid new construction. To image a new Soviet first-of-class submarine when it emerged from, say, the Admiralty Yard in Leningrad was far too late. The US Navy and the Royal Navy needed to know years in advance what the Soviets were designing and its likely capabilities.

At the heart of this complex intelligence requirement was matching baseline data with continuing Soviet research, design efforts, capabilities, and production schedules. Gaining access to the latter would involve every capability in the US and British intelligence inventories—IMINT, SIGINT, ELINT, HUMINT, MASINT, ACINT, and a range of highly specialized technical collection and analysis tools. Having the very best US satellites over facilities otherwise inaccessible to Western eyes was indeed critical, but it would take a lot more to stay ahead. Satellite data was never completely good enough, for reasons that will become self-evident.

The US and Royal Navies had a head start over the Soviet submarine force. They were able to baseline the Soviets' acoustic signatures by extremely capable ACINT collection. In the early years that collection was executed almost solely by American and British submarines on special missions. Those missions were golden, whether in the North Atlantic, in the far north of the Norwegian Sea, in the enclosed waters of the Baltic and Mediterranean Seas, or in the Pacific Ocean. Locating, tracking, and collecting ACINT against Soviet submarines constituted one of the great achievements of the Cold War. It kept the West ahead. Planning such operations required detailed a priori knowledge from all-source intelligence, along with special technical outfit and special "sea riders" (i.e., teams). US and British submarines had to be handled with the utmost care to maintain their own stealth and acoustic advantages in close-quarters collection operations.

The data from these operations provided the bedrock on which everything else was built. The logic is as follows. Knowing the signature of a Soviet submarine meant that the West knew how to characterize its opponent, hear him, locate him, and track him, whether in the deep recesses of the ocean, the littorals, or indeed in close proximity to his bases. It meant that the Soviets were naked underwater. When that ACINT had been obtained, all other collection could be conducted in a confident manner, in operations that were extremely well planned with the benefit of foreknowledge. For example, if other intelligence indicated that the Soviets would deploy a boat from Sever-omorsk (the main Soviet Northern Fleet base) area for a test sequence of a new underwater missile (particularly a ballistic missile), the ability not just to locate the boat as it left port but individually characterize it was incred-ibly powerful. The platform could be tracked to the test area, the whole test sequence observed, and critical SIGINT, ELINT, and missile telemetry obtained. None of this would be possible without superior ACINT—and one other vital technical capability.

The United States and the United Kingdom for decades had superior signal-processing capabilities. These resided in passive sonars of many types, fixed domed arrays, lateral flank arrays along the hull, and towed arrays reeled in and out astern of the submarine. Hydrophone technology and processing became more and more capable, with the advent of powerful onboard com-puters and advanced mathematical algorithms. In addition, the British and Americans developed generations of onboard sonar experts. The Soviets were up against an implacable foe in the US and British nuclear-powered attack submarines. In the airborne domain, the US Navy and the Royal Navy (with the support of the Royal Air Force) acquired very capable passive sonar buoys that would detect Soviet submarines and permit attacks by equally capable air-dropped antisubmarine torpedoes.

The above was the crucial baseline. The other parts of the intelligence process were equally complex. How do you ascertain what is going on inside, for example, the Soviet Institute of Hydromechanics, or a design bureau, or the acquisition organization in Moscow, or a shipyard production scheduling office, let alone know the intimate details of their next design and likely capa-bility improvements? These are totally nontrivial tasks. Let's look at what US Navy and Royal Navy intelligence did to meet these needs.

Espionage is not easy under any circumstances. At the heart of any attempt to compromise a foreign citizen into betraying his or her country's national secrets is the handler or trained agent, British or American, or a han-dler's surrogate. During the Cold War the counterintelligence services of the Soviet Union and its Warsaw Pact allies were at a premium. Watchdog secu-rity agencies created controls and pressures that made it very difficult for even the most diehard would-be spy, one who hated the regime, to make successful and regular contact with a handler. The Soviets could establish without much difficulty who on the US embassy staff was likely to be holding diplomatic cover for espionage operations. Their ability to monitor American and British diplomats and their staffs was prodigious. Even the most inept counterintelligence service could quickly figure out who the US CIA chief of station was and who composed his or her staff, whatever the official diplomatic list might state. The nature of their movements, contacts, and travel requests, as well as round-the-clock surveillance on them, made life very tough during the Cold War for regular, full-time members of the clandestine services operating under official diplomatic cover. Their one, but significant, advantage of official cover, of course, was that if compromised or arrested they could use diplomatic privilege to avoid trial, imprisonment, or execution. However, a person whose cover was blown would be expelled and would never be able to operate globally again; the KGB would be looking out for that person's next overseas assignment.

Naval attachés were more likely to see and hear about Soviet naval developments and activities than the "conventional" US or British agent. They could travel normally where they requested, albeit often under intense surveillance; at least, they could openly travel to Leningrad and do their best to see what was developing inside, for example, the Admiralty Yard. They could openly meet Soviet naval officials, collect open data, and take photographs unless officially restricted in advance of a visit. Of course, official restrictions did not prevent clandestine photography by attachés or random collection of whatever came their way. A classic and priceless example was a piece of titanium weld that one attaché literally picked up after it fell from a truck near a Soviet yard. That one piece of metal told US and British technical intelligence how the Soviets were managing to perform extraordinarily sophisticated welds on a new titanium-hulled nuclear-attack submarine, the Akula class. (These very lightweight, extremely strong welds, together with a new, advanced liquid-metal reactor, enabled the class to achieve high underwater speeds.)

In contrast, the likelihood that conventional embassy- or consular-based clandestine operations could successfully attract and convert, or corrupt, a Soviet citizen for espionage was very low, for all the above reasons. In fact, the most likely prospect in that line came from walk-ins or diplomatic encounters at embassy cocktail parties or other professional diplomatic gatherings where a Soviet citizen could make an advance. These encounters were very few and far between.

Successful classic espionage was most likely via other means: surrogates, commercial and industrial connections, academic contacts, travelers and tourists, and well-trained long-term "plants." Surrogates included citizens of other countries, often with neutral or benign relations with the Soviet Union, who had greater access and could travel more freely than Westerners and had good cover—professional, commercial, or sometimes diplomatic status, such as with one of the United Nations agencies. Non-American or -British business and commercial travelers, particularly those doing serious business with the Soviet defense sector, made ideal agents, as did neutral scientists, academics, and visitors attending conferences and trade gatherings. Tradecraft and discreet technology played large roles in these operations. The risks were high for such sources. If compromised there were likely to be serious consequences, from long-term imprisonment to execution after a secret trial. The reward for such high-end risk taking was significant financial benefit.

The British have tended to be very capable in these domains, and the secret of their success is self-evident: ensuring that no information available to counterintelligence agencies could connect with a British intelligence operation. A well-trained surrogate agent could not under any circumstances ever do anything that compromised his or her status. This is not the stuff of novels or the few classic UK and US espionage cases where either money, sex, or ideology (or some combination) compromised British citizens. The spying for the Soviet Union during the early post–World War II Cold War by Kim Philby, Guy Burgess, Donald McLean, and several others has been the subject of innumerable books. The real work and value added came from surrogates.

When all is said and done, one has to revert to the fundamental questions: What were the real benefits? What were the intelligence products, and how good were they? During our fifty-five-year period, high-value product was limited. However, very good material was produced that when taken with other sources and methods both illuminated overall Soviet naval capability and directed other sources and methods to high-value targets and locations that might not have been spotted by satellites.

For example, as noted, a non-US or -UK citizen with well-established credentials from another country and regular legitimate business in the Soviet Union made an ideal agent if trained and handled with the utmost care. Direct connection with Soviet navy personnel, research facilities, or higher echelons in Moscow and the ability to listen to, observe, and visit places banned to American and British personnel, and later record it all, was indeed golden. The same applied to non-Russian Warsaw Pact citizens who traveled to parts of the Soviet Union where there was critical naval activity, particularly those who had relatives in the West or other parts of the Warsaw Pact. West German, Czech, or Hungarian citizens with families in Russia had the permits necessary to visit them. Such people could act as information couriers for individuals there so disaffected with the Soviet regime that they would risk spying for the United States and the United Kingdom. Such agents had to be handled with the utmost care by either surrogates or undercover handlers with well-developed, long-term deep cover. The British in particular were masters of these particular brands of tradecraft, with decades of experience that started before World War II. No British handler would ever have been seen by Soviet watchers in the United Kingdom entering or leaving one of the UK intelligence facilities. The culture and modus operandi were intensely buried in layers of cover—the only way to succeed and to stay alive in the Cold War espionage business. We will address later the demands placed on the United States and United Kingdom by a rising China and Islamic fundamentalism and the impact on both navies and their intelligence machinery.

So this raises the question: Where and how was the real gold mined if not through classic espionage, or at least what the man in the street conceives as classic espionage? A good start is life cycle of a Soviet submarine: R&D, design, acquisition process, construction, commissioning, initial sea trials, and eventual deployment. What are the key intelligence issues?

The life cycle of either a nuclear or nonnuclear submarine starts in R&D in laboratories, research institutes, and in the industrial base that would actually construct the submarines. Almost all such centers were well known during the Cold War and have been since. However, finding out what was transpiring inside these far-flung establishments, separated in many cases by thousands of miles, was a huge challenge. Second, and very important, were the design bureaus and acquisition authorities that integrated R&D, executed the detailed design work across all the key domains (hull, propulsion, quieting, combat system, weapons and loadout, communications and sensors, mechanical and electrical systems, and habitability, or "hotel functions," as they are termed in the United States) and then managed the construction programs.

This complexity was heightened when the Soviets began to plan, design, and build multiple submarine classes in parallel—an extraordinarily ambitious goal that they did in fact achieve and that gave US and British intelligence decades of concern. As a new class was being constructed not only was a modernization program on the drawing boards for that class but development of a whole new, separate class would be progressing. The United States never tried to emulate this Soviet model. US and UK submarine classes were developed and built in well-conceived sequence as single classes. They were never built in parallel, except that British diesel-electric work ran in parallel with the nuclear program. That occurred in the cases of the *Porpoise* and *Oberon* classes

Soviet Sierra-class nuclear-powered attack submarine   US Navy, courtesy Royal
Norwegian Air Force

and, toward the end of the British employment of nonnuclear submarines, the
Upholder class, eventually transferred to the Royal Canadian Navy.

This complex Soviet process had to be understood and then penetrated, key
intelligence on it garnered, and the information fed back to user communities.
Intelligence is of zero value if it does not provide actionable information—
in this case, data, of whatever kind, that enabled strategic planners, operators,
designers, scientists, engineers, and budgetary authorities in both governments to understand and then make the right decisions to counter the Soviet
threat. Congress and Parliament had to be briefed and given the best data that
existed if they were to authorize and fund the necessary programs. (The same
applies today with respect to the emergent Russian threat, cyber, the Chinese
threat, and Islamic extremism.) Combined US and UK intelligence plans and
operations for this whole process were well thought through; perhaps in no
other domain throughout the Cold War did such a rigorous and dynamic
capability exist, nor does now.

The starting point for all the above was also where it ended, at sea. From
1960 until today the United States and the United Kingdom have amassed
and, almost without exception (which we will discuss later), shared operational intelligence at sea. Simply stated, it takes a very capable submarine to
locate, track, identify, and then collect intelligence on another submarine.

Without this baseline, this major advantage, the United States and the United Kingdom would have been in a totally different situation; the history of the Cold War might have been very different. As we have seen, the United States and United Kingdom together built a data base on every Soviet submarine class and every hull within each class. No two submarines have exactly the same profile. How was this feat achieved?

Very early in our period the round-the-clock locating and tracking of Soviet submarines enabled several critical tasks to be carried out. A Soviet submarine would be picked up in egress from or ingress to its home base, a foreign port, in an anchorage (perhaps one of the much-frequented Soviet anchorages in the Mediterranean, in company with surface assets), or geographic choke point through which the Soviets had no choice but to transit. The latter included the GIUK gap, the Danish straits (the Kattegat and Skagerrak), the straits of Gibraltar, and the key straits in the Indonesian archipelago—Sunda and Malacca. There were many other locations or often-used routes where the Soviets could be detected, and then tracked, as well.

Over time the United States and United Kingdom developed a profile of each Soviet submarine, in particular its acoustic signature across a range of frequencies. ACINT, as we have seen, is arguably a far more valuable intelligence source than many of the classic espionage sources. Speed, depth, operating characteristics, and crew performance could all be observed and recorded; also, very significantly, Soviet sensor data could be collected, and active and passive sonar could be assessed from direct operational experience as to whether the target knew or not of the presence of the US or UK submarine. In addition, communications could be monitored and recorded, noting modes and frequencies used and any hitherto-unknown techniques. Soviet naval interactions with other assets, such as strike and antisubmarine aircraft, were monitored. (Such aircraft included Bear Ds and Fs, in their NATO designations, flying from well-known and monitored bases in the Kola Peninsula in northern Russia.)

Most of all, the tactical procedures ingrained in Soviet submariners were analyzed by US and UK submariners and played back in the Western submarine schools. The United States and the United Kingdom acquired firsthand experience of the training and operational cultures of Soviet submariners, what they were used to—especially their marked dependence on centralized command, control, and communications. This dependence created many vulnerabilities for them, notably in preventing onboard command teams from developing independence, self-confidence, quick thinking, and tactical innovativeness. Deviation from strict tactical procedures by Soviet submariners was almost unknown. As a result, the Americans and British became able to anticipate the Soviets' every move.

New Soviet submarine weapons were high on the collection list. The superior stealth of well-handled US and UK submarines permitted penetration of the most sensitive and dangerous areas to observe and record weapons trials. It was essential that NATO already have intelligence of new Soviet weapons by the time they went on sea trials. Such collection was a high-risk task, but it was accomplished for decades, and the product was first-class. The operating characteristics, ranges, and key sensor frequencies of new Soviet weapons could be distributed to the NATO community under secure umbrellas that never revealed sources or methods of collection. Classic SIGINT and ELINT played heavily; they entailed passive listening and interception of Soviet communications by multiple means in special collection suites.

Translation was an essential part of this process, and back in the United Kingdom and United States a small body of highly trained translators made sense of technical and verbal intercepts. These translators were the natural successors to the Bletchley Park and US Magic cryptanalysis teams of World War II fame. In many cases, technical translators were deployed when real-time onboard intelligence was necessary to understand fully what the Soviets were doing. These "sea riders," as they were called, often spent weeks at sea in precarious operational scenarios.

The next stage in this process was to penetrate programs' bases inside the Soviet Union, the centers in Moscow where R&D and design came together—the acquisition authorities, which, as noted, managed the implementation of plans for new submarine classes. Penetration of these centers by classic espionage was extraordinarily difficult; the likelihood that officials would betray such secrets was very low, and so little reliance was placed on HUMINT. US overhead sources, although critical, have limitations. Satellites cannot see inside buildings or shipyard construction halls. They can listen—considerable SIGINT and ELINT can be obtained from space.

However, in our period—a predigital era before cell phones, microwave towers, or international transfer of massive amounts of data—the United States and the United Kingdom relied on classic communications technologies, frequencies, and procedures associated with the RF spectrum, involving a multitude of methods, platforms, and geographic locations. In addition to RF transmissions the Soviets, the Warsaw Pact in general, and NATO extensively used landlines, many of them secure and separate from those operated by governments and corporate users. The same applied to transoceanic cables and satellite communications, which became more widely available and used during the second half of our period. The United States and the United Kingdom had to use intercept technologies and procedures that dated from World War II, combined with increasingly advanced ones. Soviet communications were naturally highly secure, to avoid penetration and decoding of classified messages. The weakness of centralized Soviet military acquisition management was like that of many other aspects of the USSR's military and intelligence machinery—its centralization revealed its very organization.

Success in breaking into the communications of the central Soviet acquisition process, together with the operational intelligence discussed earlier, enabled the United States and the United Kingdom to make very informed assessments of what was likely to emerge from Soviet building yards and its likely capabilities. But the picture was not always rosy. US intelligence in the 1970s tended to underestimate future Soviet capabilities. The United States based assessments to a large extent, though not completely, on the Soviets' failure to master advanced computer-based digital signal processing, particularly in the low-frequency, narrow-band domains. The Americans argued that this weakness prevented the Soviets from resolving the critical issue of submarine quieting and that the Soviets' investments in active sonar and nonacoustic antisubmarine technologies was all due to this failure. By contrast, the United Kingdom showed, in very detailed intelligence reports, that the generations of Soviet submarines likely to appear from 1980 onward would be significantly more capable in all regards, particularly quieting and weapons. In the event, the launch of the cruise-missile-firing Oscar and ballistic-missile Typhoon (both NATO names) classes proved the United Kingdom correct. The UK assessments had been made on the basis of all-source collection on Soviet R&D, procurement system, open-source data that was clearly not deliberately deceptive, and baseline data bases. The British saw that by 1980 the Soviets would demonstrate a step change in capability, that their nonacoustic ASW programs were indeed running in parallel with new, advanced passive acoustic signal processing.

By 1982–83 the United Kingdom and the United States had divergent assessments. Operational intelligence would quickly prove the British correct. All the evidence added up, from a British perspective, to significantly new Soviet capabilities for the 1990s. The Victor III– and Akula-class SSNs joined the ranks of the Oscars and Typhoons as fundamental advances on their predecessors. A highly sensitive British "harmonized threat paper" that I published with a British colleague at about this time made totally accurate assessments of the new classes' capabilities, with one notable but minor technical exception, which the Soviets corrected after initial sea trials. The

Russian Oscar-class nuclear-powered guided-missile submarine   U.S. NAVAL INSTITUTE
PHOTO ARCHIVE

discrepancies from the late 1970s to the early 1980s between the United States
and the United Kingdom were most likely caused by the diversity of the massive US intelligence agencies, which often could not agree—cooperation was
not always their hallmark. The British enjoyed the benefits of being smaller
and better integrated: with extremely close working relations among collectors and the analysts and harmonization of final assessments within a much
tighter-knit community.

    Once the new baselines had been established the United States and the
United Kingdom could get back to amicable business-as-usual modes, but
to say there was no friction would be to gloss over a critical transition phase
in Soviet capabilities. As the 1990s progressed this would become patently
clear. On the operational intelligence side, in both collection and analysis,
extraordinary fine work continued between the US and Royal Navies. The
use of US SOSUS is illustrative. The location of SOSUS monitoring stations
in the United Kingdom from where they could track the deployment (both
egress and ingress) of Soviet submarines from the Kola Peninsula through
the GIUK gap was not just vital but critical in view of the vastness of the
Norwegian Sea, the North Sea, and the northeastern Atlantic. The US-UK
coordination of airborne ASW assets (US P-3 aircraft and UK Shackleton
and later Nimrod ASW aircraft) with surface and subsurface units was highly
organized through the UK maritime headquarters at Northwood, England,

and the outlying subordinate echelons (such as the Flag Officer Scotland and Northern Island), and other NATO centers (such as Norwegian operations from the Lofoten Islands). The US base at Keflavik in Iceland was another key link in this chain. The Royal Air Force bases at RAF Kinloss on the Moray Forth, east of Inverness in northern Scotland, and at St. Mawgan, in Cornwall in southwestern England, were sites where US aircraft could land for refueling and rest for crews. The Royal Navy's air station at Lossiemouth, east of RAF Kinloss, was the Royal Navy's center in northern Scotland for interdicting Soviet reconnaissance and bomber aircraft.

In addition, the United States maintained intensely discreet SIGINT stations in various UK locations. A legendary one, now closed, was on the far northeast coast of Scotland near a small village where the locals kept the station's secrets for several generations. This US intercept station, together with GCHQ UK-based stations, provided invaluable real-time intercepts. They also covered the communications activities of the AGIs, together with Soviet and Warsaw Pact merchant ships that were elements of the Soviet Ocean Surveillance System (SOSS). To provide intelligence to the motherland such vessels had to communicate; even their messages were highly encrypted, the descendants of Alan Turing at GCHQ, Cheltenham, their counterparts in the United States at the NSA, and the naval cryptologic centers were there to unravel them.

However, this successful monitoring of every stage of Soviet core naval capabilities and operations was being challenged in two key domains. One was the extraordinarily damaging consequences of the US spy ring led by John Anthony Walker (1937–2014). The other was the internal efforts of the Soviet navy R&D community to challenge the US-UK acoustic advantage by other means. At the same time, the Soviets began programs that sought to challenge the US and UK strategic deterrent postures. These included techniques very different from the well-established pattern of AGIs standing off US and UK bases and attempting to provide the SOSS with intelligence that could help vector Soviet SSNs, such as the new Victor IIIs, to locate and track US and UK SSBNs, the very heart of the Western nuclear deterrent posture. The Soviets' aim was destabilization. They also made strategic decisions to go under the northern ice cap and develop alternative technologies to active and passive acoustic signal processing. The Walker spy ring in the United States very much supported these endeavors.

For its part, the United Kingdom had not been bereft of Soviet spies in the naval sphere. The Portland spy ring from a generation earlier had made significant inroads into UK naval programs at the Admiralty Underwater Research

Establishment at Portland in Dorsetshire, on the south coast of England, but it had been nothing like as damaging as Philby, Burgess, and McLean, who had infiltrated the highest echelons of MI6 and betrayed countless HUMINT secrets and agents. The devastating effects of Philby in particular on MI6 were comparable to the disastrous consequences for the US Navy and its associated intelligence agencies of the Walker spy ring. In the next chapter we will discuss and examine and analyze these consequences.

In the contemporary world, the recent betrayals by Edward Snowden (born June 21, 1983) highlight the effects of the betrayal of critical intelligence sources, methods, and content. With this comes serious damage to public perception of the United States and United Kingdom and their NSA-GCHQ operations. The one positive aspect is that Snowden, who had, woefully, never been detected by counterintelligence, clearance investigators, or fellow employees, still does not know what he does not know. This is a huge credit to the highly secure, tightly knit community in key parts of US-UK intelligence, to which he did not have access. The US and Royal Navies' intelligence collection programs were successfully protected during our period. Some of their products were betrayed by the Walker spy ring, but the key critical operational aspects were never compromised, because both navies reduced the number of need-to-know personnel to an absolute minimum, while, critically, *not* sharing information with other agencies inside which were weak links such as Edward Snowden. It is to the lasting tribute of both navies that for our fifty-five-year period the inner workings of navy collection programs remained sacrosanct.

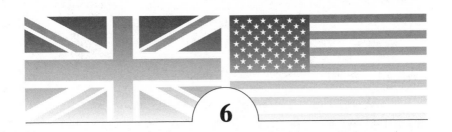

6

The Soviets Shift Gears and Make Serious Challenges at the Time of the Walker Spy Ring

The Soviet Union was seen by many in the Western intelligence community until the 1980s as floundering in a technological catch-up race with the United States and Royal Navies. The US-UK preeminence in underwater warfare, specifically in the acoustic realm, existed because of advanced narrowband signal processing, noise-quieting technologies, propulsion, and other sensitive advantages that culminated in an aggressive and highly effective antisubmarine-warfare posture. This was a commonly held view, and there was much evidence to support such assessments. However, inside the Soviet Union, within its elite R&D establishments, several major initiatives were about to challenge the Western lead. Behind these initiatives lay hard-core Soviet strategic thinking that coupled the navy of Admiral of the Fleet of the Soviet Union Sergey Gorshkov (February 26, 1910–May 13, 1988) to a wider Soviet strategic posture.

The work of eminent American Soviet analysts, such as James McConnell and his colleagues at the US Center for Naval Analyses in Arlington, Virginia, painstakingly demonstrated from multiple open Soviet sources, together with more sensitive intelligence sources and methods, that the Soviet navy would withhold its strategic submarine force in the Northern Fleet. McConnell called these "bastions," or safe havens, where Soviet SSBNs could hide undetected by Western ASW systems and where American and British attack submarines would find difficulties penetrating Soviet ASW barriers. The Soviet decision to go under the Arctic ice cap was a key element of this strategy. The Soviets' operational objective, as noted, was for their SSBNs to fire intercontinental strategic missiles from polynyas, or weak spots in the Arctic ice cap. The United States and United Kingdom tracked Soviet Arctic missile tests that landed on the Kamchatka Peninsula. These tests sent a clear message that from under the Arctic ice the Soviets could strike any major target in the United States and Europe.

The Soviet "bastion," or "withholding," strategy confused many analysts and furthermore led to findings of Soviet weakness and inability to fight in the open ocean. Nothing could have been farther from the truth. In fact, the Soviets had begun planning as early as the 1970s an aggressive technical strategy that sought to gain parity with the West in every aspect of underwater acoustics and all associated systems and, secondly, to make aggressive advances in nonacoustic antisubmarine-warfare technology. The most alarming aspect of these decisions was not just their inherent technical complexity but the operational requirements and goals that underpinned them. Unlike the Northern Fleet SSBN force, the Soviets did not plan to "withhold" antisubmarine and antisurface-warfare forces but forward-deploy them aggressively, to challenge US and UK strategic and tactical naval forces. The most ominous component of this strategy was the presumption that the Soviets at some stage in the 1980s would be technically in a position to challenge US and UK strategic submarines, a hugely worrisome aspect.

The key Soviet R&D establishments, such as the Institute of Hydrodynamics in Leningrad, began well-conceived and energetic programs, directed from the center in Moscow. The goal was to find the technical means to locate and track Western naval forces, especially submarines and aircraft carriers, together with amphibious assault forces, by unconventional and nonacoustic means. The Soviets wanted to direct their forward-deployed assets to positions where US and UK locational information could be passed, to set up trailing operations in peacetime or, in the event of war, attack and destroy Western assets. These operational concepts focused on a combination of several aspects of war-fighting doctrine: Soviet forces were to be in locations where they could preemptively attack if necessary, where surprise could be tactically achieved, and where massive strikes or concentration of force would overwhelm Western defensive systems by multiple attacks by the latest long-range antiship cruise missiles, such as the SS-N-19 (NATO designation).

These were ambitious goals. The Soviets systematically implemented programs to accomplish them. The key technical domain was ocean science and its effect on new detection mechanisms, as well as technologies that could capitalize on new understandings of the ocean and of the performance and passage of surface and submarine hulls through the ocean. The Soviets went back to fundamental oceanography and ocean physics to find new signatures to exploit. Parallel to these initiatives, Soviet scientists recognized that all means should be examined to protect Soviet submarines from acoustic detection.

They were going to address not only acoustic signal-processing improvements but also additional ways to quiet their submarines. These included technologies beyond traditional hull- and machinery noise–quieting approaches that had kept Western submarines quiet for decades and were still being improved. The Soviets embarked on ambitious, and occasionally almost far-fetched, research programs to shape submarine hulls and achieve engineering advances that would reduce drag and noise while increasing underwater speed. The technical relationships were well understood by Soviet submarine designers, and there were many people in all the necessary disciplines at the Soviet Academy of Sciences level to lead these programs.

Also, as we have seen, the Soviets planned to run parallel design and building programs of different classes. The Soviets wanted to implement quickly all major improvements, and they had multiple missions that required different classes. There were also bureaucratic reasons too, plus the need in their state-run economy to provide work to yards spread from the far north to the Far East. The discipline of a capitalist industrial economy operating in a democracy was at odds with the needs and mechanisms of a communist, noncompetitive economy.

The economics that drove US and UK submarine building at Electric Boat in Groton, Connecticut, and Vickers Shipbuilding and Engineering, in Barrow-in-Furness in the United Kingdom, were as unlike as chalk and cheese from what drove, for example, the Admiralty Yard in Leningrad. The Moscow-driven design bureaus and the communist bureaucracy behind them made for processes that had little or no resemblance to how a US or UK submarine was produced. In the United States and United Kingdom, a new submarine program passed through an intense operational-requirements assessment to the design, acquire, and build processes. In the United States, congressional oversight was pervasive. From a budgetary perspective, it seemed, from appearances alone, as if the United States and the United Kingdom had their hands tied, compared with the relative ease with which one submarine program after another passed through the halls of the Kremlin.

Let us step back for a moment and address the fundamentals of science and technology that the Soviets were seeking to apply. Soviet ocean physicists were familiar with well-known Western means of detection other than classic active and passive acoustic sonar arrays and sonar buoys. It was common knowledge that, for example, the magnetic signature of a hull can be vulnerable to detection by airborne magnetic anomaly detectors (MAD) booms on the after end of maritime patrol aircraft, such as the US P-3 Orion, and that a nonnuclear submarine when snorkeling to take in air and recharge batteries was perhaps vulnerable to "sniffer" devices that detected exhaust emissions from diesel submarines. Submarines, like all vessels, have heat signatures: when a submarine is on or very near the surface a heat signature can be detectable against the ambient background. Microwave infrared radiometers were designed and built to find these discrete temperature variances, ideally correlating to a nuclear submarine rather than a school of whales.

Various biological mechanisms were investigated, with the goal of detecting environmental changes caused by the passage of a submarine. This was a very ambitious concept, for reasons that we will address generally in a moment. Electro-optics were also favorite systems, using various types of lasers to penetrate the ocean and discriminate between the ocean background and a moving target. Work done in the mine-detection domain with blue-green lasers, later embedded in the US ALMDS (airborne LIDAR [light detection and ranging] mine-detection system), seemed to bear fruit for detecting relatively shallow submarines. The technical case was that if you can find a small mine at depth, why not a submarine? LIDAR was a very clever means of using laser technology in the ocean to differentiate targets. Classic SIGINT and ELINT were also added to this cornucopia, detecting emissions, whether communications or other, and also periscopes exposed for surveillance or navigation.

One overriding operational constraint on the use of these systems and technologies, particularly in the deep ocean or at choke points distant from US, UK, and NATO bases and airfields, was the time factor. How long it would take, say, a US P-3 or UK Nimrod aircraft to launch, fly to the last known area of contact, and begin to search, using these types of localization sensors? The variables were many and complex, and the probability of detection was very low, unless such a platform could reach a point within its localization accuracy before it became no longer detectable, and therefore untrackable.

All these technologies and operational systems had an additional major and inherent weakness: their search rates were extremely low, particularly in the vastness of the deep ocean. The most likely successful use of such systems was localization. If another system, such as submarine-mounted passive sonar or SOSUS, made an initial detection, tracking could produce actionable intelligence for localization. Then, perhaps, there was some utility in these technologies. But experience over several decades taught the West that the likelihood of such detections was extremely low. Also, countermeasures worked against these systems and technologies. Magnetic signatures can be marginalized by degaussing. Acoustics appeared therefore to reign supreme, because of the ability of passive sonar and narrowband signal processing to discriminate targets at considerable ranges, characterize their signatures, and then plot them. The huge investment in acoustics seemed to be the very best way to go, and to all intents and purposes the Western decision was correct in all regards—with one possible exception, and the Soviets were on to that.

In their search for other detectable signatures the Soviets realized that when a body moves in water it creates a displacement, its own volume, the simple fact on which Archimedes' Principle is based. For a submarine, or any vessel for that matter, the larger the vessel the greater the displacement, and that volume of water has to go somewhere. Therefore, disturbance and movement will cause change, not just volumetrically but in terms of the ambient ocean conditions. That is, there will be variances in all the parameters that have been measured for decades by oceanographers, whether for scientific research or for defense applications. The United States and the United Kingdom learned in the very early days of acoustics that understanding the oceans and collecting data from the main operating areas were crucial for applying sonar technology and adapting to the ambient ocean environment. Salinity, temperature, density, sound-pressure levels, and acoustic paths vary by location.

However, Soviet oceanographers and ocean physicists had determined one other key fact, one that would lead to both controversy and at some level, resolution, over the decades from the 1970s. Some of the finest minds in the West and the Soviet Union would address this issue, including, for example, Dr. R. V. Jones, Winston Churchill's prime special programs scientist during World War II, and the American Dr. Walter Heinrich Munk. Their counterparts in the Soviet Union were equally distinguished—Dr. Victor Etkin is a name that we shall return to later.

What then was the point that taxed the fine minds of these Soviet scientists? They were looking for a strategic capability with a very high search rate, localization capability, and ability to discriminate and then track. This was a tall order indeed, analogous to the challenge facing Allen Turing at Bletchley Park during World War II. The Soviet academicians had to solve a most intractable technical problem by sheer brainpower and inventiveness. However, Turing had been motivated by not only the intellectual challenge but the need to save his country and the world from Nazism; most of the Soviet scientists who worked for these programs were motivated by scientific challenge only, particularly those who were not ethnic Russians. The Ukrainian Institutes were populated, for example, largely by non-Russian scientists, many of whom detested the regime in Moscow and the Soviet oligarchy.

We noted earlier that a vessel creates a volumetric displacement that has several key characteristics. The most significant in terms of signature characterization is the body of water displaced. This water's characteristics will vary with the actual volume and the speed at which it is displaced. Volumetric propagation occurs both on and under the surface, with one qualification. In the case of the submarine, the volumetric displacement and speed of dispersal will also be associated with the submarine's depth. Surface or subsurface speed will also cause variations in the above parameters. In addition, the volumetric displacement will be affected by local ambient ocean conditions, depending on location, time of year, season, and diurnal variations, in addition to, in the case of the submarine, depth. Ocean currents increase complexity where tides are a factor, and ocean mixing occurs where various massive ocean movements interact, such as near archipelagoes, entrances to major ocean areas, and around capes and other channels and funnels. Ice is a factor in the Arctic north. On the surface, key state factors such as wind speed and wave height interact with more esoteric factors such as sun glint and sun angle.

So, what could Soviet scientists make of all this? The phenomenology at the heart of their initial research at both the theoretical level and in the laboratory was the displacement volume itself, called the "internal wave." The Soviets found that the internal wave had its own dynamics. The internal wave produced physical observables that they sought to measure and quantify, and indeed embody in new rule sets or theory. In simplistic terms, let us take two moving bodies: a six-thousand-ton-displacement nuclear-powered attack submarine transiting at speeds between ten and twenty knots and a hundred-thousand-ton nuclear-powered aircraft carrier at both cruising speeds and aircraft-launch speeds, between twenty and thirty knots. Both hulls will create internal waves. In addition, both hulls will also create other well-known and understood wave forms, such as Kelvin wakes and turbulent wakes.

A wake is understandable and easily observable by any layman. We have all noted wakes from various vantage points, such as looking out a passenger aircraft window and seeing the wakes of boats below. The bow wake is a displacement of water, and like all wave forms it will disperse from the bow and hull until the energy that is generated within the wave is overcome by a dispersion effect, combined with friction, in the ocean. The various types of wake can be modeled by computational fluid dynamics.

What the Soviet ocean physicists and their colleagues in the hull-hydrodynamics domains were most interested in was the much less understood internal-wave wake created by surface ships and submarines. There were several reasons for this. One important reason was that the internal wave (proportional to displacement and speed) was much larger and more persistent than, say, the classic Kelvin wake. In simple terms, the internal wave or wake lasts longer and is more widely dispersed. Its volumetric impact on the surrounding water is much greater than the relatively simple passage of the bow through the water. The other, somewhat obvious, fact is that the phenomenon, or signature, cannot be hidden, camouflaged, or reduced to imperceptibility. From the detectability aspect, it is a signature that will not go away.

Furthermore, the Soviet scientists made the simple deduction that if you can see a vessel's wake from a bridge overhead or from the stern of the vessel, you will be able to see the wake from not only an aircraft, as was common, but also from a satellite with the right sort of sensors. This fact excited attention in the Kremlin and the higher echelons of the Soviet navy. If all this was so, a wide-area search capability was possible, limited only by the swath of a satellite's or aircraft's sensors. For the Soviet scientists the surface mode was relatively simple; tests in wave tanks could be conducted using models in various configurations and speeds. Wave tanks quickly proliferated in many centers of Soviet ocean and hydrodynamics research, and from the data produced, mathematical models were developed.

A challenge lay with the submarine's internal wave, because of the simple fact that the submarine is submerged. Technical issues related to the physics of the dispersal of the underwater-generated internal wave are more complex, volumetrically, regarding the speed and depth of the submarine, and how and for how long the wave disperses until the collapse of its energy. The interface of the wave with the surrounding body of water and the effects that this produces are complex. The Soviets theorized that a large, persistent internal wave generated by a submarine could have effects not just on the underwater environment but also on the surface, creating surface phenomena that might be measurable by a variety of sensors. Their key point was, at one level, and quite simplistically, that the large displacement at speed of the internal-wave wake could be the key to a whole new area of submarine detection.

We will revert to this situation shortly, but we will sidestep for a while to address where Western intelligence was in its knowledge base and cultural affinities while the above was going on. We have seen that until about 1980 the West enjoyed a serious qualitative advantage over the Soviet Union and its allies in acoustics—the gap was significant and made for a high level of confidence. When the above programs were first detected by both American and British intelligence there were varying degrees of skepticism and doubt as to the true intentions and long-term technical goals of the Soviet Union. One view in the United States saw the programs as signs of a nation grasping at straws. This view argued that the Soviets were unable to narrow the acoustic gap because of their inherent weaknesses in ocean physics, narrowband signal-processing, noise-quieting technologies, and sensors. In other words, the Soviets were looking for all and every means for a solution to their capability gap. This type of assessment was all well and good if its facts were accurate, that the Soviets were struggling to catch up while the United States and the United Kingdom were improving across the board. If the Soviets did not have the necessary computer knowledge and technology, how could they execute the massive processing that was required to model and understand the acoustics of the ocean, let alone move into the whole new, totally unexplored domains of wake phenomenology?

There was a growing gap between US and UK assessments. The United Kingdom was much more open-minded, concerned that US intelligence was being overoptimistic. The United Kingdom was concerned lest the latest operational intelligence data was a false foundation for confidence that the Soviets would never catch up. This growing disagreement was kept under wraps while the facts were monitored, evidence assembled, and notes compared, with no one claiming absolute knowledge of the true Soviet position. There was also a natural desire to prevent rifts from occurring in a community that was unassailably joined at the hip.

However, unknown to the US government there was another major agenda at play, and it was having a significant impact on Soviet plans, policies, programs, and operations. Between 1968 and 1985 a US Navy chief warrant officer communications specialist with access to the most sensitive technical and operational information and intelligence spied for the Soviet Union. His motive was entirely financial. There were no ideological or sexual motivations or blackmail. During this seventeen-year period John Anthony Walker gave the Soviets an extraordinary amount of information. The Walker spy ring was still spying for the Soviets when the Oscar and Typhoon classes were launched in 1980—a point to retain as we analyze the roles and impacts of Walker and his collaborators, Senior Chief Petty Officer Jerry Whitworth and Walker's son, Seaman Michael Walker. Several distinguished Americans, including Secretary of Defense Caspar Weinberger and Secretary of the Navy John Lehman, went on the record to state how massive was the damage done to US national security by the Walker spy ring. The key point that emerges from all the public evidence is that the betrayal of crucial communications information, particularly cryptologic code cards, enabled the Soviets to break into and understand US capabilities at many levels, both operational and technical. The heyday of Walker, Whitworth, and Walker's son in the 1970s gave the Soviets all the insights that they needed as to where and how they should concentrate their efforts.

Their spying did not simply enable the Soviets to catch up. What these three men did to US security, and therefore that of the United Kingdom, was equally devastating: they provided the Soviets the means (not the actual data itself—they were communications specialists, not operators or technologists) to understand what they needed to do in order to catch up and then go one step farther. In addition to catching up, which was likely to be a fifteen-to-twenty-year effort in 1970, what should the Soviets do in order to steal a lead? Knowing how to address each of these questions was extraordinarily beneficial. It determined the plans, policies, and programs needed to catch up and what might be done to circumvent the advantages that the United States and United Kingdom clearly enjoyed. This crucial point links the sorry and appalling story of Walker, Whitworth, and Walker's son to the programs to which we will now return.

There was considerable shock in the US intelligence community at the launch of Oscar and Typhoon. The British were not at all surprised, having predicted in a highly classified document the capabilities of both these platforms. I was the coordinator and author-in-chief of that report. The Soviets had, in other words, turned the corner. They were on an upward trajectory to narrow the acoustic gap and other critical underwater capabilities while also working in parallel and alternate domains. The United States and the United Kingdom would quickly be introduced to Soviet titanium submarine hulls powered by liquid-metal nuclear reactors and a whole new generation of underwater, subsurface-to-surface, and surface-to-surface naval weapons. All these weapons not only worked as advertised but had serious consequences for Western aircraft carriers, amphibious groups, and other high-value units, if they could be targeted accurately.

The Soviet nonacoustic programs moved forward. Meanwhile, the United States and the United Kingdom began parallel cooperative programs. I was involved in one of the key programs. A senior representative, Les Aspin from Wisconsin, then chairman of the US House Armed Services Committee (he would in due course become secretary of defense), went on the record in the *Washington Post* that the United States would investigate what the Soviets had achieved in nonacoustic ASW programs. On Thursday, June 6, 1985, the *Washington Post* went public about Soviet nonacoustic ASW programs, on the front page and on page A16. The front-page headline read, "CIA Studies Sub Vulnerability: Soviets Apparently Tracked Strategic Missile Vessels." Inside, bold headlines announced, "CIA Studies Vulnerability of Missile

Submarines." The statements alarmed many in the US and UK intelligence communities and, naturally, the leadership of the two navies. Even to those who thought that they knew about Soviet programs and threats, these public revelations came as a major surprise. Clearly, only a few in the intelligence community and US Navy were truly aware of the detail of these Soviet programs. One particularly broad statement resonated, one that was undoubtedly read in the halls of the Kremlin and KGB and GRU headquarters: "The study is to focus on advanced techniques, particularly involving radar and satellites, that the Soviets might be using to detect US submarine under the sea." The article specifically addressed the impact of "the alleged Walker family spy ring that is being pursued by federal law enforcement authorities." It is of note too that the *Washington Post* announced that the CIA deputy director for intelligence, Mr. Robert Gates, would be in charge of the program.

The article weighed many different opinions and assessments, which were at considerable variance. Most significantly, the article mentioned the possibility that the Soviets might be using synthetic aperture radar (SAR) "housed in the Salyut 7 space station to bounce radar signals off the ocean and then process them into computer-generated images that might show up as a track on the ocean surface caused by the passage of a submarine below." These were bold and heady statements. The report cited the countervailing arguments of the special Department of Defense "JASON" group, and also the views of the technical director of the US Navy's submarine security program (Dr. Edward Harper), all claiming that Soviets had no such effective capabilities. The *Washington Post* also stated explicitly that the motive of the US Air Force was to gain support for its MX missile program versus the strategic submarine program, implying that the Air Force had reasons to try to undermine the Navy's key program. However, the article stated, the CIA had previously disagreed with the Navy about possible vulnerabilities from Soviet nonacoustic systems: the CIA "dissented from the conclusion on the basis that the Navy studies had not been thorough enough." This was strong, authoritative language, and its accuracy was not publicly challenged by any department or agency of the executive branch.

What this article revealed was dissension within the US intelligence community about assessments of Soviet capabilities and also political factors within the United States that might be driving assessments—that is, pressure from those protecting existing programs. The public perception was one of skepticism and concern, and naturally so, since the Poseidon and *Ohio* (Trident) submarine force was, as it still is, the backbone of the US strategic deterrent force. Reactions were similar in the United Kingdom, where the ballistic-missile submarines were and are indeed the sole source of national strategic deterrence. At the time of the *Washington Post* article the United Kingdom was planning and funding the replacement of its strategic submarine force. (It is noteworthy that over thirty years since the *Washington Post* article both the United States and the United Kingdom are planning and funding the replacement of their *Ohio-* and *Vanguard-*class strategic submarines. Thirty years is surely an ample period in which to determine whether or not the Soviets did indeed have the capabilities that Representative Aspin sought to investigate.) We will return shortly to the issues and arguments regarding possible vulnerabilities. Meanwhile, let us revert to the Soviets' side of things— what were they really about?

In their pursuit of the ideal nonacoustic detection mechanism the Soviets were highly efficient technically and intellectually. They immersed themselves in drag reduction, having recognized from very early on, in the 1960s, the technical link between drag and noise—that a submarine with reduced drag would have a reduced acoustic signature, because the boundary layer between the hull and the water flowing along the hull mitigates flow noise. They worked on hull shaping to improve drag; drag, however, is only one component in the noise profile of a submarine. They also designed and installed anechoic tiles on their submarine hulls to improve flow, reduce drag, and control flow noise from the hull itself. They improved the design of their propulsors. From a broader viewpoint the Soviets had a holistic view of these integrated technologies.

But they were facing, like their counterparts in the United States and the United Kingdom, demands in physics that had never been addressed before. The nonacoustic challenge was massive and expensive, and the end game was uncertain and absolutely unproven in terms of fundamental physics. The Soviet objective—dream, some analysts in the West said—of eventually having a sensor in space that would be able to detect a submerged submarine was real, though far from obtainable as the 1980s moved along toward the end of the Soviet oligarchy. However, the ten years from 1980 to 1990 were a period of intense challenge and rivalry between the US-UK team and that of the Soviet Union. Where did the truth lie among the many and varied interpretations of Soviet capabilities?

A crucial turning point in the intelligence debate, as well as the possibility of submerged submarine detection by airborne or space-based sensors, came in 1979. This date is somewhat ironic, given the advances that the Soviets were found to have made when the Oscar and Typhoon classes were launched in 1980. Nevertheless, in 1979 there was a seminal change in the technical debate, one that would create even more concern and technical disagreement. Commercial SEASAT SAR satellite imagery of various ships in the western Atlantic off the coast of the southeast United States very clearly showed long, V-shaped markings on the ocean surface. These scars were pronounced, easily observed by the naked eye on the images without any form of advanced digital processing or enhancement. Not only the clarity of the surface effects but also their lengths were prodigious, and clearly there was a relationship with the size and speed of the vessels: the larger and faster the ship, longer and more persistent the V-shaped scar—or wake, as it was to be called. Early analysis showed that it was possible to calculate the age of each wake based on the ship's speed and course.

After the SEASAT data was initially analyzed, I attended what was to be an important meeting at the Royal Aircraft Establishment at Farnborough, England, with key US technical experts. We all agreed that this imagery was a game changer, irrespective of the impact on submarine-related programs or submarine-generated phenomenology. The reason was self-evident from the data: what we were observing was not Kelvin or turbulent wakes but their internal-wave wakes. The space-based imagery we were all looking at was totally unclassified commercial data. It showed that any surface ship in the future could be observed from space by the V-shaped surface manifestation of its internal-wave wake. To the small team at Farnborough this meant simply that any surface ship could now be tracked from space or an aircraft carrying a SAR radar similar to the one on the SEASAT. Ocean surveillance had now changed forever; the gathering at Farnborough immediately realized the long-term significance. The question in all our minds was simple: What had the Soviets seen? Had Soviet scientists working their various nonacoustic programs seen the same data? Had they drawn what we considered the same, obvious conclusions? The answers to all were resounding affirmatives.

The 1979 SEASAT data opened up Pandora's box, and in more ways than one. Both the United States and the United Kingdom were concerned that the Soviets might have known more about space-based surveillance of the surface manifestations of internal and related wake effects than the intelligence community had realized. We noted earlier that by June 1985 the *Washington Post* and the chairman of the House Armed Services Committee had openly discussed this subject. In the six years from 1979 to 1985 there was intense debate and disagreement. At this point it is useful to step back and review relationships, not between the US Navy and the Royal Navy but within the US intelligence community.

It is no secret that the US intelligence community is vast and to a certain extent unwieldy. In recent years efforts have been made to exert more control over its multifarious agencies and departments, which serve different masters and for different purposes. The Office of Naval Intelligence, headed for decades by several illustrious directors, had historically been a lead agency and, in many ways, autonomous. We have analyzed earlier why this was so—reasons much related to the highly sensitive collection programs executed by the US Navy in concert with the British. However, when nonacoustic ASW began to emerge seriously as a possible threat, intensified by the Walker spy scandal, ONI and the DNI had a natural, and very understandable, wish to deal with the issues unaided, arguing that ONI should oversee and control the response. Historically and by agreement the US and the UK Navies had not shared highly sensitive joint data with third parties, except under the strictest security controls. That meant that data was not only not shared with but that its very existence was not acknowledged to, for example, the Central Intelligence Agency.

There were very good security reasons for this, and they were not political or bureaucratic. The issue was genuinely about protecting hugely sensitive information. The British, for their part, would avoid at all cost becoming embroiled in any of the internecine rivalry between US agencies. The British policy was simple—always to abide by the agreed special US-UK naval security rules and play no games. By June 6, 1985, the subject had entered the public domain, with the publication of the *Washington Post* article, and the US Navy was placed in an uncomfortable position. Congressional staffs had to ensure that the key members of the appropriate committees of record were well informed, under the appropriate security rules. Within these various committees there were restrictions on who knew what. There was therefore much scope for misunderstanding, false accusations, and miss-assessments.

It is to the enduring credit of both the US Navy and the Royal Navy that they initiated and executed new programs in nonacoustic ASW. Most of all, they collaborated to ensure that the national security interests of both countries were fully protected while intelligence about the Soviet programs was thoroughly and independently analyzed.

In order to gain perspective on the above issues, let us now revert to what many readers will find most significant, the operational impact. Let us look in detail at the operational issues. We have examined earlier the considerable difficulties in employing operationally some of the intelligence advantages that the US and UK Navies enjoyed in acoustics and submarine quieting. A well-organized and integrated command, control, and communications environment and architecture would be required to exploit any advances in ocean physics and signal processing. Consider the vastness and complexity of the oceans, and also the near- or real-time surveillance required in order to monitor by nonacoustic means for a submarine. Even if the areas for surveillance are narrowed down to choke points, the likelihood of detection remains remote, owing not only to the limitations of the sensors involved but also the sheer logistics. For example, 24/7 satellite surveillance of certain ocean areas is extraordinarily challenging in terms of the number of satellites required, cost, and competing operational requirements.

Coupled to these factors is the unassailable fact that each of the major space-intelligence powers clearly wishes to know both the orbits and locations of each other's spy satellites at any given time. Knowing when a satellite is overhead is important in itself. Additionally, the tactical situation at any given moment plays a key role; we saw earlier that such factors as speed and depth are critical. Added to these variables are the ambient ocean conditions and how these will affect sensor performance and the likelihood of detection of ocean-surface phenomenology. Common sense alone must rule: for example, it would be unwise during the known passage of a satellite to raise an antenna or a periscope; if the oceanographic science behind the Soviet programs has credibility, that would be a time to stay deep and maintain a slow speed of advance (SOA).

The permutations of all these factors make for a challenge that is huge, akin to the proverbial needle in a haystack. Even supposing a detection was made, other assets would have to be vectored to the target area to begin a search. Time then becomes a factor, as was noted earlier. Transit times and vectoring of assets, whether airborne, surface, or subsurface, are nontrivial. Perhaps only in the most highly orchestrated operation could a US or UK submarine find itself compromised, and even then it could either fight back or evade.

My only qualifications to the above relate to submarine egress and ingress. Several of the key US and UK bases are on the continental shelf, which typically, but not always, extends to about the one-hundred-fathom curve (six hundred feet). The water depth then changes dramatically, dropping to often thousands of feet. In the egress stage of a submarine's deployment there is always risk, particularly for the large, strategic missile submarines; because of their size, they have less sea room and need to be well protected until they reach their diving areas. As was discussed earlier, the Soviets invested heavily in attempting to learn when such deployments would occur. For example, in the days before the US base at Holy Loch in Scotland was closed there was always risk in the egress stage, a long transit for a US SSBN, and for their British counterparts deploying from the nearby Faslane naval base on the Gare Loch. The Soviet operational objective was quite explicit: to intercept and trail during the egress phase, when both water depth and navigational factors inhibit tactical maneuvering for a deploying SSBN.

The United States and United Kingdom worked up security measures and tactics to mitigate this particular threat, but the point remains that in the fairly long transit through shallow and constricted water to deep water, a submarine may be more vulnerable than in the vast expanses of the ocean, in a patrol mode; there the Bayesian likelihood of detection is minimal. Similarly, when SSNs are forced by operational necessity to operate in shallow areas, and certainly on continental shelves, they are potentially more vulnerable. Airborne sensors coupled to satellite surveillance may then become more efficacious when networked with surface and subsurface ASW assets; particularly they create barriers and remain quiet at slow speeds. If a US or UK submarine has to transit through such a barrier, the ambush scenario is not unrealistic. However, ambush can be mitigated by good intelligence, stealth, and tactical maneuvering, so that a US or UK submarine, particularly if it is able to receive communications, should have the advantage for the foreseeable future.

Let us return to the technical debate and examine the Soviet position in 1990. Two giants of science, one American and one British, were involved in remote ocean imaging and sensing as applied to nonacoustic ASW. Professor R. V. Jones is legendary, and rightly so. He was, under cover of working for the Royal Air Force, the key technical and scientific adviser to the British Secret Intelligence Service through World War II. Winston Churchill considered him a national asset. R. V. Jones was at least in the same league intellectually and in terms of achievements as Alan Turing at Bletchley Park. Neither was fully recognized until their extraordinary work was released by the British government beginning in the mid-1970s.

Jones—subject of a vast literature and author of *Most Secret War: British Scientific Intelligence 1939–45*—may not have been quite the genius Turing was, but he was not far behind in achievements. Professor Jones was very apt to quote Crow's Law: "Do not believe what you want to believe until you know what you ought to know." Jones became involved in the technical issues of remote sensing of the ocean surface because of the strategic issues at stake. Born on September 29, 1911 (he died December 17, 1997, age eighty-six), he was in his late sixties and seventies in the 1970s and 1980s but as intellectually alive and capable as in World War II.

On the American side the giant was Professor Walter Heinrich Munk, professor of geophysics at the Scripps Institution of Oceanography in La Jolla, California. Munk's credentials are impressive. Born on October 19, 1917, in Vienna, Austria, Walter Munk found his way by a circuitous path to the California Institute of Technology (BS in physics) and to the University of California, Los Angeles, where he earned master's and PhD degrees in geophysics and oceanography, respectively. His career is well described in a myriad of sources. Suffice here to say that Walter Munk became intimately involved in the technical issues.

However, he did not quite have the pedigree of Professor R.V. Jones and absolutely nothing like Jones' experience or achievements during and after World War II. Jones simply knew more about the whole world of secret intelligence; he had an extraordinary record of knowing not just fact from fiction but also when to stay alert for unforeseen threats, such as the Nazi program to develop an atomic weapon and the V-1 and V-2 rocket programs, as well as how Ultra data from Enigma could be utilized. Munk knew nothing of this world and those kinds of technical challenges, but he was an absolutely brilliant oceanographer of great distinction. He was also very much the US Navy's man, holding the Secretary of the Navy and Chief of Naval Operations chair of oceanography at Scripps; his allegiances and funding sources were directly tied to the US Navy. Jones, in contrast, had a long-term reputation for total independence from government influence and for absolute intellectual integrity. He was never anyone's captive, one reason why Winston Churchill not only trusted him but at times during World War II totally relied on his technical judgment and wisdom.

Jones and Munk were very different people. After several years of research and experimentation into the phenomenology that we have just examined, Walter Munk's technical judgment was that detecting a submerged submarine by means of surface effects was beyond the laws of physics. R.V. Jones' riposte was characteristically simple and to the point, to the effect that whenever someone states that it is against the law of physics, be assured that in due course the laws of physics will be changed. Jones was saying that physics has never been static but has changed, in some cases quite dramatically, over time. His observation is clearly quite axiomatic, on a line drawn from Isaac Newton to Albert Einstein to Roger Penrose to Stephen Hawking. Modern quantum mechanics bear no relation to the physics of Ernest Rutherford or Henry Cavendish—they were giants indeed, but only "for their time."

In the forty-plus years since remote sensing of the ocean surface has become a scientific quest, computational power has increased almost unbelievably. The revolution in data and information processing will inevitably continue to levels that we cannot envisage today. Moving from ASDIC to passive narrowband signal processing was a massive leap. Common sense tends therefore to lead us to the R. V. Jones' view of the world, which is not to diminish any way the great achievements in ocean science of Walter Munk and many others. The fact is, science changes.

Let us take one illustration within the field of remote ocean sensing, the issue of how effective radar can be not just in imaging the ocean surface but in converting data to actionable information. The ocean surface is so complex and changeable that any usable pattern-recognition algorithm may be impractical. Research in the 1970s relied on Bragg scattering theory, the ways in which radar waves and energy are likely to react and scatter on the ocean surface and be reflected.

This domain is very important, because it addresses the ability of a space-based or airborne SAR radar to provide ocean-surface data with intelligible information embedded. Two very capable American physicists, Dr. Dennis Holiday and Dr. Nancy Woods, assisted by a sizeable team, did what Professor Munk had said was impossible, change the laws of physics—seriously modifying Bragg scattering theory. The main point here is that nothing remains static; in an age of computational revolution and subatomic particle modeling, we should "watch this space," both literally and metaphorically. The Russians and Chinese have fine physicists, and we should not be complacent in watching their developments over the next decades.

But to return to the Soviets: How far had they advanced in science, technology, and operational application by the time the Soviet Union imploded? Just as Werner von Braun and others were brought out of Nazi Germany at the end of World War II to support US rocket programs, the United States and the United Kingdom sought to bring out scientists who had been prominently involved in Cold War programs that had given most concern; they might have capabilities the West did not or where intelligence was inadequate. One such domain comprised nonacoustic ASW and remote sensing of the ocean surface to track submarines.

I was involved in a program to examine the accuracy, indeed truthfulness, of the scientific and technical claims made by various former Soviet scientists who had relocated to the United States with the help of the US government. Several had been preeminent in R&D establishments and in Moscow. One of them, Victor Etkin, will serve to illustrate what we generally learned about where the Soviets had been headed when the Berlin Wall came down. He was distinguished, academically very capable, and had been involved in Soviet space-based nonacoustic ASW programs. Victor Etkin was most forthcoming, and what he revealed was not dissimilar to where the United States and the United Kingdom had thought the Soviets might be. However, some claims caused surprise, relating to detection of NATO submarines from space. The Soviets had built space-based SARs for this purpose but had appreciated that the deep ocean is, if not opaque, not transparent either; the operational challenges of detection were substantial. I led a team that reconstructed the data on which Etkin and his colleagues based their claims. At one level, we concluded that he and others had wanted to impress us; the data did not support several important claims. However, the Soviets' programs had been extensive, and there is no question that they were seeking a breakthrough in strategic ASW. They had most certainly not found one.

Very able former Soviet scientists emigrated to the West, where many have worked alongside North American defense and intelligence specialists as coequals, having become naturalized American or Canadian citizens. One such person with whom I have collaborated is Dr. Vassili Proudkii, a Ukrainian who was born in 1932 and at the time of writing is in excellent health and continues to work in physics. His master's and doctoral degrees are from the Moscow and Dnepropetrovsk State Universities. He has written over 150 scientific articles and papers and holds sixty-two patents, some of which are still classified by the Russian Federation. He received the Order of Honor, the highest civilian award made by the former Soviet Parliament, for "Outstanding Scientific Excellence" in September 1986. Dr. Proudkii was involved in the most sensitive Soviet programs, and his ability and integrity have lent considerable credibility to assessments of where the Soviets had reached when the USSR collapsed. As a Ukrainian, Dr. Proudkii was no lover of Russia and has given outstanding service to Western science and technology since arriving in North America.

In conclusion, the Soviets found the innumerable operational, environmental, and space-time factors militating against them in nonacoustic ASW, just as US and UK programs did. The book is most certainly not closed, however, on the issue. The peace dividend and the reduction of the former Soviet navy under the new Russian leadership led to the atrophy of former Soviet programs; that situation has now changed, and we will examine the turnaround in the Russian navy later. Suffice to observe here that the Russians continue to build submarines, as do the Chinese, with several new classes in parallel. They clearly do not believe that the submarine will be compromised in the short-to-medium term by any breakthrough in nonacoustic ASW. Nonetheless that contingency must be carefully watched.

The key reason lies in the nature of scientific and technical advance. In 1945 ASDIC was king, and technical advances helped win the Battle of the Atlantic. If antisubmarine warriors of World War II could have lived another thirty years, to, say, 1975, they would not have recognized ASW, thanks to extraordinary advances of which they had no knowledge. Looking ahead to 2045, a similar span of time, where will computational power be then? Subatomic particle physics and quantum mechanics have modified both relativity and classic Newtonian physics within the past ten years, and the Higgs boson is a proven, not theoretical, reality. The ability in the future to process the most complex ocean data may be beyond our ken today. What we do know is that science will march onward. The operational challenge will be to adjust to its advances as they are made and keep abreast by changing tactics.

In the February 9, 2015, *Defense News,* reporter David Larter described comments made by Admiral Jonathan Greenert, then Chief of Naval Operations, that "stealth may be overrated." Larter wrote, "Greenert has expressed skepticism about stealth technology's value before, arguing in a 2012 paper that improving computer technology will render even the most stealthy aircraft more detectable." The point is well made, specifically and generically. Computational power will find the most discrete signal in massive background noise. In the oceanic remote-sensing environment we should assume that the same will apply. Meanwhile, Russia remains confident of the benefits conferred by a strong submarine fleet, laying down five new submarines in 2015: *Borei*-class nuclear-powered ballistic-missile submarines, *Yasen*-class nuclear attack submarines, and Kilo- and *Lada*-class diesel-electric submarines. In 2015 the Russians were building six Kilos for Vietnam and offering more for export elsewhere. The message is clear that submarines remain unchallenged for the foreseeable future. At the same time we should closely watch the scientific front; remembering how Admiral Sir Max Horton and Captain "Johnny" Walker and many others figured out how to defeat the U-boat menace in the Battle of the Atlantic, we should never assume that science will not find the solution to the issues with nonacoustic ASW.

A Real Shooting War at Sea
The Falklands Campaign of 1982

The 1982 Falklands campaign was pivotal for many reasons. It came at the height of the Cold War, when no end seemed in sight and not one soothsayer, let alone intelligence analysts in London or Washington, would predict that the Soviet Union would start imploding within seven years and the Berlin Wall would come down. We will not examine here the antecedents to and fine details of the campaign, simply because there are many fine works on the Falklands. The official history of the campaign written by Professor Sir Lawrence Freedman of King's College, London, is a magisterial and thorough account, and there is no need to repeat it. The intent rather is to examine several domains that have hitherto been unexamined or even unreported because no authors were close to them.

The 1982 campaign is unique in post–World War II warfare. It covered every domain of naval warfare, unlike such wars as Korea and Vietnam. Space systems existed during the Vietnam War, but space in Vietnam did not have the same impact as in the Falklands, not least because the Soviet Union had an interest in the South Atlantic in ways that differed from Vietnam. The first Mideast Gulf war was the next war in which space played a significant role. Antisubmarine warfare was not part of Korea or Vietnam, nor was maritime antiair warfare in the context of carrier defense. So what overall were the domains in the Falklands conflict? Let us summarize first off what was in play.

When the Argentine junta planned the seizure of the Falklands, beginning on April 2, 1982, and of South Georgia on April 3, the dictator General Leopoldo Galtieri and his military staff may not have foreseen the magnitude of the operations that would follow. His two principal military supporters of launching the invasion, Admiral Jorge Anyana in the navy and General Basilio Lami Dozo in the air force, were likely either unaware of or did not anticipate the intricate and complex dynamics of the ensuing conflict. The Argentines successfully invaded the islands with a sizeable ground force led by Brigadier

General Mario Menendez but had then to maintain logistics between the islands and the mainland: fuel, supplies, ammunition, and personnel. Other than light aircraft, such as the Pucaras, which they landed on the islands, the Argentine navy and air force would rely on mainland-based fixed-wing aircraft for attacking the British fleet and ground forces. The Argentine aircraft carrier ARA *Veinticinco de Mayo* (formerly HMS *Venerable*, launched in December 1943 and sold to the Netherlands in 1948 before being acquired by Argentina) was old, in port, and clearly a target for Royal Navy submarines. The Argentines would have to fly round-trip sorties from their main bases. These were located in Trelew (580 nautical miles, or nm, from Port Stanley), Comodoro Rivadavia (480 nm from Port Stanley), San Julian (425 nm from Port Stanley), Rio Gallegos (435 nm from Port Stanley), and Rio Grande (380 nm from Port Stanley).

These numbers were mathematical factors that would drive Royal Navy thinking, strategy, and tactics: the speed, time, and distance calculations for the Argentine A-4s and Super Etendards flying to the islands, attacking their targets, and returning before running out of fuel. These calculations reflected the maximum operating radius for each of these main aircraft types given their known operating envelopes. By the same token, these calculations would determine the safe havens for the two Royal Navy light, Harrier-operating aircraft carriers: HMS *Hermes,* the flagship, embarking the task force commander, Rear Admiral John "Sandy" Woodward; and HMS *Invincible.* The weather and daylight would be huge factors in determining when the Argentines could fly. The aircraft that could attack the British units would have no in-flight refueling; typically, Argentine pilots had only a few minutes over the islands to attack before they had to leave.

There was the possibility that the enemy would send aircraft, particularly those armed with the French Exocet antiship missile, on a one-way mission, extending the range at the expense of ditching or landing on the short runway near Port Stanley. The payoff, however, could have been a successful attack on a major British unit, such as one of the two carriers, or one of the amphibious ships carrying units of the Royal Marines 3 Commando Brigade, its command echelons, and the ground force commander, Major General Jeremy Moore, Royal Marines. These were serious concerns for the staff of the task force commander. Although the Argentine surface navy was somewhat old, it nonetheless was armed with British-provided weapons, and the older ships had US gun systems, such as those carried by the ill-fated cruiser *General Belgrano.* The greatest concern for Admiral Woodward, a submariner of distinction, constituted three German-built diesel-electric submarines armed with torpedoes. In the deep recesses of the South Atlantic, the staff of the British fleet knew, finding a quiet German diesel submarine could be difficult; the ocean environment was unfamiliar to British sonar specialists. Similarly with air defense: the British lacked organic long-range airborne early-warning aircraft and would have to rely on forward-deployed surface-ship radar pickets positioned to detect aircraft inbound from the mainland. This risky approach was the only tactical option, aside from sources and methods that we will address shortly.

To recapitulate so far: the British had a significant task force of two light carriers, protected by a sizeable force of destroyers and frigates to provide air defense, antisurface warfare, antisubmarine warfare, and land attack/shore bombardment. In addition certain units were designated to provide recon-naissance and scouting, akin to classic Nelsonian frigate operations. Others would land special forces from the Special Air Service and from the Special Boat Section of the Royal Marines. These invaluable operations provided crucial tactical intelligence in near real time via satellite link to fleet head-quarters in Northwood, England. They were also means to destroy targets particularly worrisome, including the Pucara aircraft, allegedly armed with napalm, on the ground. The core of the amphibious assault force comprised the two landing platform dock ships (LPDs) HMS *Fearless* and HMS *Intrepid,* as well as a plethora of what the British termed STUFT ships, "ships taken up from trade," merchant vessels requisitioned for wartime use under the Royal Navy's war plans. Included in this category were such ships as the liner *Can-berra* and merchant ship *Atlantic Conveyor.* The headquarters staff of 3 Com-mando Brigade was embarked on the LPDs. The LPDs and STUFT ships would penetrate San Carlos Water undetected and land the amphibious force, a huge achievement given that the nearest British base was Ascension Island, six thousand kilometers away.

Among the aces in Admiral Woodward's hands were Royal Navy nuclear-powered attack submarines. The SSNs were under the direct operational control of Northwood (something that Admiral Woodward criticized subse-quently, correctly). They were invaluable for several reasons, not least the col-lection of key tactical intelligence using their SIGINT and ELINT antennas. One factor that was to affect both SSN intelligence operations and those of GCHQ and the National Security Agency in the United States in supporting the British task force was that all threat communications were in Spanish, to which the collective intelligence community had to adapt quickly. As a deter-rent against the deployment of the Argentine aircraft carrier, the SSNs were totally successful. Admiral Anyana knew that a British SSN or SSNs would be waiting as soon as the Argentine carrier left her home base, a sitting duck for British torpedoes. In this he was correct. The acoustic signature of this carrier was not difficult to detect and track.

After the breakdown of all hopes of a diplomatic solution and the apparently aggressive posturing of the Argentine surface action group led by the cruiser *General Belgrano* on the edge of the two-hundred-mile total exclusion zone (TEZ) created by the British government around the Falkland Islands, Prime Minister Margaret Thatcher personally authorized an attack on *Belgrano* by the SSN HMS *Conqueror*. The attack was tactically successful, as it resulted in the Argentine surface fleet returning to port and never reemerging for the duration of the conflict. Whatever the controversies regarding the position of *Belgrano* at the time, and whatever impact this had on Argentine determination to seek revenge, the fact is that one SSN effectively put pay to a surface action group. *Conqueror* could have picked off other targets one by one, but this was considered tactically unnecessary and also not appropriate under the rules of engagement that the British had set for themselves, which included minimizing casualties. The power of the SSN was exemplified—the only attack by a submarine on a warship since the conclusion of World War II.

The SSNs could also launch and retrieve special forces and could close the Argentine mainland to collect SIGINT and ELINT regarding impending aircraft operations. If in hindsight the British SSN had any weaknesses,

The Argentine cruiser Belgrano *sinking after the attack by the nuclear-powered attack submarine HMS* Conqueror   MIRRORPRESS

HMS Conqueror *returns to the submarine base at Faslane, Scotland, at the conclusion of the Falklands campaign.*   ASSOCIATED PRESS

these lay in the lack of two alternative weapons. Had the SSNs had Tactical Tomahawk (TACTOM) in the spring of 1982 they could have destroyed the Argentine command headquarters at Port Stanley, ammunition and supply sites, and land-force command sites. Moreover, if they had had a fifty-plus-nautical-mile-range precision gun system to augment the expensive and scarce missiles, and a large weapon load, they could have quickly inflicted prodigious damage, and without the risks associated with Harrier sorties. The same applies to naval gunfire support from the British surface ships. Covert gun missions from an SSN would have been minimally risky compared with deploying ships close to shore; the destroyer HMS *Glamorgan,* delivering naval gunfire support, was badly damaged, with casualties, by a shore-based Argentine Exocet missile.

However, in 1982 these options were not available, and neither was the near- or real-time tactical intelligence to support precision strikes on land targets from British SSNs. This is a good point to examine the intelligence implications of the Falklands campaign and their impact on US and Royal Navy thinking, planning, and acquisition. The strategic intelligence failures prior to the invasion have been exhaustively examined. These failures cost the capable and astute British foreign secretary, Lord Carrington, his job. He resigned in acknowledgment that he was ultimately responsible for not reading all the indications that the Argentines would actually invade, that their threats were not patriotic demagogy to assuage the Argentine public at a time when the Galtieri regime was in trouble. London failed to assess that the dictator was seeking to draw attention away from domestic chaos with a popular invasion of the "Malvinas," a distraction that was geared to holding up the faltering regime.

The British naval planners and command teams reacted extraordinarily quickly to the initial invasion. The Deputy Chief of the Defense Staff for Intelligence (DCDS [I]), and subsequently the Director General of Intelligence, was Vice Admiral Sir Roy Halliday, always known as "Gus." He was a World War II naval aviator of distinction, winning a Distinguished Service Cross flying against the Japanese during the concluding months of the Pacific War. Gus Halliday had been the British naval attaché in Washington and was well known, liked, and connected with the leadership of the US Navy and all the intelligence agencies. He was also doubly fortunate in that President Ronald Reagan and his defense secretary, Caspar Weinberger, gave their total support to Margaret Thatcher. They did so in spite of the perception that some in the United States, including the ambassador to the United Nations, Jean Kirkpatrick, were prone to neutrality, and indeed British capitulation. The outcome was total support and responsiveness to British needs. President Reagan knew that he could not see his primary ally suffer a defeat in the South Atlantic when the eyes of Moscow were firmly fixed on not just the military outcome and how well the British would fare but also whether the US-UK relationship would hold up. At one level the United States and United Kingdom were suddenly at geopolitical crossroads. The United States was never wanting, and at the center of what became total US-UK commitment to a British victory and the end of the Argentine dictatorship were the two navies, which stood the test in magnificent fashion.

The Royal Navy Harrier aircraft flying from HMS *Hermes* and *Invincible* needed more of the highly capable US air-to-air missiles immediately; without them the air war would not be possible. The US Sidewinder missile became a principal determinant of the war's outcome, along with the successful amphibious assault and march on Port Stanley. A worry from the American side was the survival of the two British carriers: the destruction of or serious disabling damage to one could be a major problem; the loss of or damage to both could be catastrophic. It was critical, from an American perspective, that this could not be allowed to occur. Sensitive plans were drawn up for what the United States would do to alleviate severe losses. These plans, which are still not in the public domain, exemplify the commitment made by the United Kingdom's major ally at a time of intense stress. They also reflect the binding relationship of the US Navy and Royal Navy. In the event, Admiral Woodward and his staff brilliantly improvised. They used tactical superiority coupled with tenacity, science, courage, and endurance to come through at the end of the longest lines of communication and logistics since the British had engaged the German navy in the same area during both world wars.

There was one other winning factor: intelligence. The British improvised here too, to make up for their total lack of long-range airborne surveillance, reconnaissance, and intelligence. The Sidewinder missile would give the British air superiority, provided the Harriers could position themselves well and engage in time. They did so, inflicting extraordinary heavy losses on the Argentine air force. What drove US-UK intelligence operations, and what were the American contributions?

In 1982 the US agency responsible for space-based and aerial collection of intelligence was still covert, an entity totally unknown to the American public, and indeed to most of Congress and almost all of the nation's military. In 1982 the existence of the National Reconnaissance Office, formed on August 25, 1960, was highly classified. Only a small percentage of the intelligence community's personnel were cleared into its material, which covered various imagery sources, SIGINT, ELINT, and other multispectral material. Prior to the highly classified space-based collection program, the NRO had been dependent on manned aircraft at high altitude; when Argentina invaded the Falkland Islands, the U-2 aircraft was still very much a part of the NRO collection program. The NRO's highly compartmented program and its small, tightly knit, cleared community seriously inhibited the ability of operational users to obtain actionable information. The US sentinels in space were indeed in orbit as Argentina made its fateful moves. What value were they for the United Kingdom?

The United States shared space-based intelligence data with the United Kingdom in 1982, but on an extremely limited basis: only those with a need to know and had been intensively vetted could have access. How could such information be disseminated? It could not, except after intensive sanitization so that sources and their quality could not be discerned. This produced dilemmas. Added to all this were issues of the complexity of US satellite orbits, the number of satellites in space, and coverage prioritization at a time when the Cold War was hot elsewhere. In spring 1982 the South Atlantic was not high on the lists of the NRO, the US National Security Council, or the unified commanders-in-chief. The CIA, the Navy, and the Air Force had their own competing priorities at the NRO, all highly classified. When General Galtieri made his decision to invade, the NRO could not simply reorchestrate its symphony in space overnight to meet British needs. Indeed hardly any British planners and operational leaders had any idea that such sources and methods even existed, any more than did their counterparts in the United States.

This scenario was compounded by other operational processes that inhibited space intelligence from reaching the end users most in need. In 1982 space-based intelligence data was not disseminated in or near real time. The data, particularly imagery, was typically downloaded and then analyzed by specialists. This all took time. In addition, the imagery analysts tended to focus on technical assessments in addition to current operational needs. Many naval specialists would spend significant periods ensuring that accurate measurement and analysis. The war fighter needs less emphasis on exhaustive review and classification, which inhibits transmission and who can see the actual data; as it was, the number of cleared people on the British side who were involved in current operations was absolutely minimal. In hindsight, the operational intelligence most needed in the South Atlantic in 1982 were Argentine order of battle, unit compositions, dispositions, movements and intentions, indications and warnings of attacks, tactical modus operandi, and associated technical capabilities. Let us address some of the most needed requirements.

The British task force sailed on April 5–6, 1982, in itself a masterpiece of logistics combined with high-end leadership. Rear Admiral Woodward and his staff, together with the fleet headquarters staff at Northwood and the Defense Intelligence Staff in London, knew that there were several threats to successful amphibious landings of 3 Commando Brigade and other echelons. The Argentines had both air and ground variants of the capable French Exocet missile. They had three German Type 209 submarines, built by Howaldtswerke Deutsche Werft. These boats displaced 1,285 tons submerged, could cruise at 21.5 knots submerged, had a crew of thirty-one, and were armed with eight 533 mm German SST-4 torpedoes. These submarines had an operating endurance of about fifty days, long enough to do significant damage to high-value elements of the British task force. In the event, only two of these boats deployed, but they became a considerable problem for British ASW forces.

Fortunately for the task force, one of these boats, ARA *Santa Fe,* had technical problems and was forced to put into South Georgia, where she was captured and scuttled on April 28. The other, ARA *San Luis,* was a totally different matter. She was operational, at sea, and a serious threat. Once the

Argentine surface navy retreated to port, *San Luis* was the prime naval threat, combined with air force jets. Where was *San Luis?* For a navy that prided itself on its ASW capabilities against the Soviet Union, this became a non-trivial question. Subsequently the Argentine navy claimed *San Luis* had made two attacks on the British, one on May 1, against HMS *Brilliant* and HMS *Yarmouth,* and one on May 10, against HMS *Arrow.* (The British later knew that the *San Luis* returned to Puerto Belgrano on May 17 for repairs and never deployed thereafter in the conflict.) From the task force commander's perspective, the submarine *San Luis* and the Exocet missile–armed aircraft could create havoc if things went badly.

The British casualty list mounted after the sinking of *Belgrano*. HMS *Sheffield* was attacked on May 4, two days later, by an Argentine Super Etendard aircraft firing an air-to-surface antiship missile. The frigates HMS *Ardent* and *Antelope* fell victim also to air attacks, as did the destroyer HMS *Coventry*. One of the most grievous losses was the merchant ship *Atlantic Conveyor* on May 25, taking with her all the large, heavy-lift Chinook helicopters that were to fly the Royal Marines across the main island to Falkland's capital, Port Stanley. Three Commando Brigade had to march, as a consequence, carrying heavy packs and weapons, and after a considerable feat of endurance engage the Argentine ground forces dug into the hills overlooking their approach to Port Stanley. Several other ships suffered serious damage and casualties from bomb and missile attacks. Toward the end of the conflict, as noted, *Glamorgan* was badly damaged by a shore-based Exocet fired from well within the missile's arc and range, significantly larger than those of the destroyer's 4.5-inch guns. We will examine these losses in the context of actionable intelligence, but first let us address another major British concern, which began immediately after the invasion occurred: Was the Soviet Union involved in any shape or form with the Argentines? Were they providing intelligence, however clandestinely?

At the time of the invasion I was closely involved in addressing a highly sensitive Soviet operation that received the highest attention in London. The details are still highly classified, and there has been no reporting of these events. There was deep concern that somehow the operation was associated with the Argentine invasion: perhaps as a distraction, perhaps as pressure on the United Kingdom, and perhaps a message that the Soviet Union would not stand by and let the British task force move against the islands. There was much conjecture and little hard fact, except that the Soviet moves were seriously real. I was equally concerned at the time that the Soviets would provide direct intelligence support, particularly targeting information, to the Argentines via their clandestine sources in Buenos Aires. Any of several ocean-surveillance assets could follow the British fleet or monitor British positions in the operational area, in due course: Victor III–class submarines, an AGI, and a range of merchant vessels that were part of the SOSS.

The passing of near- or real-time location data to the Argentines would have been extraordinarily serious, potentially destroying the element of surprise after the British leadership chose San Carlos Water for the amphibious landing and base from which to attack the main Argentine force at Port Stanley. Aside from surface ships, the Soviets might provide satellite imagery, ELINT, and SIGINT to the Argentines, in particular if they programmed their satellites to collect locational and tracking data to alert the Argentines. In any event, there is no evidence that I know of from British and American sources that the Soviets attempted to intervene directly. There is no question that they watched with intense interest, no doubt hoping that the British would fall on their swords in the South Atlantic. Soviet activities during the week of the invasion appear to have been nothing more than coincidental. In fact, the Soviets were both surprised and impressed with how quickly the Royal Navy and Marines responded and how they fueled and supplied the task force at such great ranges.

Looking back at the total Soviet ocean surveillance system in 1982, it is clear that the USSR was much worse off than the United States in ability to convert intelligence data into actionable information of immediate, direct value to a commander at sea. The Soviets were highly centralized and not as efficient as some believed. The concept of the real-time flow of intelligence to the frontline user had not entered the Soviet lexicon. But it would be another decade before the United States addressed classification and making operational intelligence arrive in the right place at the right time to influence outcomes. The Falklands campaign was a short, hugely dynamic event; much that happened occurred on the fly, with operational commanders making tactical choices based on whatever weapons and information they had. No one in London or Washington could suddenly change that mix, except in a few limited, if crucial areas.

The provision of additional Sidewinder missiles for the British Sea Harrier aircraft has been mentioned earlier: these were crucial for winning the air war, without which the Falklands might not have been retaken. Both GCHQ in the United Kingdom and NSA in the United States provided invaluable SIGINT on Argentine activities. The ELINT data bases had information on the Exocet parameters, other main emitters, and means to aid British radars in detecting inbound aircraft. HUMINT sources revealed that the Argentine

Exocet missile inventory was almost pitifully small—a major factor in favor of the British task force. A large inventory of Exocets might have proven overwhelming in spite of jammers and chaff. The tragic demise of the *Atlantic Conveyor* shows that radars, jamming, and chaff can pull a missile off a high-value unit—but that a good one then heads for a less well protected target.

Many "what if" games may be played about the Falklands campaign, and certainly one of them is what the British would have done if the Argentines had had a large Exocet stockpile or posed a large submarine threat? The effects on the British fleet of, for example, twenty Exocets could have been devastating. What if the three 209s had been in a good state readiness, their command teams had had German Bundesmarine training, and their SST-4 torpedoes had worked as advertised? It is generally believed that poor Argentine maintenance had reversed the polarity of cables between the torpedoes and the submarines' combat systems. If the reverse had been true, the consequences for British surface units might have been very serious. Three well-handled and quiet German 209s in the acoustic environment of the South Atlantic might have had as devastating effect on the task force as HMS *Conqueror*'s attack on *Belgrano* had on the Argentine surface fleet.

The campaign showed that navies go to war with what they have, not what they should have had or what they had asked for; they simply have to make do. It then comes down to leadership, tactical expertise, training, experience, courage, and endurance, plus improvisation and the ability to understand the situation quickly and effectively and adjust accordingly. Admiral Woodward and his staff did a superb job of allowing for British deficiencies. Two other factors that also came into play and will always do so: the fog of war and luck. HMS *Sheffield,* for example, was tragically unlucky in the way in which she was attacked and badly damaged and subsequently sunk. Her commanding officer was on a satellite communications link to the fleet headquarters when, late in the day (when, the fleet had been informed, the likelihood of an air attack was very low), she was attacked by an Exocet missile. *Sheffield*'s electronic support measures (ESM) equipment had to be offline while satellite communications were in progress. Luck had it that an Argentine Super Etendard pilot caught *Sheffield* on her outer-ring air-protection station with EW systems and released the missile. The Exocet, a highly capable sea-skimming missile for its day, homed in at very low altitude; the first the ship knew of it was when the bridge team made visual contact—too late to fire chaff, maneuver, or engage with surface-to-air missiles. *Sheffield* had all the right defensive systems, including Abbey Hill, an excellent ESM system. She was simply unlucky and caught in the fog of war.

One domain where the near- or real-time flow of crucial tactical intelligence would have been vital was in support of British special forces. The Special Air Service is highly competent. In late April to early May 1980 they had caught the world's attention when Prime Minister Thatcher ordered the SAS to retake the Iranian embassy in Princes Gate, South Kensington, London, from a terrorist group. The operation was a major success. In the Falklands the SAS was used for covert insertion, reconnaissance, and reporting via satellite link on the tactical situation. It also provided kinetic solutions to a variety of threats. However, SAS teams were themselves vulnerable to being surrounded and overrun; overhead imagery and SIGINT (which today can be received in handheld units) would have been invaluable, to pinpoint the movement of nearby enemy units.

As we discussed earlier, if the British SSNs had been fitted with underwater-launch gunfire systems the SAS could have called in fire support and much reduced the threat before the landings at San Carlos Water. Almost ten years later, in Operation Desert Storm, the American and British intelligence communities had still not provided their special forces with the types of capabilities envisioned here. The British SAS general Sir Peter de la Billière would become the deputy to American general Norman Schwarzkopf, and both would complain about the lack of high-value, real-time tactical intelligence. We will examine these issues later when we look at the 1990s.

A final observation before we leave the South Atlantic of 1982 is that in war much depends on the interaction between opposing units and the tactical decisions that commanders make. There are also strategic decisions at the theater level. Let's look at Argentine theater-level decisions. When the British responded the way they did, the Argentine appreciation of the situation, to recall a well-known staff college adage, may have been less than adequate. For example, it did not note a crucial point, that the whole British task force, with the exception of the nuclear-powered SSNs, required fuel oil, aviation gas, ammunition, and supplies. A fleet that must be sustained represents a possible weak link; if a chain is only as strong as its weakest link, the fleet's supply ships and oilers are it. They are highly vulnerable unless kept well out of harm's way and can rendezvous with the surface fleet without compromising their location to the enemy. The timing and location of underway refueling and resupply in a high-intensity combat area requires much coordination.

The same vulnerabilities apply to the STUFT ships. Merchant ships used in combat are typically unarmed and vulnerable, particularly in amphibious assaults. Because they carry highly valuable troops and weapons, they are major targets. The Argentine high command made a crucial strategic mis-judgment in not recognizing that it would not be frigates and destroyers that retook the Falklands but ground forces in STUFT and amphibious assault ships. Those ships too would be supplied by replenishment ships and refueled by oilers. Although the British frigates and destroyers posed serious threats to inbound aircraft, the targets should have been the noncombatants. The almost accidental destruction of the *Atlantic Conveyor* proves this point; 3 Commando Brigade had now lost its helicopter transport.

The Falklands campaign had far-reaching consequences beyond the retaking of the islands and the restoration of British governance. The US Navy had watched with intense interest as the campaign unfolded. So too had the Soviet Union. The impact on the latter was significant; the USSR real-ized that the primary ally of the United States would not be shaken by sabre rattling or violations of international norms. Moscow watched with concern as the British successfully executed every major domain of expeditionary war-fare, taking setbacks apparently in stride while inflicting resounding losses that led to the overthrow of a dictatorship. This was a salutary lesson for a single-party state with a purported Marxist economy. The Soviets absorbed also the same lessons that the British and Americans did, many self-evident to the astute observer of military operations and technology. Perhaps most of all, there was deterrent value: it became obvious that neither the United Kingdom nor its chief ally could be meddled with without consequences. This was at a time when Soviet naval diplomacy was at its height; naval planers in Moscow could now clearly see that there were boundaries to what they could do in remote locations like West Africa, the Mediterranean, or the Far East.

The lack of long-range organic reconnaissance and surveillance was a major problem for the British fleet. It had no fixed-wing carriers—the light Sea Harrier carriers did the job, but only just. When the Royal Navy decom-missioned HMS *Ark Royal* (R-09, an *Audacious*-class fleet aircraft carrier launched in 1950) on February 14, 1979, the service lost the ability to fly its F-4 Phantoms and Buccaneer fighter-bombers or its airborne reconnais-sance aircraft. All were significantly more capable than the short-range/low-endurance Sea Harriers. In a worst-case scenario, a fixed-wing carrier could have launched air strikes against the main Argentine airfields before the Brit-ish reached the islands and could be attacked in San Carlos Water.

It is one of the great ironies of this campaign that in spite of its great success and enormous national pride that it generated, the reduction of the Royal Navy begun by Secretary John Nott before the invasion, with the concurrence of the Prime Minister Thatcher, continued. The Royal Navy garnered enormous popularity, and President Reagan saw as his best friend and ally the "Iron Lady," a sobriquet that was not lost on the Soviet Union. However, after the campaign there was no plan to bring back fixed-wing naval aviation on fleet carriers. The long-range strike on the airfield near Port Stanley by Royal Air Force V-bombers had been superb and gallant but had achieved almost nothing; all but one of the iron bombs missed the runway. By 2020, when the Royal Navy plans to have its first new fixed-wing carrier, HMS *Queen Elizabeth,* in service, it will have taken thirty-eight years to learn and for the British acquisition and funding process to make right what was palpably clear to all analysts and military observers in and after 1982.

The extraordinary value of the nuclear-powered attack submarine was self-evident; it consigned the whole Argentine surface navy to port by sinking *Belgrano.* We have seen that if the UK submarines had had Tomahawk cruise missiles in 1982, let alone submerged-fired guns, the campaign would have been shortened. What the British submarines would require in the coming decades, in addition to the Cruise Missile Targeting Center data provided by the United States as part of the Tomahawk acquisition, was a near- or real-time flow of tactical targeting data that extended capabilities beyond fixed targets with clearly known geographic coordinates. We will address this issue later in the context of improved satellite surveillance and targeting and the value of such assets as Joint STARS, unmanned aerial vehicles (UAVs), and drones.

The SAS and the Royal Marines Special Boat Section provided outstanding surveillance and reconnaissance data. As was indicated earlier, what these forces needed most was satellite-based tactical intelligence. This required a whole new architecture on the American side, and this would not come until the 1990s. Meanwhile, classic capabilities paid off. These included prior knowledge of the beach profiles and terrain, particularly of East Falkland, collected by well-trained Royal Marines before the invasion. Although the US National Geospatial Agency three-dimensional terrain imagery is excellent, especially if up to the moment and accurate, there is still the human factor—that is, local knowledge from having been on the ground already. Input from Royal Marines who knew East Falkland was absolutely invaluable, particularly in the final decision to land at San Carlos Water rather than elsewhere.

We have discussed at some length the lack of real-time intelligence, in a complex multisource sense. It was made up by great leadership; Rear Admiral Woodward adapted, improvised, and adjusted his campaign plans in the light of evolving contingencies. Above all else, he and his outstanding staff anticipated the enemy's moves. They did not permit the enemy to get ahead of them. Losses that occurred were the direct results of tactical engagements, the dynamics of conflict, the interaction of military systems, and, as we saw earlier, the fog of war. We examined earlier the discovery in SEASAT imagery in 1979 that any surface ship's wake can be seen from space. In 1982 this phenomenology was not yet available to space systems, but no surface ship is stealthy or ever can be if it moves and is observed by a space-based synthetic aperture radar. The 1982 British deployments could, theoretically, have been monitored if such capabilities and the necessary communications architecture had existed. None did, but in future expeditionary warfare, groups will have to allow for this form of surveillance from space. Commercial satellites can now provide data that was once the sole preserve of agencies of the United States and the USSR. Today numerous international commercial providers can orbit such sensors over the oceans, often for oceanographic, weather, resource related, or environmental purposes.

The Falklands campaign was certainly not the last hurrah of a postcolonial Britain, seeking a new identity. Neither was it just about the precipitous actions of a failing dictatorship. Nor was it just about sovereignty and maintaining the international order from chaos. There were also implications for international law and access to resources. The two-hundred-mile exclusion zone that the UK government declared around the Falkland Islands during the conflict corresponded to the two-hundred-mile economic zone embodied in the United Nations Convention on the Law of the Sea. The economic zone around the Falkland Islands contains deepwater oil reserves, potentially vital for the United Kingdom when cost and technology make exploitation worthwhile.

In addition, the fishing rights are nontrivial at a time when the demand for fish is increasing globally and the supply is diminishing. Now apply this to East and Southeast Asia and the islands and island chains that China and almost all of its Asian maritime neighbors are disputing. The US Navy is the primary peacekeeper in this region. The Seventh Fleet is the mainstay of naval presence there, around the clock; on-station nuclear attack submarines, along with other sources and methods, provide the necessary tactical intelligence. The analogy with the Falklands becomes clear. Nations often make rash and irresponsible choices, but often for perceived reasons of national self-interest. Resources will be a major source of conflict as the twenty-first century progresses, most analysts agree. The Falklands campaign should be much studied today, as showing what it takes to conduct across-the-board naval operations in a harsh environment. Preparation is always wise, and war games now use the Falklands scenario.

Also, the campaign was a glaring demonstration of the failure of deterrence because of the lack of presence. In the South Atlantic there was only the ice patrol ship HMS *Endurance,* whose commanding officer sent reports that warned of an impending invasion. The Foreign Office reacted too late. Had a Royal Navy nuclear submarine or surface group been deployed in the South Atlantic and the United Kingdom had made it known, it is most likely that sabre rattling by Galtieri would not have been translated into invasion. The point is clear: the presence of credible naval forces acts as a major deterrent to unbridled actions by possible adversaries.

The role of merchant ships in the campaign has been much underestimated. Without the aptly named STUFT ships the Royal Navy could not have performed its missions. They were essential for transporting ground forces and supplies over and beyond those conveyed by the Royal Fleet Auxiliary (RFA), whose oilers and supply ships were inadequate for the magnitude of the task. However, and although many of these ships, such as the ill-fated *Atlantic Conveyor,* had Royal Navy liaison officers on board, the mere presence of naval expertise could not make up for the lack of close-in weapon systems and chaff launchers. This is a major lesson for both the US Navy and Royal Navy, perhaps requiring load-on/load-off packaged systems stored appropriately for use in emergencies. Reservists who in time of conflict might command such ships could undergo training in the use of such systems in peacetime. The contemporary Automatic Identification System (AIS), on most merchant ships and many oceangoing yachts, provides real-time locations and permits AIS ships to be distinguished from non-AIS ships. Merchant ships can now benefit from global communications, data sharing, and a variety of situational-awareness applications via satellite systems.

It may be a stretch to suggest that the British take a leaf from the former Soviet Union's book on the noncommercial use of merchant ships. However, the British found in 1982 that they had no effective tactical methods of their own for SIGINT and ELINT collection in real time. By their very nature, GCHQ and NSA sources and methods are never 100 percent capable. Merchant ships can have eyes and ears, as the Soviets showed the United States and United Kingdom in spades. Non-UK-flag ships in foreign ports could report all that they see and hear, with imagery, SIGINT, and ELINT. Ships off the Argentine coast where fighter aircraft attacking the British had to transit could have provided critical warning. Emission control and encryption can sometimes reduce warning time to naught, but in fact many communications with shore-based activities simply cannot be easily hidden or obfuscated.

As just one example, during the Cold War, Soviet- and non-Soviet War-saw Pact–flagged ships and other merchant vessels flying flags of convenience but under Soviet control could transit inside the twelve-mile international limit by exercising their right of innocent passage. Ships could listen to RAF activity at the maritime reconnaissance station at Kinloss and to the nearby Royal Navy air station at Lossiemouth. SIGINT and ELINT systems on these ships could discern indications of flight operations. The same would have applied with respect to the Argentine air force bases near the coast.

In addition, merchant ships can land and retrieve agents and special forces clandestinely and covertly, particularly at night, to report movements and forces by handheld LPI satellite devices. Clearly there are risks associated with such operations, but they are second nature to SAS, SBS, and US Navy SEAL units. Insertion by helicopter, special surface craft, or underwater swimmer delivery vehicles from merchant vessels is a good option, provided the tactical conditions and threat detection systems are well known. Long-range helicopter flights over water run many risks, as the British found during the campaign, when all personnel were lost in such a helicopter operation. Merchant ships positioned in key locations, close in, can mitigate such tragic losses.

Unfortunately, however, the implications of the Falklands campaign were lost on the secretary of defense in the United Kingdom, John Nott. The strategic imperative was lost sight of in the haste to meet Cabinet Office demands to cut budgets at a time of squeeze on the national exchequer. The patriotism and loyalty of John Nott can never be called into question: he served as a commissioned officer in the 2nd Gurkha Rifles in Malaysia (1952–56). But on becoming secretary of state for defense in the British cabinet reshuffle of January 1981 he issued a white paper that cut back significantly on naval forces. The Royal Navy leadership reacted accordingly but to no avail. Nott had no experience at all of maritime strategy, and his critics lambasted him for his apparent ignorance of not only British naval history but also the basics of maritime expeditionary warfare, which had been the core ingredient of Britain's security since medieval times. His apparent intransigence (many said arrogance) having led, after the Falklands campaign, to much public criticism, he decided not to seek reelection to the House of Commons and was replaced by Michael Heseltine in January 1983.

However, the damage that he had done to the Royal Navy endured. The cuts that he oversaw were not redressed. There would be no new fleet carriers; improvised permanent defenses of the Falkland Islands after the fall of the Galtieri regime was considered sufficient. In October 1982, John Nott was interviewed by the legendary correspondent Sir Robin Day, who famously provoked Nott to wrath by asking, was he "a here today and gone tomorrow politician?" Nott threw down his microphone, called the interview "ridiculous," and precipitously left the studio in high dudgeon, before millions of British observers. But still, the damage to the Royal Navy had been done.

A factor that complicated national budget issues was the replacement of the submarine-based strategic deterrent. Thatcher had faced on arrival at 10 Downing Street in 1979 the dilemma that the British government faces today: how to pay the extraordinary costs of four ballistic-missile-firing nuclear-powered submarines. To build what became the four *Vanguard*-class submarines was as big an issue then as the replacement of the *Ohio*-class SSBNs is today. How do both navies pay the replacement bills and still maintain a viable shipbuilding and naval aircraft programs? This issue is in the process of resolution in both countries. The cost consequences are enormous unless strategic-deterrent replacements are funded outside naval budgets. Thatcher opted for the *Vanguard*-class replacement, but with serious consequences for the rest of the Royal Navy. The 1980s saw a steady decline in critical force structure, experienced and highly trained manpower, and deployment cycles.

Our last chapter will immerse us in maritime strategy issues and attendant strategic defense reviews in the United States and United Kingdom, but for now suffice it to observe that in spite of the patently clear strategic value of the sea services, the British Defense Review would not save the Royal Navy and Royal Marines from major reductions. The 1980s and 1990s were decades when US naval supremacy was fortunately at its height, under the leadership of President Ronald Reagan and his Navy secretary, John Lehman. What Reagan and Lehman created in the 1980s endured until the apparent peace dividend benefits of the 1990s, after the demise of the Soviet Union, and the US Navy began its own force-level reductions.

The Changing Tide

The Demise of the Soviet Union and the End of the Cold War

The 1980s and 1990s were marked by a preeminent US Navy and a Royal Navy with a reduced force level. They were golden years of the US Navy's support to Pax Americanus, culminating in the fall of the Berlin Wall, the demise of the Soviet Union, and a new order in the 1990s in Eastern Europe, with hope for a new way of life for millions. This was not just a geostrategic change but a massive cultural and economic shift. The latter was reflected in the rise of newly liberated free-market, capitalist economies. In due course there followed the liberalization of latter-day Marxist economies that would now operate under state-run capitalist economic principles, under the umbrella of single-party communist regimes. The tide had turned in world events in an extraordinarily massive way.

The US Navy had a significant part in this world-changing scenario. The six-hundred-ship Navy was not just a shipbuilding program. It was a geostrategic plan that had the full support of the White House. Indeed, it was one of President Ronald Reagan's prize initiatives, challenging the Soviets in a duel that was not just about technology, orders of battle, or who had more submarines, aircraft carriers, cruisers, destroyers, amphibious ships, and, of course, battleships, on which President Reagan placed his personal imprimatur. It was, rather, about a power struggle. In this way the United States demonstrated to the Soviets that they could never win a conventional war and that the United States would outmatch them not just in technology and war-fighting skills but also in a more sophisticated battle over national will. The six-hundred-ship Navy made a huge statement: the United States can outbuild you and beat you at the technology race. It can challenge you in ways that you can never match, because the American people are simply too strong for a Soviet-style, one-party, highly bureaucratized, communist state. The Star Wars initiative, whatever its technical merits, made the same statement.

However, the six-hundred-ship Navy was not just a real prospect but a fact: it was out there, forward deployed in the ocean areas where the Soviets made their challenges. The indomitable power of the US Navy was manifest, and by now the Soviets understood, courtesy the Walker family, the power of the US submarine force. There were many factors in this process. One was clearly political resolve in the United States. The other can be stated in three letters: GDP. The gross domestic product of the United States in the Reagan era permitted the United States to invest heavily in defense. The percentage of GDP spent on the six-hundred-ship Navy showed not just national resolve but the strength of the American economy. Underpinning GDP was a technological edge that stemmed from the very nature of a free market and the competitive edge that allowed the intellectual wealth, or capital, of the United States to be harnessed.

This national policy was implemented in an era when congressional representatives of both parties could work together, not necessarily in perfect harmony but in a spirit of mutual respect, courtesy, and devotion to a single cause, outflanking the Soviet Union. There was no bitter partisan strife; multiple states and congressional districts benefited from the downward flow of taxpayers' dollars to industry. However, one point may not receive sufficient recognition. The US Navy's six-hundred-ship goal cost a measurable number of dollars, a public accounting of what it took to challenge the Soviet Union. It is not an argument to put the clock back to state the fact that strategic defense, in this case in the strategic maritime domain, comes at a cost. This raises a question: What price, what percentage of GDP, do taxpayers wish to invest in their navy in order to obtain the greatest protection for the United States, its friends and allies, and the international order?

We will return to this critical issue in later chapters. Nations that have been bloodied and financially exhausted by war can have short memories. The cold, hard facts of the international regime, however, militate against the understandable sentiments to avoid further embroilments. That was at first the British reaction to the rise of Hitler, to avoid any repetition of the war to end all wars.

The contrast between the US Navy and the Royal Navy in the 1980s is stark in retrospect. The great irony of the Thatcher years, the running-down of the strength of the Royal Navy, was not lost on Washington. This wariness was perhaps softened by President Reagan's, and then President George Herbert Walker Bush's, personal ties with both Margaret Thatcher and her successor, John Major. Neither American leader wished to chide the prime ministers publicly about the drawdown of the Royal Navy, incongruous as it was after its resounding success in the Falklands. The Falklands campaign had been a "close-run thing," as the British ground force commander, Major General Sir Jeremy Moore of the Royal Marines, paraphrased the Duke of Wellington's recollection of Waterloo. However, if one compares the states of the British economy that Margaret Thatcher inherited in 1979 and when she left office, the facts speak for themselves: she had, in essence, saved Britain from itself. She did so by draconian measures, and she paid a price when she finally left office. How best to invest GDP in defense at a time of financial stress is not an easy question to answer, though the need may be clear.

This is probably the nub regarding the Thatcher years and the cuts to the Royal Navy. The Navy continued to punch above its weight through the 1980s and into the 1990s. However, a trend was set toward strategic confusion, leading to what most analysts regard as a series of poorly conceived and executed strategic-defense and security reviews, none of which reset the clock positively for the Royal Navy. The much-quoted fact that the United Kingdom contributed more GDP on defense than many of its NATO partners during this period is not the point: the issue is that UK GDP was likely misapplied, based on flawed analysis of national interest and strategic needs. The seeds were sowed for a decline of the Royal Navy.

By contrast, the US Navy made enormous strides in almost all domains, many of which were passed over to the Royal Navy. The 1980s for the US Navy can be best characterized as a time of innovation. In retrospect, it was a golden age. The Vietnam War era was replaced by a new energy and determination to stay way ahead in the Cold War. We will not dwell on the minutiae of systems and technologies, which have been well documented. What we will do here is address systemic issues and factors that bear on today and the future—not just lessons that we may relearn but also the cultural and organizational issues that helped shape actions inside the US Navy, public opinion, and Capitol Hill.

Congress was right behind the expansion of the US Navy order of battle and capabilities. There was a deep and abiding appreciation by many former naval persons on Capitol Hill of the Navy and Marine Corps as national assets. They understood how both services fit into the global interests of the United States. These individuals were of both parties but were united in a common Navy–Marine Corps cause, whatever their day-to-day disagreements. The sea services had a way of uniting Congress in the 1980s.

We will take just one example: a representative from San Diego, California, the Honorable Duncan Hunter, who had fought with great distinction as a Ranger in Vietnam. He fully understood the value of the Navy and Marine

Corps and as a member of the House Armed Services Committee supported their programs. As he moved up in seniority he became in due course the chairman of that committee, one of the most powerful in Congress. The nurturing that he received in the 1980s from congressional veterans from the 1960s came to fruition when he became the House lead on defense. His son would eventually replace him in his House seat. Duncan Hunter Jr. was a Marine Corps company commander in action in the Middle East at the time of his election to replace his father, who had served for thirty years in Congress. The younger Hunter is today a senior member of the House Armed Services Committee and a strong proponent of not just maintaining the strength of the sea services but of stimulating the US merchant marine and commercial shipbuilding industries. The members of the House and the Senate in the 1980s and into the 1990s who fit the Duncan Hunter mold are too numerous to mention. In short, political leadership counted at every level, and the harmony between Congress, the White House, and public opinion was essential.

The drive and energy on Capitol Hill was manifested in innovations. The decade of the 1980s was the dawn of the digital era in military systems. Relevant for today's US and Royal Navy is that innovation and acquisition in the 1980s worked well. Change could be implemented relatively quickly, and technology did not overtake systems before they were fielded, as commonly happens today, when the commercial sector is better at keeping ahead of technical change than is the government.

A system that takes ten years to bring to initial operating capability (IOC) will be outdated before the initial production unit appears. Chief of Naval Operations Jonathan Greenert's public statement mentioned earlier about the obsolescence of various stealth applications (not in submarines) shows that keeping ahead, and staying ahead, of the threat is now much more difficult than it was when major threat nations were significantly behind the technological curve. In an era of technological as well as global communications, innovation is ever more critical for the US and Royal Navies, provided that they can bring its fruits to production quickly. Long acquisition time lines could cause loss of the technical edge. Production by competitors of several parallel and "stepped" (i.e., with improvements quickly embedded in the next generation) systems renders military technical advantages even more difficult to maintain. However, the good news is that in the 1980s and into the early 1990s the US Navy set in motion ways and means from which the contemporary US and Royal Navies can learn.

The Tomahawk land-attack cruise missile, fired from US surface ships and submarines and, in due course, Royal Navy submarines, is a classic example of both innovation and timely acquisition. The missile entered service in 1983 and has a future that will persist for decades. One of chief reasons is a modular design that has permitted a wide range of core missions, warheads, ranges, guidance systems, and targeting. For example, the nuclear and antiship versions went out of service as requirements changed. However, the core technical concepts—DSMAC (digital scene matching area correlation), TERCOM (terrain contour mapping), INS (inertial navigation system), GPS (global positioning system), and active radar homing, plus variable launch systems (vertical-launch and torpedo-tube launch)—demonstrate the enormous flexibility needed to modify systems without a whole new program, a new acquisition process, and attendant costs.

The history of the program shows a Navy/contractor partnership to reduce cost while increasing capability and inventory—an apparent contradiction. The Block IV Tomahawk can be retargeted in flight via satellite communications, carries warhead variants based on the mission, and can loiter for significant periods, sending back vital information from its sensors. The 1980s six-hundred-ship Navy saw armored-box launchers in the reactivated *Iowa*-class battleships, the eight *Spruance*-class destroyers, the four *Virginia*-class cruisers, and USS *Long Beach*. The vertical-launch system has been installed on numerous other surface ships, including those of major US allies, and both American and British submarines use torpedo-tube and vertical-launch systems.

A naval platform, indeed any military platform, is only as good as the weapons that it fires and the targets that it can destroy over the life of the total system—that is, a total through-life cost of ownership in terms of what it can inflict on the enemy. This is a weapon/target-centric view of naval systems rather than a platform-centric view. Tomahawk has amply supported this paradigm. During the 1991 Gulf war, 288 Tomahawks were launched; in Operation Deliberate Force, the Bosnian Serb conflict, thirteen Tomahawks were fired; seventy-five were launched against targets in Afghanistan and the Sudan in retaliation for the East African embassy bombings; in 1998, Tomahawks were fired at Iraqi targets in Operation Desert Fox; a Royal Navy submarine fired Tomahawks in 1999 against targets in Serbia and Montenegro, together with the US Navy's 218 Tomahawk strikes against similar targets; in October 2001 the US Navy fired approximately fifty Tomahawks against critical al Qaida targets in Afghanistan in Operation Enduring Freedom; in 2003 in excess of 725 Tomahawks were fired against Iraqi targets as the invasion of Iraq got under way; in 2009, two Tomahawks were fired at Yemeni targets; the Royal Navy's submarine-based Tomahawks (twelve fired in total) were in action against targets in Libya—the US Navy fired 112 Tomahawks on March 19, 2012, alone; attacks by Tomahawks against Islamic State of Iraq and Syria targets from the Red Sea and Persian Gulf numbered forty-seven in September 2014.

The Tomahawk missile program is at the apogee of US Navy–Royal Navy cooperation on weapons procurement, as is the ballistic-missile program, both reflections in particular of the special relationship in submarine warfare. Among US allies, only UK submarines carry the Tomahawk missile. The first British Tomahawks were acquired and test-fired in 1998. Today all UK submarines are Tomahawk capable, including the new *Astute*-class SSN. The Royal Navy has acquired the Tomahawk Block IV TACTOM missile, a highly capable weapon. It remains to be seen whether the latest British destroyers, those of the Type 45 class, will be retrofitted with the Tomahawk Block IV and its successors or whether the new Type 26 frigate will be Tomahawk equipped.

The US Navy is now in a position to make smart technical and acquisition decisions regarding the next generation of ship- and submarine-based weapons. One aspect that is certain is that it will leverage technologies embedded in Tomahawk for weapons across mission domains, not just land-attack but also antisurface. This technical flexibility will maintain the war-fighting edge without extraordinary new start-up costs. However, a dilemma may be lurking for the industrial base in the maintenance of the Tomahawk inventory. If the Navy considers its stockpile sufficient, production is not likely to continue beyond 2016. This would naturally affect the industrial base and its core competencies and workforce. Recent operations though have shown that unforeseen contingencies tend to diminish the inventory and that missiles have to be replaced.

The Navy's planning for new-generation, multimission TACTOM derivatives also remains to be seen. The advocates of advanced electromagnetic launch systems have made range and flight-time estimates that water the eyes of traditional cruise-missile experts and users. However, alternative technologies and totally new approaches, perhaps hugely beneficial over the long haul, have the short-term disadvantage of new programs: with high front-end R&D costs and long learning curves. Such systems could take to the middle of the century before reaching full maturity, absent of course is the drive, innovativeness, energy, and political clout of a Hyman Rickover to push them through. It has happened before, and the US Navy's nuclear submarine force and its surface ships now entering the fleet with electric drive have the reserves of power needed for revolutionary long-range and high-speed electrically launched weapons.

Before leaving the Tomahawk missile, one remaining critical observation should be made, regarding the targeting of Tomahawks in Royal Navy attack submarines. The US Navy developed multiple targeting facilities that were combined in the Cruise Missile Support Activity (CMSA). The United States transferred the CMSA systems and technologies and the command-and-control functions associated with Tomahawk attacks to the United Kingdom. The US Navy CMSAs in the Atlantic and Pacific are replicated at the UK maritime and joint warfare headquarters at Northwood. This arrangement permits the Royal Navy and US Navy to coordinate Tomahawk strikes. Data are passed from the CMSAs to US and Royal Navy submarines (and also US Navy Tomahawk-firing surface ships) that permits accurate strikes. The Block IV TACTOMs purchased by the United Kingdom will give the Royal Navy that missile's superior capabilities. The early versions of Tomahawk restricted attacks to fixed targets. This paradigm has changed significantly with the improvements mentioned above.

The choice between revolutionary versus evolutionary systems has always been a dilemma for planners and budgeters. Do the advantages over time outweigh the heavy initial costs of making change palatable to all the key players? Revolutionary technical change is perhaps less easy to accomplish in the United States than in the United Kingdom, because consensus building across the political spectrum is not as necessary in a cabinet-run, parliamentary democracy. However, the United States has historically had one advantage that has been demonstrated by several systems that have emerged from "black" programs, highly classified and not visible in materials released to the public. Advanced programs can be hidden from view until their operational existence becomes difficult to hide from professional journals like *Aviation Week*.

The British Harrier aircraft, the precursor of the US Marine Corps AV-8B, set a trend for technology transfer. The British made their mark in the 1980s and into the 1990s in several areas parallel to Tomahawk development. The *Trafalgar*-class nuclear-powered attack submarine was not just a linear development from its predecessors. The Royal Navy had had excellent intelligence on Soviet submarine improvements and realized that its next-generation attack submarine would have to be a very much improved platform to stay ahead of the Soviets and remain an equal partner with the US submarine force. Vickers Shipbuilding and Engineering (today part of the British Aerospace company) had naval architects and engineers who could innovate in harmony with the Royal Navy's ship department in Bath. Every aspect of reducing noise was addressed, as were the critical issues of propulsion, underwater speed, and n cavitation at high propeller RPMs. Cavitation not only reduces energy and therefore speed but also induces noise to unacceptable levels, even with the most sophisticated propeller designs.

The British solution was the water- or pump-jet propulsion system, another breakthrough akin to the British angled flight deck and ski jump. In parallel, the Vickers team addressed drag reduction and boundary-layer control across many domains: hull form and shaping, surface coatings, and the power-density ratio of the total system. One of the objectives was to create additional space for weapons and other war-fighting systems without increasing volume and therefore cost and yet being quieter than before. The UK government/Vickers team created in the *Trafalgar* class an extraordinarily capable submarine, one that was indeed weapon/target-centric as well as stealthier even than its fine antecedents. The impact on the US Navy came about in ways that perhaps no one could have predicted or anticipated.

The *Seawolf*-class submarine was planned to meet the new Soviet submarine threats represented by the Typhoon, Oscar, and Akula classes in bluewater operations. *Seawolf* was the successor to the *Los Angeles* class, and twenty nine were planned. In the event only three were constructed: USS *Seawolf, Connecticut,* and *Jimmy Carter.* The first was laid down in October 1989 (design work had begun in 1983), and the last was commissioned in February 2005. All three are still very much in service. By June 1995, when *Seawolf* was launched, it had been realized that in the post–Cold War budget-constrained world the *Seawolf* class, at approximately three billion dollars per unit ($3.5 billion for *Jimmy Carter*), was unaffordable. *Jimmy Carter* was more expensive than her sister submarines because of her special multimission fit—particularly for SEALs and launch and recovery of remotely operated vehicles. Special intelligence facilities over and beyond those in most American SSNs were also fitted. *Jimmy Carter* took over from USS *Parche* her unique-to-platform special intelligence collection.

The dilemma now facing the US Navy was not so simply resolved: what would replace the *Seawolf* class? The answer had to be much less expensive but also have capabilities that would match any threat submarine into the 2020s and beyond. The basic design would have to be modular and open-architecture so that over time improvements could be introduced without fundamental and unaffordable changes. The *Trafalgar* class offered the Americans insight into what an alternative might look like. It was smaller and much less expensive than the *Seawolf* class yet highly capable.

HMS *Trafalgar*, the first of class, was laid down in April 1979 and commissioned in May 1983. She was decommissioned in December 2009. The remaining six boats of the class were commissioned between April 1984 and October 1991; four boats are left in service in 2016 (HMS *Torbay, Trenchant, Talent,* and *Triumph*). The last of the class, HMS *Triumph,* is expected to serve until 2022. It is of note that all the actual war-fighting actions of the *Trafalgar* class have involved firing US Tomahawk cruise missiles, at targets in Afghanistan, Iraq, and Libya. Like their US counterparts, all the "T boats" have been involved in sensitive intelligence collection. At 5,300 tons submerged (4,800 tons surfaced) the seven submarines of the class are significantly smaller than the *Seawolf* class (9,238 tons submerged, 8,600 tons surfaced, except *Jimmy Carter* at 12,139 tons submerged). However, size did not inhibit the capabilities of the class.

For example, in 1993 HMS *Triumph* sailed to Australia submerged, a total distance of 41,000 miles, without any form of forward logistics support. The *Trafalgar* class was larger than its predecessor, the *Swiftsure* class, with several improvements to reduce radiated noise: pump-jet propulsion, a quieter, more capable reactor system, and anechoic tiles on the hull (to absorb sound rather than reflect it), along with other, classified features. The *Trafalgar*s were a major

The fast-attack submarine USS Virginia *(SSN 774) arrives at Her Majesty's Naval Base, Clyde, Scotland, for a scheduled port visit March 22, 2016.* US NAVY, COURTESY ROYAL NAVY

improvement over the *Swiftsures*. In keeping with joint US Navy–Royal Navy operational plans in the Arctic, the *Trafalgars* had their fins strengthened and their hydroplanes made retractable, permitting surfacing though the polynyas. The Type 2076 towed array made the class a formidable opponent for Soviet submarines.

What did the above suggest for the *Seawolf* follow-on? Could a platform that was smaller than the *Seawolf* class and less costly be much more capable than anything the Russians can produce? The answer was an undoubted affirmative. Time has proven this correct not only from a technical perspective but also in terms of the annual build rate and force structure necessary to meet national strategic needs and the unified commanders' war-fighting requirements. Today the answer, the *Virginia*-class SSN, is being built two per year, an absolutely impossible scenario for the *Seawolf* class. Future modifications to the *Virginias* will likely be added to the *Seawolfs*. The *Trafalgar* class showed that it could be done.

The *Virginia,* or SSN 774, class will replace the *Los Angeles*–class attack submarines. Because of their modularity and through life updates in each of the successive acquisition "blocks," *Virginia*-class SSNs could be in service past 2060, possibly as late as 2070. However, that depends on the total number built and future acquisition. The study that initiated the 7,800-ton *Virginia* class was started in 1991, building commencing in 2000, and USS *Virginia,* the first of class, commissioned in 2004.

The open architecture and modular design of the *Virginia* class has permitted many innovations, notably non–hull-penetrating photonic masts that use optical fiber to transfer information from sensors (high-resolution cameras, infrared and light intensification sensors, a laser rangefinder, and an ESM array) to the control room. Improvements to these systems will be made with each block; in due course, it is anticipated, the class will have a full, simultaneous, 360-degree view of the sea surface. *Virginia*-class boats have in addition tactical communications masts, satellite communications masts, a radar mast for surface search and navigation, and ESM equipment. The sonar fit is formidable, including a bow-mounted spherical active/passive array; a wide-aperture fiber-optic array along each side of the hull; high-frequency active sonars in the sail (conning tower) and bow; low-cost, conformal, high-frequency arrays providing coverage above and astern of the submarine; and low- and high-frequency towed sonar arrays. The combat system is modular too and can be upgraded with each block, and the control systems on board are of the optical-fiber fly-by-wire type, with no electrohydraulic systems as in previous boats for actuating control surfaces.

The *Virginia* program has won awards for excellence, on-time and under-cost delivery, with very few glitches in production quality. Sound-damping tiles on the hull have presented some problems, but overall, given the massive technology changes, *Virginia* is an overwhelming success. Its payload tubes and modules will enable integration of a wide range of mission-dependent plug-in/plug-out capabilities. Block V includes a range of new, networked innovations in unmanned undersea vehicles and sensors, with an architecture more sophisticated than, for example, SOSUS at the height of the Cold War.

Numbers and force structure are important, and a submarine can only be in one place at a time. However, the high unit cost of production, resulting in a force structure small enough to be discernible and therefore predictable in its operational deployment pattern, can be mitigated by the use of lower-cost systems. The US submarine will not be a stand-alone unit, even where it would not be wise to position surface units. Off-board systems networked with *Virginia*s will pose in due course formidable threats to any potential adversary.

The Royal Navy connection with *Virginia* has been beneficial in a twofold sense. British Aerospace provides the pump-jet propulsors for *Virginia*, replacing the bladed propeller for main propulsion and, as designers of the *Trafalgar*-class SSN found, reducing cavitation.

For several decades after the US Navy decommissioned the last of its diesel-electric submarines, a lively and on occasions contentious debate went on about the relative merits of nonnuclear boats. The arguments for and against have been thoroughly aired in the literature. Suffice to say here that the United Kingdom did for a while envisage continuing with diesel-electric submarines, in the shape of the 2,455-ton-displacement *Upholder* class. These submarines were planned to replace the British-designed-and-built *Oberon* class. The four boats of the class—HMS *Upholder, Unseen, Ursula,* and *Unicorn*—were completed between 1990 and 1993. By 1994 the British government, ostensibly as part of the peace dividend, had decided to go the all-nuclear route; the four *Upholder*s were decommissioned and passed to the Maritime Command of the Royal Canadian Navy for $750 million Canadian dollars. There they became the *Victoria* class: HMCS *Victoria, Windsor, Corner Brook,* and *Chicoutimi,* recommissioned between 2000 and 2004. The Canadian boats have been much modified and improved since acquisition yet have endured a large measure of technical malfunctions.

Many other nations have gone the nonnuclear air-independent-propulsion (AIP) route. A quiet, well-handled nonnuclear submarine in the littorals, such as the South China Sea, offers many navies a positive answer to the affordability-versus-capability dilemma. In possible shallow-water scenarios the American and British SSNs will have to maximize the network centricity that the United States in particular has initiated to offset the capabilities and numbers of such potential adversaries.

Before we move to surface warfare innovations, it is interesting to recall from chapter 7 that since the last submarine action of World War II there has in the public record been only one victim in open warfare casualty of submarine operations, the Argentine cruiser *Belgrano,* sunk by HMS *Conqueror.* There have been no submarine-on-submarine combat encounters, no live-fire ASW actions of any description except in the Falklands campaign, though there have been multiple combat launches of cruise missiles against land targets. These generalizations, however, gloss over the reality of the Cold War and the 24/7 nature of forward-deployed US and UK submarine operations then, as close to actual combat as any other military assets of either side.

The jewel in the crown of the US surface navy is Aegis. It was a visionary system, an attempt to get well ahead of the curve, in anticipation of emerging threats that would in due course replicate advanced US systems and technologies. As an integrated weapon system, Aegis (the shield of Athena in Greek mythology) combines powerful computers and radars to guide advanced missiles to their targets. Aegis has achieved another "first" in recent years in successful testing in anti-ballistic-missile defense. Accordingly, as such it constitutes a critical shield for NATO and the continental United States. Aegis' virtues are enhanced greatly by the simple but inalienable fact that the high seas are international space, where Aegis cruisers and destroyers that make up the shield are not restricted by boundaries or territorial limits. The only limitations placed on Aegis are navigational constraints in enclosed waters and, of course, the maximum range and altitude of the system's missiles.

The Aegis weapon system is a family of integrated subsystems, at the heart of which is the family of successive SM-2 missiles, with upgrades developed alongside improvements to the AN/SPY-1 radar (an automatic-detect-and-track, multifunctional, three-dimensional, passive, electronically scanned array system), the Mark 99 fire control system, and the command-and-control suite. The impetus for Aegis was the growing Soviet antiship missile threat; its long development culminated with the first Aegis guided-missile cruiser, USS *Ticonderoga* (CG 47). The introduction of the vertical-launch system (VLS) on board the sixth of the class, *Bunker Hill,* was a major milestone, permitting wider missile selection, more firepower, and greater survivability. USS *Princeton* had the first improved AN/SPY-1B radar, and *Chosin's* AN/UYK-43/44 computers had vastly increased processing power.

USS Arleigh Burke *(DDG 51)*   US NAVY

The US Navy next adapted the system to the *Arleigh Burke*–class destroyers, with the first of class commissioned in 1991.

The key to the success of these two classes of US Navy cruisers and destroyers has been the ability to upgrade via a modular architecture, a huge cost saving. Excellent platforms with fine seakeeping qualities and endurance can be built with regularly upgraded Aegis systems, a point sometimes lost in the haste to introduce new hulls based on stealth design concepts. As we have seen earlier several Navy programs did not heed what has now been publicly articulated by Admiral Greenert—stealth has been matched by counterstealth. Moreover, as we have also seen, a surface ship, however low the signature of its hull shape and materials, cannot hide its wake. The Aegis cruisers and destroyers are therefore weapon/target-centric systems in the best sense of the concept—they are about attacking and destroying the enemy, and their hulls simply transport the deadly force with which they do so.

The proliferation of the Aegis system to allied navies has been prodigious: the Japan Maritime Self-Defense Force, the Spanish navy, the Royal Norwegian Navy, and the Republic of Korea Navy have all been beneficiaries. The Royal Australian Navy's new *Hobart*-class destroyers will have the Aegis system. We will address strategic issues in a later chapter but we note here that Aegis has been a unifying part of the US maritime strategy, embodying a common system and architecture that enables joint operations and interoperability with major allies.

All of this is not just visionary planning coupled to innovative and world-class technology but a reflection of the United States as a whole, as an alliance of the industrial base, the Navy, and Congress. This alliance forged a sea-based, totally mobile, and forward-deployed deterrent to emerging threats. This contrasts with the inability of the Soviet Union to outmatch and outplay the United States and its allies. Aegis is a key part of both the legacy and of the future, a military-strategic paradigm that cannot be forgotten in the haste to reduce defense spending and spread investment across a wide spectrum of platforms and systems of doubtful efficacy. Aegis remains today and will be for the foreseeable future an insurance policy worth its weight in gold.

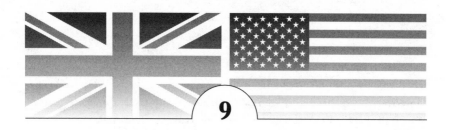

9

The 1990s

A Decade of Rising Threats in the Middle East and
a Period of Retrenchment with the End of the Cold War

The decade of the 1990s has been seen as one of transformation, fleet battle experiments, and "peace dividends," but combat quickly set the tone. The Iraqi invasion of Kuwait galvanized the Western nations to united action in support of President George Herbert Walker Bush's aim to remove Saddam Hussein's forces from Kuwait and restore order in the Middle East. A library of works record and analyze the events surrounding the conflict that became known as the first Gulf war. What ensues is an examination of the maritime strategic issues and connotations of Operation Desert Shield: an analysis of alternatives, not for "Monday-morning quarterbacking" but rather to look objectively and realistically at how the US Navy and the Royal Navy could have provided alternative solutions.

This is an important exercise, not an academic analysis but a serious look at how maritime forces can jointly be employed in alternative strategic modes in similar conflicts in the future. The stress is on "strategic," because often in the haste to resolve an international crisis perfectly workable solutions that arise may not be the optimal ones. "Optimal" implies military-strategic efficacy: What is the best course of military action to meet the primary strategic objectives? Clearly, any Western leader will want to achieve such objectives, and with minimum loss of casualties, the lowest economic cost, in the most realistic time scale, all coupled to political actions to garner support and convert this support to actual military deployments.

To recapitulate briefly: Iraq invaded Kuwait on August 2, 1990. There was genuine and realistic fear in Western governments that Saddam Hussein would not stop at Kuwait but would challenge the Kingdom of Saudi Arabia (KSA). Owing to Saudi Arabia's role as a prime oil supplier, the economic consequences could have been catastrophic. The West's air campaign began on January 17, 1991, as Operation Desert Shield, with the United States in the lead and supported by a formidable coalition. On February 1, the ground offensive began against the Iraqi invasion forces; it ended successfully after a short, sharp, and highly mobile and agile ground offensive: Operation Desert Storm. The offensive was led by General Norman Schwarzkopf, with a British second in command, Lieutenant General (later General) Sir Peter de la Billière, who was also the commander-in-chief of British forces in the war.

General de la Billière, a seasoned SAS veteran of great military distinction, had been a Margaret Thatcher favorite since the Iranian embassy siege of 1980. During the Falklands conflict he had planned the controversial Operation Mikado, a SAS operation to destroy their home base in Rio Grande, in Argentina, the three remaining Exocet missiles that Argentina possessed, the aircraft that carried them (five Super Etendards), and their pilots. (The operation was abandoned in due course for several reasons, not least of which was poor real-time, tactical intelligence.) De la Billière had experience fighting in the Gulf region, knew the people and cultures, and had good language skills. He was to become a most important voice during the war recommending the use of special forces. On November 28, 1990, before the fighting began, Prime Minister Thatcher was replaced by John Major. This change did not affect the British position or commitment; Major was as dedicated to Hussein's ouster as his predecessor. Prime Minister Thatcher had ordered two additional warships into the Persian Gulf to supplement the destroyers that made up what was designated Operation Armilla by the United Kingdom. Later, Prime Minister Major stepped this commitment up with the deployment of another destroyer, three minesweepers, and various support ships to work with the US Navy in the Gulf. The key role of the British naval forces was to support the US Navy carrier, battleship, and amphibious forces by providing additional air defense.

Let us now address an aspect of this short and decisive war—the strategic options—because this debate will play most importantly as we move farther into the twenty-first century and examine the US Navy and Royal Navy in the global maritime strategic context. The war became primarily, but not entirely, a land campaign, presaged by an air campaign to destroy command, control, and communications infrastructure. The precursor was the destruction of all air defenses, to allow manned aircraft to ingress to their targets without fear of surface-to-air missiles. The key to the destruction of these initial targets were Tomahawk missiles fired by the US Navy. They made the air as safe as was practical for carrier-based aircraft, Air Force fighters and bombers, and Royal Air Force Tornado and Buccaneer aircraft. The land war was a tank war, one of encircling and outflanking the Iraqi army and destroying it, rather like the classic tank battles of World War II—for example, the second battle of El Alamein in October 1942.

The US Air Force, US Navy, and Royal Air Force so harried the retreating Iranian forces that the chairman of the Joint Chiefs of Staff, General Colin Powell, recommended a halt to the slaughter. Besides the humanitarian and tactical issues, Powell and his commander-in-chief had sound reasons for calling a halt: the strategic and international objective of ejecting Iranian forces from Kuwait had been achieved. It was clear that Saddam Hussein would be unable for the foreseeable future to mount any form of counterattack or threaten his neighbors. His forces had proven inept and would take serious rebuilding.

The US Navy, the US Marine Corps, and the Royal Navy had made critical contributions but had not been the sledgehammers of the war. That had been the US Army, supported by the British Army's last armored division in service. The British had originally committed their 7th Armored Brigade in September 1990, largely for political reasons and because bureaucratic status was measured by force contributions. The British realized that a brigade was insufficient if they wished to be a major player and in November 1990 the tank commitment was increased to their one remaining armored division. (The division, in the event, performed magnificently in what is likely to have been the last hurrah of a full British armored division, certainly in a desert war.)

No alternatives were ever seriously explored in Washington or among the "coalition of the willing." President George Herbert Walker Bush and his military-political leadership team had clear political objectives. With General Powell's deft hand on the tiller, it became clear that a short war was in order, with minimal casualties for the coalition. There had to be a substantial buildup to give the coalition side overpowering capability. This was a major logistical operation for all the countries involved, and sealift was the primary means, given the volume, the nature of the loadouts, and access issues. The KSA was a natural source of access and facilities, in view of the geopolitical threat Hussein potentially posed to it. However, from a larger strategic viewpoint, the invasion of Kuwait demonstrates that assault from the sea may be credible only given certain factors, involving basing issues, overflight rights, airfields with good runways, and access to deepwater port facilities, and communications.

The US Military Sealift Command and the US Marine Corps' amphibious lift capabilities were designed for assault from the sea. The availability of a friendly country near the target diminished the risks inherent in amphibious assault. However, there are qualifications. The Tomahawk missile combined with carrier-based strike aircraft EW can decimate a threat. Any assault over a beach would be preceded by massive air and sea-based firepower. A combined barrage of naval gunfire, Tomahawks, air-to-ground attacks, and electronic jamming can have devastating effects in short order. If the enemy concentrates to resist at possible beachheads, it facilitates targeting; by contrast, dispersal weakens shore defenses and ability to resist penetration and encirclement.

Against the combination of airborne assault by helicopter with traditional landings from assault ships (LPDs and LHAs), tank landing ships, and other transports, underscored by advance special-forces operations, an enemy that has been barraged by shore bombardment and air-to-ground weapons is likely to be seriously disadvantaged unless it possesses capable missile systems. The Iraqis did have a capability to fire at US warships relatively close inshore for shore bombardment. This is where escorts play a critical role, defending high-value units from missile attack. The Royal Navy's destroyer and frigate force became part of a US carrier battle group's protective screen and escorted US and UK amphibious assault forces. As we move toward 2020 those same ships will be the defensive screen for the two new British aircraft carriers, HMS *Queen Elizabeth* and HMS *Prince of Wales*.

In the event, the US Marine Corps' offshore activity in the Gulf was a deception, while the land force readied a rapid pincer attack that quickly destroyed Iraq's armor and infantry. Had a US Marine Corps attack at MEF (Marine expeditionary force) level been launched, supported by Royal Marines, SEALs, SBS, and SAS, the Iraqi forces would likely have been overwhelmed in short order. Surprise, deception, and sabotage would have all played their parts against the Iraqis.

The question of armor in amphibious assault is always a critical question: How much? How capable (versus threat armor)? How disembarked to the beachhead? And how to support logistically? The other key factor is the beach profile: Is it suitable for a landing? How many choices are there if more than one is needed? The US Marine Corps and the Royal Marines are well equipped to answer to all these questions. Strategic expeditionary warfare is the heritage of both US and Royal Marines. The combination, with a MEF-level Marine Corps force, is an extraordinary capability, particularly when supported by US Navy carrier battle groups, to be joined in the 2020s by a Royal Navy carrier and amphibious battle group.

This is not simply a war college "what if" exercise. It is meant rather to ask, one level higher, "What are the strategic alternatives available to the US president and commander-in-chief, the British prime minister and his/her National Security Council and chiefs of staff, and their allies when the military-political factors are not as favorable as in 1991?" This question comes down to strategic planning, strategic options, the resources, and the choices. Bear these points in mind as we thread our way through the next chapters and end with the future of US-UK maritime strategy and resourcing. Much depends on the political-military mix of leadership, thought processes, strategic-studies training and education, and a complex set of vested and inherited interests that can impact and slant decisions. Later we will try to analyze conclusively what is most in the national-security interests of the United States and United Kingdom, without fear, favor, bias, or skewed data.

Let us now return to more tactical issues associated with the first Gulf war. We have seen how increasingly precise weapons like Tomahawk can play pivotal roles early in a conflict. Weapons improvements since 1991 make precision ordnance even more effective. However, the 1991 war exposed several weak links that military commanders on the scene recognized early on. Simply stated: however good the weapon, it can only be as good as the targeting system and the timeliness, accuracy, and reliability of the targeting data. Near- or real-time data is necessary in fast-moving tactical situations or where units are unaware of it. The immediate tactical situation can include the disposition of civilians, because rules of engagement, the Geneva Conventions, and simple humanitarian concerns issues can quickly come into play.

We discussed in an earlier chapter the issue of intelligence data dissemination to the frontline war fighter. In 1991 several factors inhibited its free flow, particularly from overhead/satellite sources. Security restrictions prohibited the wide dissemination of valuable intelligence and degraded the timeliness of what was distributed. By the time intelligence had been collected, analyzed, and passed through special channels to a limited few, it was often "time late" and therefore irrelevant. As we noted earlier, in the 1990s the National Reconnaissance Office was unacknowledged, totally covert. Disseminating overhead data to a frontline war fighter in or near real time was unheard of, totally at variance with the culture, organization, and communications systems of the intelligence community.

To say that intelligence was poor during the first Gulf war is well off the mark, but it certainly was not good enough. Nowhere was that truer than in the "Scud hunting" operations by special forces, attempts to locate and eliminate Iraqi Scud missiles before they could be fired into Israel and against coalition targets. The Iraqis played several games to disguise the Scuds' locations and movements. Placing a precision weapon on a camouflaged and mobile Scud battery is not as simple as it may appear. Dealing with threat mobility requires the real-time overhead IMINT, SIGINT, and ELINT to locate and confirm the Scud, and then maintain contact while an attack is prepared. All these factors presuppose satellite availability; correct positioning in terms of the orbit, trajectory, and swath of the satellite; downloading, to analysis to command center to war fighter. None of this is easy. As a result, in 1991 many war fighters were badly served, with intelligence either inadequate or late.

The US intelligence community took great pains and made a significant investment later in the 1990s to rectify the situation. The architectural and communications solutions were imaginative and sophisticated. In addition, the community recognized the need for other systems besides satellites: the requirement for unmanned aerial vehicles to track mobile targets became axiomatic. Systems and platforms such as the Predator and Global Hawk UAVs and the US Air Force's Joint STARS were born of war-fighting experience. The Joint STARS radar is a prodigious system, but the aircraft that carries it has the usual limitations of range and endurance. Joint STARS can image at considerable ranges in benign environments, within the constraints of crew endurance and the availability of inflight refueling and friendly airfields.

The first Gulf war taught the intelligence community important lessons about the need to take fundamental cultural strides to sanitize intelligence to make it usable at the secret level by any user with a need to know and a clearance. This called for clever ways to change highly classified material so that its inherent value was not lost but the true capability of the collection system could not be deduced if the material was ever compromised.

I was directly involved in the key programs that provided the solutions to the weaknesses exposed in the 1991 Gulf war. One that to this day requires attention is special-forces operations—in the case of the US Navy, the SEALs. SEALs are placed in highly dangerous situations and are well trained to cope. However, SEALs always need the best, up-to-the-minute tactical intelligence. Providing it is not easy, because even the lightest transceiver is an additional weight, carried at the cost of weapons, ammunition, water, and food. In the 1990s there was no tested and approved means to send a satellite image in real time to a SEAL. The digital-communications and iPhone eras were getting into gear, but only in the most modest ways.

The issue was not just compact, light, and secure hard drives and small displays but bandwidth: an issue that continues to trouble conventional US military communications, particularly satellite systems. The successor systems will transmit massive amounts of data, voice, and imagery that will make the intelligence issues of the first Gulf war look as antiquated as Nelson's bouncing "Yorker" shots. Even when it reprograms satellite orbits to support special operations, it has taken the US intelligence community a long time to provide real-time intelligence to SEALs except via satellite voice, and this has not always been efficient. The well documented SEAL Operation Red Wings in Afghanistan, which began on June 27, 2005, went wrong for several reasons, but one was poor and unreliable communications. Images or video of where the threat is located are absolutely critical to avoid being surrounded and attacked, a no-win situation. Threats on the ground need to be identified in plenty of time; there is no substitute for persistent, reliable, real-time IMINT, SIGINT, and ELINT. This applies to ingressing and egressing helicopter lifts for special forces; the UAV helps shift this paradigm.

There were no such networks in the desert in 1991, when British SAS units were up against not just the environment but the unknown. Handheld transceivers can obviate much stress in dangerous tactical situations, provided the hardware is reliable, there are backup systems, and the information needed is actually available. In the Falklands campaign, operations planned for the Argentine mainland were frustrated by unreliable information, though satellite voice communications worked—these are ineffective if there is no actionable information to pass. The worst of all worlds is a distant command center with overall operational control over special-forces units in the thick of things but possessing no intelligence of value to them. In such a situation the unit on the ground learns the local picture by direct contact with the enemy and finds that the intelligence assessments at the last predeployment briefing were inaccurate, incomplete, or both.

There has been a critical shift in the civilian-military/industry-government mix in the twenty-five years since the first Gulf war, one that is important for ensuring that the US Navy and the Royal Navy stay ahead of the threat curve. The American and British governments' acquisition processes and cycles are now well behind commercial R&D; businesses can survive only by keeping up with technology and ahead of the competition. For the military, the "competition" is a possible future enemy; clearly, military-government procurement time scales must not invalidate technical leads by causing IOC to be reached too late.

For example, a system that takes ten years or longer to reach the field may be out of date when it does. This is a major issue in the digital era, particularly in the command, control, communications, intelligence, surveillance, and targeting domains: industry will necessarily be ahead of the American and British governments if they continue to follow current acquisition practices. Nowhere is that truer than in communications, particularly in the non-high-end satellite systems. Global, networked 4G LTE systems can carry massive volumes of data, and contemporary encryption can provide full cyber protection, indeed built-in cyber offense-defense systems, to the US and Royal Navies. We will address this issue further.

Let us go back now to the post-first-Gulf-war 1990s and moves by the US Navy to recognize what was becoming a new phrase in the military lexicon: asymmetric warfare. At the center of change was the Third Fleet, US Pacific Fleet, whose commander flew his flag on board USS *Coronado,* based in San Diego, California. Third Fleet was not the only element concerned with asymmetric warfare, though it should get credit for drawing attention to it. Several people on the Third Fleet staff were well ahead of the game and recognized that the US Navy, and US military forces generally, would face asymmetric threats.

There was nothing new in itself about "asymmetric warfare," defined as conflict in which opponents are mismatched and the resource weaker adopts tactics and lesser technologies to offset its shortcomings. The weaker player typically resorts to unstructured and informal means to undermine a more formal, better equipped and structured force. Military and naval history offer many examples in modern times—the American Revolutionary War, raids by the Confederate colonel John Mosby during the American Civil War, the methods of the Boers during the Second Boer War in South Africa, Lawrence of Arabia's attacks on Turkish forces, and the tactics of the French Resistance and Yugoslav partisans during World War II.

What Third Fleet recognized, as did the Marine officers on its staff, was that the world was changing, that it was becoming asymmetric rather than structured and bipolar as in the Cold War. The evidence for this was collected by such organizations as the International Institute for Strategic Studies (IISS) and the Stockholm International Peace Research Institute (SIPRI), as well as by government intelligence. The "peace dividend" was slowly being eroded by a less publicized but relentless surge of violent extremism in the Near and Middle East. What was emerging had been experienced in recent years in the United Kingdom (the Irish Republican Army) and in the Middle East (the attack on the US Marine barracks in Lebanon and countless outrages in the Palestinian-Lebanese-Israeli territories); all these had decisive asymmetric characteristics. Later would follow the East African embassy bombings, the routing of US conventional forces in Mogadishu, Somalia (the "Blackhawk Down" incident), and the attack in Aden on the USS *Cole*—all precursors to September 11, 2001. Third Fleet staff perceived that the Navy had to be trained and prepared to counter such threats.

There was no response from Washington in terms of funding for training, doctrinal statements, or other signals of recognition of global change.

Fundamental Islamic extremism was gaining momentum, but there was no official reaction. In hindsight, what happened then in San Diego was quite revolutionary, in conceptual as well as practical terms. The Third Fleet team did not wait for Washington to lead: they initiated and provided the lead themselves. Third Fleet found a way ahead through a combination of leadership, ingenuity, resource capture, and a remarkable coalition whose members fully understood what they advocated. The Third Fleet staff did this without any formal action on the part of the Department of Defense or Congress; its achievements led in due course to massive changes in maritime strategy and tactics.

Third Fleet found two principal means to create change: Fleet Battle Experiments (FBEs) and Limited Objective Experiments (LOEs). No US Navy fleet could have achieved what this one did in the nine years from 1994 to 2003 without outstanding personal and engaged leadership from its commanders—in this case, two extraordinarily capable ones: Vice Admiral Herbert "Herb" Browne, from October 1996 to November 1998, and Vice Admiral Dennis "Denny" McGinn, from November 1998 to October 2000. Both were the lineal successors of illustrious Third Fleet commanders back to "Bull" Halsey. There was an impressive lineup of four-star support for these Third Fleet commanders. For instance, Commander-in-Chief Pacific Fleet from November 1996 to October 1999 was Admiral Archie Clemins, himself an innovator, leading his fleet into the digital era with network-centric concepts and technology. He took a personal interest and involvement in implementing change. There was therefore a crucial period before the 9/11 tragedy when the US Navy had what can only be called an "A team" in the Pacific Fleet.

Both Admiral Browne and Admiral McGinn were distinguished naval aviators; Admiral Browne had received the Navy Cross for valor in Vietnam and commanded Navy Space Command. Admiral McGinn would later become Deputy Chief of Naval Operations for Warfare Requirements, a most appropriate position following his innovations at Third Fleet.

There was no official, "line item" funding for Third Fleet's initiatives or any "earmarked" indirect congressional funding (that is, additions by defense and appropriations committees or subcommittees to the president's Navy budget). The fleet drew funds from various budget line items that were broadly enough defined to allow it. At the same time, senior Navy flag officers in Washington who were supportive of Third Fleet's goals were proactive in moving funds to legitimately support FBEs and LOEs, which were nowhere provided for in the official budget. One such admiral was Vice Admiral Arthur

"Art" Cebrowski, who during this period of innovation was the "N6" on the Navy Staff, responsible for all future requirements affecting Navy command, control, communications, computers, and related domains across all warfare specialties. Admiral Cebrowski, the father of Navy transformation, was the Navy catalyst for change back in Washington, while Vice Admirals Browne and McGinn led at sea.

Cebrowski as N6 realized that large-scale integrated circuits permitting the network-centric flow of information that he advocated would be game changers for naval warfare. He saw what the civilian sector was doing in information technology and that the Navy, indeed the US military as a whole, needed to get on board. As a member of the Strategic Studies Group in 1981 at the Naval War College, in Newport, Rhode Island, he looked out to the future. He and colleagues like Commander William Owens (later vice chairman of the Joint Chiefs of Staff) argued that a networked environment sending information to war fighters from multiple sources, would establish "information dominance" in the battlespace that would lessen the need for massed lethal kinetic force. A white paper, *Joint Vision 2010,* issued in 1996, a look ahead into the next decade, became the template for how things would work.

Not everyone supported this philosophy of radical change. In fact, when Cebrowski's two leading champions (the chairman and vice chairman of the Joint Chiefs of Staff, General John Shalikashvili and William Owens, respectively) retired in 1998, there was a definite push-back from the Joint Staff and the Navy. Some were skeptical of the new lexicon; some used more pejorative terms, such as "jargon" and "buzzwords." More sophisticated educated analysts argued that Cebrowski did not see that the technological impetus from the commercial world and its military impact were evolutionary, not revolutionary, and that the Navy should exploit the new capabilities as it had on many occasions before. Some considered the change from active to digitally enhanced passive sonar as an analogue. Cebrowski concluded his military career as president of the Naval War College on October 1, 2001, just days after the 9/11 attacks, and took up the civilian position of director of the Office of Force Transformation, at the personal request of Secretary of Defense Donald Rumsfeld.

Admiral Cebrowski succumbed to cancer on November 12, 2005, before he could consummate his influence over the wider Department of Defense. However, he left an intellectual legacy. He had shown that military power could come from information, that this can lead to new strategic thinking, concepts, and advocacy, and that networked forces could wield kinetic power with overwhelming effect. Attrition might even be superseded by the effects of information dominance, thus providing the political leadership with a whole new array of options. The Cebrowski philosophy championed the notion that information dominance would always win over brute force. The counterarguments were that such change was part of the evolution of military technology; that such issues as the invasion of Iraq and nation building are political-military strategy in nature, not products of changes in information technology; and that strategy had historically been unaffected by changes in the information-technology base. Some argued that the flaring up of the historical clash between Muslim Sunnis and Shia in the Middle East was a fundamentally unrelated strategic issue.

Many held that information dominance was part of classical electronic warfare, evolving in ways that had been seen before—from direction finding and communications intercept, through the Ultra and Magic in World War II, to contemporary SIGINT and ELINT. The electromagnetic spectrum was still what it always was, and technology was evolving through new exploitations of it. The same argument was applied to digital communications and the whole microwave environment: evolutionary, not revolutionary.

Nevertheless, the impact of "network-centricity" on the tactical level of naval warfare was not only significant, it was here to stay. One reappraisal that the supporters of change pushed hard for in this period was how the industrial-military community did business. The status quo of program development—lengthy acquisition and contracting processes and long waits for initial operational capability—combined to stifle innovation. The Department of Defense was simply not keeping pace with commercial information technology; in fact, the military was several years behind. In retrospect, this seems a powerful case for simply keeping up with the commercial world. However, that view overlooks the need for rapid acquisition and implementation. Admiral Cebrowski wanted a cadre of naval innovators to emerge from the Naval War College. This may indeed be his lasting legacy: that education is the true catalyst of change, and that the opportunity to think through, in an unfettered environment, the implementation of change is a powerful advantage.

On the waterfront, at Third Fleet in San Diego, there was a different approach, a different tempo, and real action. The coalition of the willing in the Pacific Fleet turned words into deeds. What did they do, how did they do it, and what did they achieve? First, let us define the "it." Third Fleet was very much aware of network-centricity, and the three-star leadership was read into the latest highly classified programs at the National Reconnaissance Office. The "it" was to take both new and innovative network concepts and existing systems and command, control, and communications architectures and translate them into new, advanced operational applications. Let us take a look at Fleet Battle Experiment Bravo, which had a subtitle, "The Ring of Fire." This took place between August and September 1997 and involved the Navy, Marine Corps, and Navy special forces. Bravo was sponsored by the Chief of Naval Operations. The key units involved were the Third Fleet flagship, USS *Coronado,* and two other major surface units, the amphibious assault ship USS *Peleliu* and the guided-missile destroyer USS *Russell,* with support from Naval Air Station Fallon (F-18 aircraft), Naval Air Warfare Center China Lake, and Naval Air Warfare Center Point Mugu. The NRO provided services. The concepts of operation (CONOPS) centered on a new battlespace local-area network (LAN) architecture that connected sensors and other information sources in real time via satellite links.

The objective was to test whether a target could be attacked and destroyed and real-time battle-damage assessment obtained by the network architecture. One scenario involved a small SEAL reconnaissance team inland sending real-time intelligence data, including imagery, via satellite; that imagery was exploited on board *Coronado* and then transmitted in real time to an F-18 aircraft, which destroyed the target—flares indicated a direct hit. The flagship built a command tactical picture (CTP) from multiple sources, including IMINT from the forward air controller (FOFAC) who had designated the target. The *Coronado,* many miles out to sea, was able to pair weapon to target. In this the F-18 aircraft delivered the coup de grâce, but there were several choices available, including a SEAL attack and a Tomahawk launch. The US Marines provided the FOFAC, from the 13th Marine Expeditionary Unit.

Another subset of Bravo included Operation Silent Fury, a highly successful test and demonstration of a national-level C4I (command, control, communications, computers, and intelligence) architecture, with the NRO providing both systems and direct support. This was the first time in naval history that the breadth and magnitude of national satellite systems were brought into play. This FBE led to major fleetwide changes that were to reap dividends soon after the 9/11 attacks. The use of the new architectures and real-time sensor data via satellite links and the US Navy SIPRNET (the classified variant of the unclassified NIPRNET) has borne fruit and has given the service a massive advantage over its potential adversaries. Since 1997 the Navy has made further strides.

Let us look at an interesting, and at one level amusing, episode that occurred during an FBE in Herb Browne's time. It involved a US Air Force Joint Stars (JSTARS) aircraft and its revolutionary radar tracking system. Before the FBE series, no one had thought through the potential of JSTARS to support fleet operations, in particular so that Navy aircraft could attack mobile targets "on the fly." The fighter would get real-time updates on the way to the target and when within weapon range employing the latest to engage, while the JSTARS aircraft remained well outside the range of known threats. Third Fleet conducted a unique joint operation involving a JSTARS from Warner Robbins Air Force Base in Georgia. The plan was to fly JSTARS from Georgia to California and then out some distance over the Pacific Ocean, taking station at high altitude and in contact with *Coronado*. Time on station was a function of fuel load, fuel consumption rate, and crew endurance. The aircraft would pass its detailed tracking data to *Coronado*, which would then use it to direct live-fire air-to-ground attacks.

Unfortunately, the aircraft developed mechanical problems and had to land in California. The Air Force repaired the aircraft, and it circled just west of the coast imaging and tracking mobile targets in the area of the Marine Corps base at Twentynine Palms, well inland. At 0100 the Third Fleet staff was huddled in the flagship operations center. I was standing with Vice Admiral Browne and a senior US Marine Corps visitor and observer, Major General Charles F. Bolden (who later would become the administrator of the National Aeronautics and Space Administration, NASA). The data from JSTARS flowed in, and a series of targeting evolutions took place. At one point the *Coronado* operations team and I were puzzled by vehicle traffic around one particular building: What was going on at this time in the morning? General Bolden laughed aloud: in all those cars were Marines getting their early-morning Big Macs at the 24/7 McDonald's on the base.

But a serious tactical innovation had just taken place, one that meant real-time attacks on mobile targets in urban environments, over and beyond the capability to attack fixed targets with predetermined coordinates using expensive weapons such as Tomahawk. It meant that an aircraft could launch from a carrier at considerable distance, be updated in flight and vectored to the area, and use precision weapons to engage mobile targets—a huge step forward. Other, classified scenarios that Third Fleet simultaneously explored with national satellite systems added to this capability, which quickly became known as "sensor-to-shooter operations."

Let us now address Fleet Battle Experiment Echo (FBE-E) and Limited Objective Experiment Zero (LOE-0), which had a seminal impact on the US Navy, the Department of Defense, the US national intelligence community (NIC), and the nation's allies. The objectives and outcomes of the other FBEs from March 1997 to September 2000 (FBEs Alfa, Charlie, Foxtrot, Golf, and Hotel) are available from various Navy websites and publications. FBE-E and

LOE-0 are not so well documented publicly, because of sensitivities and the involvement of other agencies of the US government. We will restrict ourselves here to outcomes and impacts.

FBE-E took place in March 1999 in and around the San Francisco Bay area, the sea approaches to the West Coast, and the airspace above San Francisco and offshore. Innovative intelligence sources and methods were employed. The overall scenario examined advanced command, control, and communications, naval "fires," and sensor-to-shooter networks, specifically addressing actual and simulated asymmetric and terrorist attacks. Information superiority and the real-time movement of information for quick reaction were at a premium. FBE-E was visionary and reflected excellent insight into the mind-set and likely operations of al Qaida and other Islamic extremists. FBE-E placed the US Navy in a remarkably well prepared position; most American citizens were not aware of the threat of al Qaida or of the existence of Osama bin Laden, but people who worked FBE-E were singularly aware of them. What they did in and around San Francisco was a portent of things to come. What did they do, and what lessons did they learn?

One observation is important: the methodology employed was, as the title implied, experimental. The essence of Echo was operational experimentation, of kinds different from what the Navy's Center for Naval Analyses (CNA) had conducted for decades since World War II. CNA's Operational Evaluation Group (OEG) conducted systems and tactical evaluations at sea. In addition, CNA conducted paper and computer simulations and analyses, such as Sea War '85 in the mid-1970s (of which Captain John Underwood and I were the principal architects). Echo had all the hallmarks of good science: it recorded data in real time and devised apt metrics. It showed in a controlled environment what asymmetric and terrorist threats could achieve and what it might take to anticipate and defeat them.

The "Red Team" (that is, opposition) made extremely accurate predictions of how Islamic fundamentalism could threaten not just Third Fleet but also American and allied interests. One domain the Red Team explored that has fortunately not so far reared its ugly head (unless the Syrian Assad regime is an exception) was the use of weapons of mass destruction. WMD, particularly chemical and biological warfare, combined with explosives and in certain meteorological conditions, could be exploited with formidable effects. Only in a real-time, fast-moving, live environment could such threats be examined. No simulation could replace the real world.

Vice Admiral McGinn gave introduction to the video the Navy produced on FBE-E. He stressed that major shifts in doctrine and in the underlying

Vice Admiral Herbert A. Browne, USN, as a rear admiral   US NAVY

tactics, techniques, and procedures (TTPs) were now necessary to address
the changing nature of asymmetric warfare, and specifically in the maritime
environment. The live operations shown bore out his comments: attacks on
large fleet units by small boats, combat swimmers, jet skis, the stealth ship
Sea Shadow. One of Third Fleet's most able intelligence officers, Lieutenant
Commander Dan Shanower, stressed in the video that Aegis-type systems
would not be appropriate for discrete, mobile, asymmetric targets, particularly
in urban settings.

Vice Admiral Dennis V. McGinn, USN, as a rear admiral (select)   US NAVY

Most significant of all was the use of two low- and slow-flying aircraft to deploy simulated chemical and biological weapons, including anthrax. The concept of civilian aircraft being used for the deployment of WMD and in suicide missions was not lost on senior observers from the NIC on board *Coronado*. (This was a lesson that was not later shared with the Federal Bureau of Investigation.) The aircraft involved, one of which I piloted, had a Navy cameraman on board recording events in the air and communicating with

Vice Admiral Arthur K. Cebrowski, USN, as a rear admiral   US NAVY

JSTARS over the Pacific. JSTARS was to locate and track the aircraft as it mingled with radar "sea return" from the ocean and urban traffic. With the full approval and under the operational control of the Federal Aviation Administration, I flew my aircraft under the Golden Gate Bridge. I then followed, at low altitude and at low speed, vehicle traffic in downtown San Francisco, attempting to make it difficult for JSTARS to distinguish my aircraft and for Third Fleet missile systems to track and engage it. I climbed up and over the Oakland Bay Bridge and then attacked units of the Third Fleet with simulated chemical weapons. GPS coordinates at every stage were recorded to determine how effectively JSTARS had tracked the aircraft and how in the future it could do so.

New defensive systems with the latest integrated, networked information systems were examined to see how effective they could be against such targets. A wide range of platforms were involved, including P-3 aircraft, UAVs, and JSTARS. The Office of Naval Research "SLICE" boat was used for special asymmetric purposes, and the Marine Corps conducted live operations ashore to see how effectively threats could be located and targeted in a highly complex civilian setting. Small, mobile targets in an urban environment were a serious problem for the sensors and integrated real-time networks used. Highly focused elements of Echo concentrated on issues that had hitherto not been examined in a real-world, fast-moving battlespace; the Silent Fury component challenged the Navy, Marine Corps, and intelligence community to continue to operate effectively if GPS was jammed or denied.

Echo was a resounding success in terms of the lessons learned and the impetus given to facing the urgent realties of asymmetric threats. Echo took place in March 1999, and the attack on *Cole* occurred on October 12, 2000. Sadly and tragically, now-promoted Commander Dan Shanower, one of the brilliant young US naval officers who put together Echo, was killed in the Pentagon on September 11, 2001, while on duty inside the Navy Intelligence Center.

Limited Objective Experiment Zero (LOE-0) was another milestone event. The Third Fleet team, Vice Admiral Cebrowski in Washington, and a distinguished senior group from the NIC assessed that the early part of the twenty-first century would witness fewer large-scale, force-on-force wars. Rather, terrorist, brush-fire, and asymmetric conflicts arising from schisms within Islam, other ethnic and religious rivalries, energy and water disputes, and economic tensions from scarcity and high demand could play out as maritime rivalries where UNCLOS two-hundred-mile economic zones conflicted. Possible threats included WMDs in the hands of state players, surrogate state players, rogue nations, terrorist groups, or criminals. Third Fleet and the NIC recognized that a new genre of TTPs, specialized equipment, doctrine, and training would be required. In the changing world order China would play a dominant role and Russia perhaps a more shadowy one, seeking to reestablish its place in the sun.

In Zero, the combined capabilities of Third Fleet, the NIC, the Naval Air Systems Command, (c) and the emergent Center for Asymmetric Warfare

(CAW) at Naval Air Station and Naval Air Warfare Center Point Mugu were joined to look at locating, tracking, and targeting various WMDs in complex scenarios that reflected real-world discord. Most of Zero was classified; the unclassified essence was about combining integrated intelligence with targeting. The collaboration between the Navy and the NIC and the panoply of intelligence systems, technologies, sources, and methods were unprecedented. If there was an omission it was the absence of the federal law-enforcement agency of record, the Federal Bureau of Investigation. This observation is, of course, made with the benefit of hindsight, but as the agency charged with domestic counterintelligence and antiterrorist operations, the FBI would have witnessed something like what bin Laden's nineteen terrorists executed a short time later. Most of all, the need for intelligence-data exchange between the CIA and the FBI at an operational level could have been not just explored but written into TTPs, memoranda of understanding, and agreements. The failure to ensure that critical threat information was shared on a multi-agency basis was, perhaps, the single most important reason why the 9/11 tragedy was not anticipated and prevented.

The US Navy implemented new ways of doing business after FBE-E and LOE-0. Vice Admiral McGinn took all this knowledge and experience with him to the OPNAV staff in Washington. By now Admiral Browne was doing sterling work at the US Space Command headquarters. When 9/11 occurred the Navy was instantly ready to respond by strikes from the sea into Afghanistan and with Navy special forces. It would be a senior SEAL commander who would, alongside other clandestine US forces, attack bin Laden's sanctuary, caves, and training grounds in Afghanistan.

We now turn our attention to several of the conflicts that occurred before and shortly after 9/11 and what was happening inside the Royal Navy during a period of cutbacks, force-level reductions, overall retrenchment, and Strategic Defense and Security Reviews. We will look later at the post-9/11 events in a different context and from new and hitherto unexplored viewpoints.

10

Conflicts, Minor Wars, and the World-Changing Event of 9/11

The US Navy and Royal Navy in a New Era

The character, locations, and roles of the US Navy and Royal Navy in the new era of conflict from 1990 through 2015 varied dramatically, a testament to the changing nature of conflict and its resolution. What many of these conflicts showed is that technology is often not enough—overwhelming kinetic force may not be the solution to complex politico-military, theocratic, and economic scenarios in which force can be only one component. We will look at this twenty-five-year period not to restate what is well known but to see naval power and the wider maritime strategic issues in terms of both actual events and alternatives. What could have been done, as opposed to what was done? Where was the strategic analysis underpinning political decision making? What were the viable choices? Where did intelligence play, or not play? What were the gaps or inadequacies in intelligence? What does this all portend for the future? What should we do in future strategic defense and security reviews? What should the Royal Navy and the US Navy look like for the next generation, and how should they work together, in the interests of both international order and their respective nations?

Let us look at Bosnia, Kosovo, Sierra Leone, Libya, the Arab Spring, the major conflicts in Iraq and Afghanistan, Syria, and the whole ISIS phenomenon objectively, in terms of what these events tell us about how we spend defense resources. If, for example, the Royal Navy is to have a close relationship with the US Navy, then we should be absolutely clear about why and how. It has been a theme of this book that the two navies have not only much in common but should be irrevocably joined to maximize mutual effectiveness, despite the much smaller size of the Royal Navy. The power of naval warfare and maritime diplomacy is much greater than the sum of that of the individual units; a combined US-UK task force has immeasurably more political-military significance than a single-nation task force. Any opponent, potential adversary, or violator of international order has to take account of US-UK combined capabilities. Additionally, two highly professional navies can do things in unison in ways outside the ken of most navies. Of course, this case was well made by Admiral Michael Mullen, former Chief of Naval Operations and chairman of the Joint Chiefs of Staff.

The Bosnian crisis in southeastern Europe, 1992–95, was a wholesale humanitarian tragedy. The protagonists were the Serb and Croat communities in the Republic of Bosnia and Herzegovina, following the breakup of Yugoslavia and secessions of 1991. The conflict was one of ethnic and religious rivalries, overlain by the ambitions of individual leaders, particularly Slobodan Milosevic, the Serbian leader. The worst atrocities centered on the massacre or ethnic cleansing of the Bosnian Muslim and Croat populations. There was considerable political blowback against US inaction; the European Union was politically committed to countering any return to the disharmony that had produced bloodshed since the Middle Ages. Once finally committed, the United States and its European allies agreed on intervention. The British government chose the Royal Navy as its instrument, sending HMS *Invincible, Illustrious,* and *Ark Royal* (the three light, through-deck cruisers, or "Sea Harrier carriers") into the Adriatic to enforce sanctions. On April 16, 1994, one of the Royal Navy FA2 Sea Harriers was shot down by a Serbian surface-to-air missile; fortunately, the pilot escaped unharmed. In addition to Royal Navy Sea Harriers, the United Kingdom also provided twelve Royal Air Force GR7s.

It was not until March 24, 1999, that the United States ramped up its own involvement, in connection with Operation Allied Force, NATO's bombing campaign to halt the internecine hostilities and ethnic slaughter in Kosovo. The targets of US Navy and Royal Navy strikes were the forces of, again, Slobodan Milosevic. This conflict was the first time that NATO had gone to war, and a milestone also in that a Royal Navy SSN, HMS *Splendid,* fired Tomahawk missiles in anger for the first time. Seven Sea Harrier FA2s conducted strikes, in somewhat stark contrast to the many airborne strikes launched by the US Navy.

During the operations in southeastern Europe a most significant event occurred back in London: the United Kingdom's 1998 Strategic Defense Review unveiled a plan to build two 60,000-ton aircraft carriers. This was twenty years since the last British fleet carrier had left service, and, somewhat ironically, it will have taken almost twenty-two years, from 1998 to 2020, before the first of the two *Queen Elizabeth*–class aircraft carriers becomes fully operational. For the time being, however, even in a minor conflict on

Europe's doorstep, the Royal Navy could offer little. But the fatal decision of Denis Healey had been reversed, and one of the lessons of the Falklands had been learned and implemented. Strike from the sea with fixed-wing aircraft would return to the Royal Navy, albeit twenty years in the future.

In 1999 the Royal Navy supported an Australian-led operation to stabilize East Timor, sending the destroyer HMS *Glasgow,* a Royal Marine Special Boat Section team, and a three-hundred-strong Gurkha unit. Similarly, the Royal Navy was the key UK component of intervention in the civil war in Sierra Leone in 2000, deploying HMS *Argyll* and HMS *Chatham,* the assault ship HMS *Ocean,* and the light carrier HMS *Illustrious,* with thirteen Sea Harriers on board.

The Royal Navy was actively involved in humanitarian support in these stricken areas. During this period the United Kingdom was also faced with the recapitalization of its strategic nuclear force, through the replacement of the *Resolution*-class SSBNs by the *Vanguard* class, embarking the latest Trident II ballistic-missile system. This was a serious drain on the UK defense budget, fortunately at a time of an apparent "peace dividend." The latter was indeed hollow, a period of retrenchment in the Royal Navy to pay for overall defense cuts and the strategic-deterrent replacement. The Royal Navy now had to compete with the Royal Air Force and the army to maintain core capabilities. There was zero fat anywhere in the British defense budget; indeed, the 1998 carrier-acquisition decision was a most welcome reprieve. A more positive aspect of this period was the maintenance of an amphibious capability. This provided the agility and flexibility inherent to maritime expeditionary warfare, and within this nexus the Royal Marines managed to survive. Their rank structure had been so reduced that promotion was dependent on joint staff appointments, NATO positions, and the occasional senior naval billet. Would a turnaround occur that would bring growth rather than decline?

Within three years of the British Strategic Defense Review, and at a time when, fortunately, the US Navy had not suffered a decline anything proportional to that of the United Kingdom's naval forces, there occurred a defining moment in history: the 9/11 attacks on the World Trade Center in New York and the Pentagon in northern Virginia. The world would likely not be the same again for generations, given the unpredicted and unplanned consequences of post-9/11 intervention and of attempts at nation building, and Western-style democratization of the Islamic world.

Of the three thousand innocent victims on 9/11, sixty-seven were British citizens. United Nations Security Council Resolution 1368 condemned the attacks and asserted the rights of both individual and collective self-defense, while NATO's North Atlantic Council invoked article 4 of its charter—that the member nations will assist one another in collective self-defense. The world had changed.

We will not analyze here the rights and wrongs of the US-led interventions into, indeed invasion of, Iraq and Afghanistan, or the intense consequences for the Islamic world as a whole. Readers will have their own opinions. What we will do here is address several abiding issues. The al Qaida group that carried out the US attacks was small in number: nineteen sacrificed themselves in the name of Islamic jihad to inflict a massive human tragedy.

The consensus of democratic nations is that the reactions of President George W. Bush's administration, culminating in the invasions of Iraq and Afghanistan, were misguided and strategically inappropriate. Here we intend to address the maritime and strategic implications. The initial responses by the United States and the United Kingdom conspicuously included naval forces. From October 7, 2001, the United States and United Kingdom launched attacks with naval aircraft and cruise missiles against Taliban and al Qaida training camps and communications. The Northern Alliance, the pro-Western Afghan forces, became crucial to on-the-ground success. On November 16 the al Qaida leader, Mohammed Atef, was killed by a US air strike. US Marines landed by helicopter, set up Camp Rhino, south of Kandahar, and occupied the main road from Kandahar into Pakistan. Crucial to these operations were American and British special forces. It is commonly held that Osama bin Laden (whose capture was the chief reason for being in Afghanistan, aside from destroying his training camps, infrastructure, logistics pipeline, and personnel) had escaped by December 2001, after the battle of Tora Bora. That month the Bonn Agreement created the Afghanistan postwar government and established the International Security Assistance Force (ISAF). On December 21 an interim Afghanistan government was sworn into office.

Let's now look at what had happened. The legitimate reason for the United States and its main ally, the United Kingdom, for being in Afghanistan was, in accordance with UN Resolution 1368, to destroy Osama bin Laden's al Qaida–related capabilities, and nothing more. The means to achieve all this was clear: maritime power supported by special forces. On the night of October 4, 2001, USS *Theodore Roosevelt*, with Carrier Air Wing 1 (CVW-1), launched the initial strikes against al Qaida from the northern Arabian Sea. She then spent 159 consecutive days at sea, without shore support, the longest underway period in the history of the US Navy since World War II. This was an extraordinary achievement and symbolic of the flexibility and sustainability of naval power. Persistent forward presence characterized American and British maritime operations to destroy a relatively small group of Islamic fundamentalists who had rocked the civilized world.

The plans to create a presence in Afghanistan, with other, non-immediate military and political objectives, remain a matter for readers to evaluate for themselves. The point is that maritime power, coordinated via new and innovative communications and real-time or near-real-time intelligence, had been the strategic answer: it had been responsive and mobile; it had required no overflight rights, no fixed runways, and no shore-based logistics. The huge investments had paid off. The US Navy, US Marine Corps, Royal Navy, and American and British special forces (together with covert CIA special forces) had demonstrated these intrinsic capabilities. The SAS and SBS worked alongside US special forces to execute attacks beyond the capabilities of air strikes, in addition to calling down air strikes from hidden positions.

The Royal Navy showed a capability that the Strategic Defense Review of 1998 had not thoroughly analyzed at the strategic level, one represented by Tomahawk strikes against al Qaida and the Taliban from the SSNs *Trafalgar* and *Triumph* during Operation Enduring Freedom. Also, HMS *Illustrious* and a Royal Navy task force was in the Persian Gulf at the time of the initial operations, a clear demonstration that global presence is critical and that response time lines will often be measured in days, not months. Assembling and dispatching ground forces for conventional combat present a completely different task, massively more expensive than having maritime expeditionary forces already at hand. In November 2001, 40 Commando, Royal Marines, helped secure Bagram airfield, and in April–July 2002, 45 Commando, together with American, Australian, and Norwegian forces, destroyed al Qaida's infrastructure in eastern Afghanistan, a remarkable military achievement.

Readers will ask, what happened then? Why was not the chief tenet of expeditionary warfare—"early in and early out"—followed? The answer comes back to the fundamental point made at the beginning of this chapter. The political-strategic objectives and plans of the United States were clearly different from what hindsight may suggest they should have been. From a solely British perspective, strategic force structure can dictate what can and cannot be done. If the United Kingdom, based on the belief that British national interests are best served in this way, has a force structure based on maritime expeditionary warfare, then nation building and long-term intervention and sustainment become irrelevant, as well as militarily impossible. In 2002 the United Kingdom did create a Joint Rapid Reaction Force (JRRF) along expeditionary lines, but this was not accompanied by a serious realignment of capabilities.

We will not dwell on the decision by the United States and the United Kingdom to invade Iraq in 2003. The US House and Senate gave their approval (The Joint Resolution to Authorize the Use of United States Armed Forces against Iraq, October 2, 2002, and enacted October 16, 2002), and the House of Commons voted 412 in favor and 149 against on March 18, 2003. So in effect few are truly blameless regarding what many see in retrospect as strategic blunder.

Some observations, nevertheless, are highly relevant nonetheless to what happened. The British facilities on Diego Garcia and in Cyprus (the sovereign base at Akrotiri) demonstrated that joint overseas basing is invaluable in expeditionary allied operations. This is a key for the future and a point to remember in our finale. The Turkish parliament voted not to allow American or British troops to invade Iraq via Turkey, a point that is not now forgotten in relations between Turkey and its major NATO allies. When the Iraq war began, it was air strikes from US Navy CVNs and US Tomahawks that destroyed Saddam Hussein's communications, air defenses, and critical infrastructure. Royal Marines, 40 and 42 Commando, inserted by the Royal Navy, secured Umm Qasr and its sea approaches. As a key task, Royal Navy and Royal Marines personnel secured the offshore and southern oil fields from possible mines and sabotage, respectively. The "regime change" objective in Iraq was hard to connect with the 9/11 attacks, in light of the faulty and misleading intelligence that had been used to justify it. However, solely at the military level, the United Kingdom clearly got out of its depth, because of force-level issues. British command of ISAF, of the Allied Command Europe Rapid Reaction Force, and of operations in Helmand Province was all well and good but the United Kingdom just never had the forces on the ground to sustain the level of effort required. This is a massive lesson learned from the British side. We will look at this issue later in terms of future US-UK naval and expeditionary operations.

As the Iraq campaign persisted over the succeeding years a whole new set of problems, characterized by sectarian upheaval and violence, occurred there. Meanwhile both navies had to deal with other, global threats. The US Navy and the Royal Navy effectively countered piracy in the Gulf of Aden and off Somalia. There were 197 pirate attacks in 2009, but by 2013 there were just 13. At the time of writing in 2015 the problem has been surmounted, though there will always be pirates in certain regions who are desperate enough, like most criminals, to take their chances. This campaign again demonstrated the overwhelming effectiveness of a multinational force.

Humanitarian relief and evacuation of nationals and others from hot spots have always been peacetime missions of US and UK naval forces. For example, the December 2004 tsunami in South and Southeast Asia and the July 2006 Royal Navy evacuations from Lebanon during the Israeli-Hezbollah conflict show their flexibility. In January 2010 came the Haiti earthquake and the vital roles played by the US Navy, without which it is difficult to see how sustained help could have been brought to bear so quickly and effectively. Then in November 2013 came the devastating Typhoon Haiyan in the Philippines. The US Pacific Fleet came to the rescue and showed, in the most arduous of circumstances, that relief from the sea is the only practical and sustainable response in such a contingency.

In the United Kingdom the 2010 Defense Review reinforced the commitment to, by 2020, both make operational the first of the two *Queen Elizabeth*–class carriers and reduce the regular army to 82,000. The plan to replace the Royal Navy's four *Vanguard*-class SSBNs was put firmly in place.

In among natural disasters came global political change, in the shape of the "Arab Spring"—a series of antigovernment uprisings across the Middle East in early 2011. Beginning in Tunisia on December 18, 2010, it spread across the Middle East, to Egypt, Libya, Yemen, Syria, Bahrain, Kuwait, Lebanon, and Oman. Meanwhile the governments of Morocco and Jordan preempted revolt by various constitutional reforms, knowing that protest could and would escalate. There were also protests elsewhere, including Saudi Arabia, Sudan, and Mauritania. By mid-2012 the "Spring" had faded to a "Winter," but by spring 2012, rulers had been forced out in Tunisia, Egypt, Libya, and Yemen. There were major civil uprisings in Bahrain and Syria. From a naval perspective, US and UK naval forces became involved in the 2011 Libyan revolt and then the civil war that ensued there. Royal Navy ships HMS *Cumberland* and HMS *York* secured Benghazi and transported evacuees to Valetta, in Malta.

On February 26, 2011, the United Nations imposed UN Resolution 1970, an arms embargo, on Libya, together with a UN-mandated no-fly zone, Resolution 1973. The Royal Navy conducted Tomahawk strikes from the SSNs HMS *Triumph* and HMS *Turbulent,* as did US Navy surface ships, in Operation Odyssey Dawn in March 2011. More than 112 Tomahawk cruise missiles attacked over twenty targets in the first assault: Libyan air-defense missile sites, early warning radar, and communications facilities, mainly around and in Tripoli, Misratah, and Surt. The United States handed off these early strikes to NATO operational control under Operation Unified Protector. Non-NATO participants included the United Arab Emirates (UAE) and Qatar. The United Kingdom's name for its military support of UN resolution

1973 was Operation Ellamy, Canadian participation was Operation Mobile, and French participation was Operation Harmattan. The overall NATO umbrella operation remained Operation Unified Protector.

The US Navy presence and level of operational support was considerable, demonstrating that forward presence enabled rapid response. The Royal Navy contribution was significant also. In addition to the two SSNs, the British contributed seven destroyers and frigates to enforce the UN embargo and provide naval gunfire support. The amphibious helicopter carrier HMS *Ocean* was also deployed.

The US Navy had had significant prior operational experience in crisis response, in Lebanon in 1982–83, in Grenada in 1983, and in Panama in 1989. These operations, together with the Royal Navy's operations in the Falklands, Sierra Leone, and East Timor, illustrate that both navies have the experience to work together in coordinated maritime expeditionary operations. We will analyze this point in the final chapter.

In some contingencies neither the United States nor the United Kingdom have become involved, and in some maritime power was not utilized or was not practical. The 2008 Russian invasion of Georgia provoked no military response from the United States or the West in general. In August 2013, the British House of Commons voted against intervention in the Syrian civil war—a resounding withdrawal from "regime change" as a strategic objective. India's invasion of East Pakistan in 1971 in support of Bangladeshi secession invoked no response. Similarly, the 1978–79 invasion of Cambodia by Vietnam to destroy the evil Khmer Rouge regime was simply observed. In 1978–79 Tanzania intervened in Uganda against the equally evil regime of Idi Amin without Western response. Perhaps tragically, the United States and United Kingdom and the West as a whole did not intervene in the terrible 1994 genocide in Rwanda.

In August 1999, Vladimir Putin, a former Soviet KGB officer, became Boris Yeltsin's prime minister. Following the second Chechnya war, Putin became president of Russia. In August 2008 he launched the invasion of Georgia noted above. The more recent occupation of the Crimea by Russia gained much more attention; US naval activity in the Black Sea showed both presence and capability. It remains to be seen whether Russia will now settle for stalemate and quiescence or become more ambitious both regarding territories on its periphery; we will discuss the resurgent Russian navy later.

What all this shows is that the United States and the United Kingdom have picked their interventions and have used naval power judiciously. In fact, in the past twenty-five years from 1990 to 2015, most of the interventions globally have been under the auspices of the United Nations. This observation somewhat undermines the often-repeated but misleading notion that the UN is moribund. Between 1989 and 2013 the United Nations directed a total of fifty-three peacekeeping operations with the support of the United States and United Kingdom, as members of the UN Security Council, supporting these actions. It is salutary to note too that the number of UN resolutions against the state of Israel is formidable—seventy-seven from 1955 to 2013, by my calculation.

Before we move back to the Middle East and the post-Iraq/Afghanistan consequences of intervention/invasion, let us address American and British strategic priorities. A fundamental concept underpins both US and UK strategic thinking in the post-9/11 period: it is better to meet foreign threats forward rather than in the homeland. Behind this clear, indeed commonsense, stance stands a fact often forgotten fact among the general publics of both nations—that their navies and marines are the preeminent instruments of forward presence and response. We have seen the freedoms from encumbrances and constraints they enjoy.

The United Kingdom, however, is subject, as a signatory, to the United Nations Convention on the Law of the Sea. UNCLOS became effective on November 16, 1994, with sixty nations signing. As of the time of writing, 166 countries and the European Union as a whole have joined the convention. International lawyers disagree as to whether the convention has in effect codified customary international practice as embodied in case law.

The United States is a nonparty, though it participated in negotiations and modifications until 1994 and recognizes UNCLOS as customary international law. In practice, however, UNCLOS is part of the law of the sea: it defines rights and responsibilities of nations, in the areas of maritime business, environmental issues, and most significantly, the management of marine natural resources. We will address this point later regarding an emergent China in East and Southeast Asia and the controversies over territorial rights and the sea resources within its territorial limits as defined by the UNCLOS and by the Chinese government. There is strong legal and intellectual support in the United States for ratifying and signing UNCLOS respectively, much of the argument stimulated by the current situation in the South and East China Seas.

We will conclude this chapter with an observation and a question regarding the United Kingdom's participation in Iraq and Afghanistan. The United Kingdom has been a great maritime power with a naval tradition to match. Its historical large-scale interventions on land have arisen from treaty and diplomatic obligations. In the past it could field large "citizen armies," led by fine corps of regulars. In Iraq, however, it may be concluded that the United Kingdom became unnecessarily overcommitted, its forces split among different missions, and, though they behaved with outstanding courage, unable owing to limited numbers to do the job fully. The United Kingdom committed itself to Afghanistan immediately after 9/11, but this commitment was made moot by commitment in Iraq beyond its capabilities. This recent experience sets the stage for a later analysis of the prospect of the United Kingdom moving back to its historical role as a maritime power, with a small, professional regular army, supported by a larger reserve volunteers.

How then should the United Kingdom's defense share of its gross domestic product be spent? The United States has a much larger economy and so wider choices, as reflected in force structure, technology investment, and global commitments. Given the history of the relationship of the US and Royal Navies, how should this relationship continue to develop, and what should the British government do to reinvigorate it after a period in which the United Kingdom allowed the strategic use of maritime power to atrophy?

The New Challenge in the Middle East, the Rise of China, and a Possible Challenge from Russia

The possible aftermath of the occupation/invasion of Iraq was clearly not adequately assessed prior to military operations, a huge lesson in itself. At the core of this issue most likely lay a fundamental lack of understanding of the history and culture of the Middle East. Coupling post-9/11 reactions to a country, Iraq, that was simply not understood in the White House, was a recipe for strategic disaster. Before we discuss how maritime power will play in the future, we need an understanding of not just why we are where we are today in the Middle East but also what systemic factors are driving regional politics and doing so in ways that no one in Washington would have predicted in 2001. Let us first look at several fundamental issues.

Over the past two years there have been many academic analyses and intelligence assessments regarding the rise of the Islamic State of Iraq and Syria (one of its several names) and its apparent successes. Interpretations have varied, in some cases quite significantly. Some researchers have assigned responsibility for ISIS to Washington, while the others have seen al Qaida in Iraq (AQI) as the driving force behind its emergence and growth. The upshot of these varying views is that what caused the emergence of ISIS in 2006 and its claims to be a state is a difficult and complex matter.

Syria and Iraq lie at a geostrategic crossroads, where the Sunni and the Shia worlds intersect. From the south to the north runs the main Sunni line, from the Gulf countries to Turkey. The Shia area stretches from east to west and consists primarily of Iran and Hezbollah-controlled territory. Syria and Iraq have mixed populations, and until the beginning of the twentieth century both had secular regimes, with mixed populations of Sunni and Shia communities coexisting in similar economic and sociopolitical conditions.

The roles of ideology and doctrine in the Middle East should never be underestimated. The struggle between Shia and Sunni Muslims has not ceased since the seventh century. The ruling regime, whether Sunni or Shia, is what determines outcomes, irrespective of population and Muslim demographics; Bahrain, for example, is a Sunni state, though it has a Shia majority. ISIS appeared just after the Iraq parliamentary elections of January 2005. The Shias obtained the overwhelming majority in the National Assembly; the two main Shia parties obtained 180 seats (the Kurds receiving seventy-five seats, the rest twenty). These results led to a wave of criticism, and the elections were repeated. In spite of an increased number of Sunni votes, the Shia United Iraqi Alliance got 128 seats out of 275 (Kurds fifty-three, the Sunnis altogether fifty-eight).

The Sunni population would not acknowledge the legitimacy of the elections, and the civil war began. The main role was played by terrorist groups that had evolved from breakup of the Iraqi army and what became AQI (al Qaida in Iraq), and later ISIS. In June 2005 Washington began a "Together Forward" operation, which finished in October, and immediately after that ISIS appeared. ISIS consisted of some elements of the terrorist groups defeated in the civil war, including AQI, and other subdivisions and generals of Saddam Hussein's army. Though distinct entities, these groups did display some similarities. Some have argued that they fought a common enemy, the Americans, and aimed to expel them from Iraq. More important is that they are all Sunnis. The very name of a new group, Islamic State of Iraq and Syria, marked a common and unifying claim: to create a Sunni state within a Sunni political elite.

Sponsorship from the Gulf countries helped them to join together. ISIS emergence is not directly related to the Washington government, to AQI, or to economic factors such as poverty, but rather support from the Gulf and, in particular, from Saudi Arabia and Qatar. Saudi Arabia has always claimed to be an undisputable leader of the regional Sunni communities. Although Qatar had intensified its connections with European countries in order to increase its GDP, it still needed a Sunni relationship to the north. Syria was ruled by the Alawi clan and showed political affinity for Iran; Iraq had a strictly secular regime and a Shia-majority population. As a consequence, Gulf countries like Qatar felt a strong need for a separate Sunni state.

The invasion of Kuwait by Saddam Hussein, August 2–4, 1990, eliminated a chance for the United States and its allies to cooperate with his regime, while good relations between the Assad family and the Iranian government did allow cooperation. The political instability in Iraq in 2006 allowed a Sunni organization with a clear political program to gain momentum toward the creation of its own state. The Sunni state between the Gulf and Turkey was needed to facilitate laying a gas pipeline from Qatar to Europe and also to divide the Shia into two unconnected parts. This view of a new Sunni state solved the Saudi problem of political leadership. Syria, primarily agrarian, and Iraq, an oil producer, would not challenge Saudi and Gulf-state economic supremacy.

Why had ISIS been waiting near Syrian–Iraqi borders, and why did it begin its expansion only in 2013–14? ISIS could not establish its state only in the Sunni territories of Iraq, as it would have to face surrounding forces, both the Shias of southern Iraq and neighboring countries and the Kurds. Also, it could not connect directly to Turkey or any sea; so from a strategic viewpoint ISIS, while solely in Iraq, had strategic limitations.

When the Western intervention in Syria began, when all conflicting parties and the population had become exhausted after two years of war, ISIS crossed the border and interfered. ISIS needed support from the local population. The idea of a caliphate was created in order to win over peoples in the newly controlled territories. It is most likely that the main aim of ISIS was to establish a state, an internally stable one that could be used by the Gulf countries as a bridge to the West. The early success of ISIS militarily can be explained not by military superiority but rather the fatigue of Syria and Iraq by civil disorders and external intervention. However, this volatile environment also prevented ISIS from gaining stable control.

The "domestic" strategy of ISIS seems to be centered, then, on creating a state. ISIS has never tried to break into Shia territories, and in both Iraq and Syria it now claims to control only the Sunni lands. It has, however, tried to capture parts of Kurdistan, in order to reach the Turkish border. Direct ISIS territorial control appears to be a basis for a caliphate ideology that would allow Syrians and Iraqis to tolerate their loss of sovereignty and influence, by offering them a theocratic self-identity as an Umar-like (to recall one of the most powerful historical caliphs) caliphate. ISIS has been criticized by various groups within Islam for direct violations of sharia. However, none of the key theologians or religious leaders have dared to publish fatwas against the regime. It has been only recently that the Muslim intelligentsia, within the religious leadership, has come out in direct criticism in response to ISIS atrocities, exemplified by the cruel murder of a captured Jordanian pilot and the violent treatment of non-Muslim women.

ISIS has claimed some success in creating state institutions. The ISIS regime provides electricity, water, a schools, hospitals, roads, and mosques. ISIS aims to control perception, to be perceived by the local populations as an organization that does the best for its people. ISIS would like to be seen by its grassroots followers, and those caught innocently in the cross fire, as the political conjunction of the material and spiritual, as the fulfillment of its people's need for stability. The reality and the perception have gone dramatically out of kilter; ISIS has spiraled into atrocity after atrocity, driven by a creed of violence and mayhem.

ISIS has drawn in professionals, such as scientists, administrators, engineers, technologists, and economists, to manage its industry, agriculture, and trade. For example, ISIS became able, with financial support from the other Sunni-dominated states in the region, to operate the dam on the Assad Lake, a thermal power plant near Aleppo, and petroleum enterprises; now it claims to be issuing its own currency. These represent critical infrastructure and logistics. Many ISIS specialists and consultants are from Western countries.

ISIS self-assessments of the internal problems it faces are difficult to gauge. If these problems are not solved, ISIS may lose most of its territories to regional forces, especially now that Jordan has joined the Kurds and independent Syria and Iraq in their struggle against ISIS. The disagreements between ISIS leaders are unpredictable, and neither Saudi Arabia nor Qatar may be able to control them. That inability may in due course be a defining factor if rifts appear and pressure from the West and the Sunni Islamic states undermines the ISIS leadership.

What evidence is there that ISIS might still exist after several years? Its main objective is to conjoin the Sunni space. Well-organized and coordinated Western and regional opposition means that ISIS is not likely to spread to the territories on its "future map."

The short-term objective of ISIS may be to establish contact with the Turkish government, with or without Saudi mediation. Cooperation with the Gulf is certainly profitable for Turkey. President Recep Tayyip Erdogan of Turkey, in office since August 28, 2014, is likely to behave cautiously, as he did during fighting between ISIS and the Kurds, while recognizing the key role of Saudi Arabia. In Iraq, ISIS may try to capture Baghdad. The latter was the capital of the Abbasid caliphate (in the eighth to thirteenth centuries) and an ideological and theocratic center of gravity. Baghdad's fall to ISIS would legitimize the "state" as a real caliphate in the minds of many Sunnis and might secure for some time the inner stability of ISIS itself. The fall of Baghdad would have an additional advantage: the Islamists would control the Tigris River as well as the Euphrates. This would give ISIS the infrastructure and fertile lands near the rivers, as well as water, a precious resource in the Middle East. An ISIS march to the Gulf, however, does not seem possible in the next few years, as Shia unity and identity are much stronger than those of the Sunnis; that population will defend its homes, security, and holy cities (Najaf and Karbala) aggressively.

ISIS relations with Syria will probably stay officially hostile. Syria seems to be safe, however, as it is impossible for ISIS, in the face of President Bashar al-Assad's forces, supported by the Russian air force external arms supply, and covert forces either to reach the coast or to capture Damascus. Although the situation continues to be unstable, the noncaptured territories are inhabited mostly by non-Sunnis. If ISIS could conquer Syrian lands, it probably could not hold them. The main aim of Bashar Assad is to exterminate local radical terrorist groups, stabilize the remaining territories, and then rebuild the economy in the context of a lost Euphrates (a symbol of aspiration evoking the four rivers, one of them "Euphrates," lost in the Genesis account of the Garden of Eden).

One critical variable will be the relationship between ISIS, Saudi Arabia, and Qatar. ISIS atrocities and divergences from Muslim teaching will leave the Islamists isolated and surrounded. ISIS may well have masterminded its own downfall, by violating all the norms of human conduct and indeed the Prophet's words. Cruelty and inhumanity have no place in the civilized world; ISIS will reap the whirlwind, unifying its enemies with all who will simply not tolerate its atrocities.

The United States, the United Kingdom, Jordan, and other allies in the Middle East and Europe have a clear moral and "just war" mandate to break the back of ISIS. Destroying ISIS infrastructure, logistics, training camps, weapons supply chain, and recruitment mechanisms will remain military priorities, with the highest priority being the destruction of ISIS leadership, command, and control. All nations that have unwittingly supplied foreign recruits to ISIS will have to intensify surveillance and detention of would-be recruits but also be alert to the dangers presented by returning converts, trained and indoctrinated. Recent brutal attacks in Europe could be repeated, with intensity proportional to the numbers recruited from the West.

The United States may have to commit special forces, which are best suited to and trained for destroying ISIS on the ground. Regular ground troops may not be appropriate, because structured forces, in easily identifiable units and in known locations, become clear targets for asymmetric opponents fighting outside the norms of the Geneva Conventions. The United States has a hugely capable special operations cadre, and ISIS is no match for it. It will need new and innovative sources and methods to provide intelligence, in or near real time, backed by ideological and other media tools. Once the leadership is decapitated and its infrastructure and logistics destroyed, the battle for the minds of those affected by ISIS will begin.

At the end of World War II the United States pursued a most far-seeing strategy to turn around a country that had perpetrated the worst atrocities and war crimes in history. This model was created by George Marshall and the American leadership. Once ISIS is obliterated, the challenge for the United States and its allies—an extraordinarily demanding one—will be to find just and equitable ways to resolve the complexities of the Sunni-Shia territorial and theocratic space. Respect for religious and cultural differences should perhaps echo the words of Admiral Lord Nelson in his prayer before the battle of Trafalgar: "May humanity after victory be the predominate feature of the British Fleet." It will require immense humanity to steer through the vastly troubled waters of Sunni and Shia, the heart of the issues in the Middle East. The opportunity lost after the Iraq intervention/invasion to separate Sunni, Shia, and Kurd into defined geographic and theocratic political territories may remain lost for the foreseeable future. The dismemberment of the Iraqi army as a stabilizing force was a clear strategic mistake. So, in essence, we are left with an ancient sectarian divide erupted in bloody conflict.

The countries committed to stopping barbarity must establish workable relations with their Middle Eastern friends and allies, some of whom are reluctant to wage war against their Sunni brothers. Iraqi ground troops have not been, to date, up to the task. Jordan has clearly indicated that it will back its abhorrence of brutality with military action, but to do so it will require US help.

The problem seems intractable considered in terms not of geography but theocratic distribution and demographics; regional loyalties and contradictions add a layer of complexity. ISIS is Sunni, and so are Saudi Arabia, Jordan, and the Gulf states (at least in terms of governance). It is ironic that Saudi Arabia, for example, is being attacked by Yemeni extremists with ISIS and al Qaida associations. Iran, by contrast, is Shia and is providing support to the Shia element in Iraq, which is fighting ISIS within Iraqi borders and overflowing into Syria. The internecine complexity of this is mind boggling, and it was all unleashed by the occupation of Iraq. ISIS may begin to lose conquered towns one by one; its opponents do not need a Sunni "state" among the lands of the Shia.

From the maritime perspective, what can the US Navy and the Royal Navy do to both contribute to stability and their national interests, and how? And why should they? Maritime power is persistent, present, and mobile, and it occupies a free and neutral space, the sea. Oil from the Middle East flows mainly by sea to Europe and the Far East, whose economies would rapidly go into free fall without it. The need to stabilize the region is therefore self-evident. With naval forces come marines and special forces, precision strike, agility, and ability to focus quickly on vulnerable areas. The fact that the US Sixth and Fifth Fleets are disposed on the east–west geographic axis of the Middle East says in itself that presence is critical. Attack by ISIS or any of a number of Islamic fundamentalist groups on the oil infrastructure in the Persian Gulf or the Saudi oilfields could be disastrous. The offshore facilities are vulnerable. The Shamoon virus cyber attack on the ARAMCO computer network on August 15, 2012, took down as many as 30,000 Windows-based machines, and it took two weeks to recover. A physical attack on the key infrastructure combined with a massive cyber attack could have a rapid global economic effect.

American and British naval forces provide a lynchpin capability to be present, to deter, and to react in the event of a crisis. The use of American and British amphibious ships as bases from which marines and special forces can operate freely would be critical against capability challenges by mines, mini-submarines, terrorists operating from merchant ships, and so on. A blockade of the main channels, though not a fatal blow, would nonetheless have a negative impact on oil flow, as would scuttling large oil tankers. The quickest and most effective defense is American and British naval power.

The problem of ISIS, as well as the other Islamic extremist groups described in detail above, is also one of recruitment and expansion and the attendant flows of people, weapons, and explosives. In addition to overland routes, such as from Syria to Turkey, much of this will occur by sea, owing to the close watch kept at airports and because weaponry is difficult to transport by commercial air. The interruption of the illicit flow of people and weaponry is a naval task, coupled with good intelligence. Naval power cannot directly change the course of Sunni-Shia rivalry, which has marked the region since shortly after the Prophet Mohammed died. What it can do is deter and prevent the spread outside the theocratic and geographic space that was described earlier. This will be an enduring task for the US and Royal Navies for the foreseeable future, just as the security and counterterrorism forces of both countries will have to be constantly vigilant to watch for returning jihadists bent on reproducing their particular form of violence in the American and British homelands.

Let us now address the issue of Israel and Palestine and how naval power in the future can impact what is one of the most serious and intractable international problems. The president of the United States, at the time of writing,

has stated that he wishes to see Israel return to the pre–1967 June War boundaries in accordance with United Nations Security Council Resolution 242.
President Barack Obama sees as a critical prerequisite to a truly long-term
solution to the Israel-Palestinian situation the fundamental UN concept that
Israel took land that was not Israel's by force and that the Golan Heights and
the West Bank must be restored.

President Benjamin Netanyahu of Israel has reacted vehemently, stressing
to international audiences that in any two-state solution Israel must have what
he defines as "defensible boundaries." He sees a return to the 1967 status quo
as giving up territory that is vital for Israel's survival. His Palestinian counterpart, President Mahmoud Abbas, and several US secretaries of state have fully
understood the reasons for his declarations. However, if the peace process is
ever to enter a substantively new era and the Palestinians are ever to become
a nation-state, more has to happen than declarations.

A brief overview of the history will help us visualize what may constitute a viable solution. There has been considerable analysis since 1967 of the
intent of Resolution 242, drafted by the then British ambassador to the United
Nations, Lord Caradon. The resolution is to most lawyers and international
specialists quite explicit, precise, and unambiguous. What has drawn most
analysis is an affirmation of article 2 of the UN Charter: "Termination of all
claims or states of belligerency and respect for and acknowledgment of the
sovereignty, territorial integrity and political independence of every state in
the area and their right to live in peace within secure and recognized boundaries free from threats or acts of force." The words that cause most disagreement are, "right to live in peace within secure and recognized boundaries."
The Israelis and President Netanyahu have insisted that any redrawing of the
pre-1967 boundaries (now essentially the West Bank of the Jordan River and
the Golan Heights, since Israel has withdrawn from the Sinai), must leave
Israel secure, with, as noted, "defensible boundaries." To most military personnel this phrase has significant and specific connotations.

The Middle East was a critical arena of the Cold War, a hotbed for the
rivalry between the United States and the Soviet Union. Israel felt naturally
threatened, surrounded by potential belligerents encouraged and supported
by Moscow. By June 1967 the situation had reached the boiling point. Israeli
preemptive strikes to seize territory from Egypt, Syria, and Jordan to extend
its boundaries and create defensive barriers was extremely successful. However, they all but plunged the United States into a conflict with the Soviet
Union; we saw in chapter 4 how the Soviet Union would have reacted had
Israel continued in toward Damascus. The world has changed with the demise

of the Soviet Union, and in its aftermath have emerged equally grave threats to Middle East stability, not least the rise of Iran and the emergence of groups that espouse terrorism for achieving political goals. Other state and nonstate players have become either directly or indirectly involved through the supply of arms, training, and other material.

It is easy to forget that terrorism is not a recent phenomenon in the Middle East but a vehicle for change since World War II. President Menachem Begin of Israel was a member of Irgun, an organization dubbed by the international community as a violent terrorist organization and one that David Ben-Gurion described as the "enemy of the Jewish people." Begin saw himself as a freedom fighter, not a terrorist. It is easy to forget too that in the Middle East the past is often prologue: Hamas and Hezbollah in their turn pursue political goals often by violent means, most often called terrorist acts by the international community. Such factions cite the same principles in working for the creation of an independent Palestinian state that the postwar Israeli "terrorists" cited to justify their violent actions in the creation of the independent state of Israel. It is easy to lose this perspective while condemning, as the world should, acts of terrorism, whatever the goal. In 1977, Begin, a Russian Jew persecuted by the Nazis and the Soviets, became prime minister of Israel. He was responsible for the peace treaty with Anwar Sadat of Egypt that returned the Sinai to Egypt and that won both men the Nobel Peace Prize. What this demonstrates is that all things are possible: in 1946 Begin had led the bombing of the King David Hotel in Jerusalem and in March 1952 an attempt on the life of Chancellor Konrad Adenauer of West Germany.

Today the Sunni Islamist group Hamas, which has run the Gaza portion of the Palestinian territories, and Hezbollah, a Shia militant group and political party in Lebanon, look much as Irgun did in 1942 when it split from the Haganah and from 1944 to 1948 waged a campaign against the British in Palestine. When on May 14, 1948, the state of Israel was created, the poignancy was clear: Israel had fundamentally been born of terrorism. How today is the spread of terrorism to be prevented and yet a solution found? The answer lies with Jordan and Israel, the support of the United States, and with capabilities provided by the US Navy.

President Netanyahu's strategy of "defensible boundaries" is driven by geography: points in Israel are only six to nine miles from the West Bank, and the Israeli population, commerce, and industry are concentrated on the coastal strip. His perfectly reasonable wish is that the West Bank provide a buffer area and site for defensive missile systems.

The key to helping President Netanyahu and the Israeli people find peace and security is Jordan, the most stable regime in the Arab world. King Abdullah leads a nation that is making significant progress in democratization, improvement in the lives of the ordinary Jordanians, and security against extremism. Israel needs to respect and trust Jordan, and Jordan's security has to be underpinned by US aid as much as Israel's does. The likelihood of a destabilizing and anti-Israel regime in Jordan is remote; the vast majority of Jordanians are loyal to their political processes and their head of state. The threats to Israel lie much farther to the east, in Iran and that country's associations with state and nonstate extremists. By the same token, Jordan too is threatened by those groups.

Modern cruise and ballistic missiles are such that the West Bank is irrelevant as a buffer zone for Israel. The most likely threat to both Israel and Jordan, other than terrorism groups, is missile attack. The worst scenario for Israel would be a preemptive ballistic-missile strike from Iran, in which case, and in other missile scenarios, the West Bank does not play as a geographic entity, except as hosting part of a layered defensive network.

A settlement with Jordan over the West Bank could include the following. First, Jordan regains control of the West Bank, both Palestinian and Israeli settlements, with US oversight. In return, Jordan should grant to Israel several sovereign air-base sites in the West Bank for defensive missile batteries and early-warning radar, with full rights and permanent access. Such sites and systems will be of equal value to Jordan. The United States can provide Jordan and Israel additional layers of defense, along with what it provides currently under the various aid agreements.

The first is the US Navy's Aegis missile system. The Navy has proven that Aegis not only works but can be flexibly stationed. The United States can cover Jordan, Israel, and NATO allies in Europe by deploying Aegis cruisers and destroyers in the Fifth and Sixth Fleet areas of responsibility. The second US Navy contribution would be attack submarines and cruise-missile submarines. SSGNs can fire Tactical Tomahawks on time scales that make preemption by an aggressor strategically foolish.

The United States, therefore, can provide in the Persian Gulf and the eastern Mediterranean the first and last layers of defense, and in between would be the defensive systems of Jordan and Israel. If an accord, underwritten by the United States, can be reached between Israel and Jordan, they can move to the next stage, an integrated, joint missile-defense system. From President Netanyahu's perspective, the strategic role of the West Bank must guarantee Israeli access and presence for these defensive systems.

Intelligence sharing would be critical. Flight times are short, and so warning time is vital. Jordan and Israel will need to build confidence with each other and with the United States in order to share time-sensitive intelligence. The United States, for its part, will want to minimize deployment costs when tension in the region permit.

The above offers a long-term solution, and not just for the issue of the West Bank. It defuses the arguments of both the extremists and the moderates of the international community who see the ongoing Palestinian situation as not only fomenting discord but providing ammunition to those who wish to destabilize the Middle East by violent means. The US Navy therefore will play a crucial role in making long-term peace in the Middle East a reality.

Now let us now turn to Asia. The emerging global power of China and its challenge to US military strength in East Asia pose fundamental questions: What is the nature, and what are the goals, of Chinese policy for the long term? How should the United States craft a strategy in its interests and those of its friends and allies, in the region and worldwide? The United States may easily slip into an action-and-reaction vis-a-vis increased and seemingly challenging Chinese military capabilities and operations. China is overtly demonstrating what its official writings convey, that the American East Asian presence will be challenged, that China is the preeminent Asian power, and that it intends to create hegemony extending in due course to the outer island chains of the western Pacific.

Action and reaction were very much phenomena of the Cold War: the Soviet Union would develop a capability, extend its influence somewhere, or establish a new base, and the United States would counter it. The "great game" played itself out until the demise of the Soviet Union. The United States must seriously consider now the potential negatives of following a similar pattern with China, of being led astray into costly and complex situations. There are other ways to address the issues, problems, and challenges that lie ahead for the new generation of American leaders, who cannot afford the luxury of a Cold War standoff.

Creating an enduring US strategy in East Asia should begin with analysis that reverts to first principles. Do China's activities resemble those that have characterized nations that have sought regional hegemony? Do the imperial models of ancient Greece and Rome, of the Spanish, British, Hapsburg, Turkish, and Russian empires apply to what we see evolving in China? Do the militarist, expansionist territorial goals of Napoleon, the Nazi Germany, Fascist Italy, or imperial Japan connect with what we observe happening with a growing Chinese military? China is an economic juggernaut that is by no means yet in top gear and has massive resource needs, particularly oil, that require overseas investment, port facilities, and political/military infrastructure.

The answer to much of the above is that China has taken an extremely noninvasive approach to international relations in modern times, with certain exceptions. The past five hundred years, since the European powers began their outward growth, exploration, colonization, and empire building, have seen China take a different track. In that time, China has never invaded and permanently occupied a sovereign state or shown imperialistic intent. Since the Chinese revolution and the conclusion of World War II, China has for the most part lived inwardly. But again, there have been exceptions.

Gen. Douglas MacArthur's 1950 foray into North Korea and to the Yalu River provoked from China a response that was not surprising. Its forces invaded south across the Yalu and drove the United States back to the thirty-ninth parallel. From the Chinese perspective, the United States posed a threat to China's sovereignty and to that of a communist client state. In 1962, during the short Sino-Indian War, China invaded India briefly as a means of letting Jawaharlal Nehru's government know that it disapproved of New Delhi's support for the Dalai Lama and the Tibetan independence movement. India suffered a defeat and China quickly withdrew, having made its point.

However, China's invasion of Vietnam in February 1979 to signal disapproval of Vietnam's invasion of Cambodia to suppress the Khmer Rouge, a Chinese client, led to ignominious defeat. The war lasted just one month. China lost about 20,000 troops, more than the United States lost in a single year in Vietnam. A Vietnamese force of a hundred thousand border troops had humiliated a Chinese army of 250,000. The impact on China's leader, Deng Xiaoping, was dramatic.

China has supplied weapons and technology to nation-states that oppose US interests. China has distinctive and clear-cut policies regarding all major international issues, whether it is the UN in the Middle East or rogue nations (of which North Korea is a leading example). China, like any other country, pursues what it believes to be its self-interest. The United States has to accept this reality, which is not likely to change any time soon.

What China has *not* done is indicate that it sees territorial expansion as a way to extend Chinese power and influence. It has mostly followed international law and agreements. There is no question that China could have marched into Hong Kong or Macau at any time, without resistance. Instead, China waited until the legal expiration of treaty agreements that, in twenty-first-century hindsight, themselves amounted to the blunt use of nineteenth-century imperial power by Portugal and Britain. Both territories transitioned peacefully to Chinese rule. By contrast, when an Argentinian dictatorship decided in 1982 to challenge Britain's long-standing rights and ownership of the Falkland Islands, it suffered consequences. China has never made such moves. If there is a deviation from this trend, it is economic and not militarist; the resource-hungry dragon could in due course prove to be the seed of serious discord.

China has repeatedly indicated that its inherent needs and destiny are bound to economic hegemony in East Asia. To that end, the People's Republic has systematically asserted claims, based on perceived historical rights, to islands in the South China Sea. China is now self-evidently an economic goliath. At some point its gross national product will equal and likely then surpass those of the United States, Japan, and Germany. The danger is not economic competition, which is beneficial in the context of a well-managed, globally interconnected marketplace, but competition for resources. China's massive population requires to be fed and sustained in keeping with its world economic position. China has precious metals, particularly for the semiconductor and space industries, but in other domains it is woefully dependent. Oil is the largest problem. The exponential growth of Chinese oil demand could reach a crisis situation by 2020–25. The country's planners are constantly looking for alternative suppliers and areas for investment and exploration.

The legal concept of a two-hundred-mile economic zone has been generally accepted into the body of international law, but has been little developed and codified. Drawing two-hundred-mile economic zones around the disputed island groups of the South China Sea creates major disputes. Vietnam has been at odds with China over island-sovereignty issues for some time, and geopolitics place Japan, the Philippines, South Korea, Malaysia, Thailand, Singapore, and Indonesia in potential conflict with China over such claims as well. The wider issue of Chinese resource needs will not fade away. There are no signs of major green-energy programs that will solve China's problems any time soon. Coupled to China's increasing thirst for oil is its parallel policy of hard-currency accumulation and ownership of foreign debt.

What then may China really want to achieve, given its military buildup, its naval exercises, and its posturing regarding Taiwan? What does China hope to gain by its new weapon systems, its growing fleet of submarines, moves into space, and other intelligence, surveillance, and reconnaissance domains? China may be planning on winning a war that it never fights.

Such a war would be about countervailing power, raising orders of battle to high levels, and posing constant challenges that require persistent US presence, deployments, and basing in response, all at high cost. It would be a war of attrition by other means, underpinned by sustainable economic growth and a Chinese military-industrial complex based on the new state-capitalist model, which even American economists have called more efficient than free-market capitalism. It would aim at a new form of hegemony, a uniquely Chinese version. The threat is not the military buildup per se but the underlying weakness in China's otherwise rosy future: its resource limitations and increasing demand for oil. By beefing up its military strength, China wins by checkmating the United States, specifically the US Seventh Fleet, the representative in Asia of American presence, intent, technology, and firepower.

So what is the best strategy for the United States? No one in their right mind can contemplate a war with China. No responsible US leader, however, can abide a Chinese East Asian hegemony that lessens US influence and hinders American economic interests. The US Navy and the Royal Navy, and allied navies, have to return to a more regular presence in Far Eastern waters. The key to keeping the economic arteries healthy is the wise use of naval power.

The solution lies within the problem itself. In the urgency of reacting to Chinese moves, essential points are likely being missed. China's quest for economic hegemony by political-military means can be addressed at the strategic level, where the United States has several critical factors in its favor. In the strategy that arises from these factors, the US Navy is a major player.

East and Southeast Asia are joined economically, and therefore politically, by the sea. It is the means by which most of Asia's trade, thus the world's, takes place. If, for whatever reason, the sea routes connecting the Asian countries with the rest of the globe cease to function, the world will hemorrhage economically. The disparate Asian nations are interdependent in this regard. The passages of the Malacca Straits and the Indonesian Archipelago are routes to the South China Sea, the East China Sea, the Yellow Sea, the Sea of Japan, the Pacific islands, and the transpacific trading nations.

The protection of that trade, the maintenance of the freedom of the seas, and the enforcement of the laws of the sea represent a strategic opportunity to bring together the United States and its allies in the region. Such common effort can foster long-term peace and prosperity and ensure that East Asia is not destabilized by misplaced Chinese hegemonic intentions. China does not then win a war that it never fights, and Asia grows with its American trading partner. That is the essence of a new US strategy in Asia, one based on trade-route protection, maritime power, and shared efforts based on shared interests. This new maritime paradigm should include the Royal Navy as a key supporter of the US Seventh Fleet. This strategy's ingredients include freedom of navigation, freedom of the seas, protection of seaborne trade, and rights of passage. What is required is a new "Asian law of the sea," either written or declaratory. Such a law would:

- Guarantee and define various maritime rights, including territorial rights, access and passage, fishing and resources, and maritime conduct.
- Provide unified policing and enforcement.
- Provide agreement-based (in due course, treaty-based) means for regular international gatherings of the member states.
- Take the Association of Southeast Asian Nations and other multilateral and bilateral agreements into a new forum for organizing and implementing a maritime code of conduct.

This new organization would be the vehicle for resolving issues associated with two-hundred-mile economic zones and island claims, for enforcing international law and human rights, and for combating piracy, smuggling, and terrorism. That is a formidable array of international activities that the United States can carry out with its regional partners. Such a cooperative undertaking could bring China into the family of Asian nations in ways that are neither belligerent nor disruptive. The strategy clearly draws lines in the sand: Not to participate would be to step away from the community of nations. If China chooses to continue its less cooperative, hegemonic course (e.g., creating and militarizing bases and airfields on disputed reefs in the South China Sea), its Asian neighbors will have built themselves a formidable maritime community.

The alliance aspects are crucial. The good news is that the region's nations are on board. The Australians, the Malaysians, the Indonesians, the Thais, the South Koreans, the Japanese, the Philippines, and now the Vietnamese (to whom President Obama made, as this book was in production, a historic visit) are increasingly joined in a common bond. At the center is the United States.

The Royal Navy can build a new relationship with the Seventh Fleet, a clear signal of the special US-UK relationship in Asian waters. Navies are unique for a number of reasons, and one of them is the brotherhood that navies show one another. Sailors are gregarious people, diplomats in myriad ways, and nothing is more unifying than port visits after joint exercises, rescue missions, disaster relief, or successful operations against drug runners, pirates, or terrorists. Navies by themselves can make progress that no amount of conventional diplomacy can hope to achieve. The United States has enough resources to make security assistance with all the participating nations a permanent of US naval diplomacy—indeed, that phrase should be the watchword of this strategy. Joint international protection of maritime trade, economic rights, and of a new law of the sea for Asia can be the means to peaceful ends. If China balks and insists on an open standoff characterized by "benign aggression," there will be little that the United States and its friends and allies can do other than make it clear that they will never tolerate any form of overt aggression. The olive branch can be continuously offered, in the hope that at some stage it will be accepted with magnanimity.

No one can realistically predict regime change in China. What one can safely predict is the confluence of generational change, the international trade that is making China great, cultural and travel exchanges, the Internet, and technological sharing will overcome the inwardness of the current Chinese leadership. The specter of Tiananmen Square still looms large. China displays a ruthless streak from time to time, and the concern for human rights is not part of its political makeup. Only time will tell if this will change. The virtues of youth and of the global economy may eventually combine to make certain political transformations inevitable in China.

One scenario can illustrate a new regional collective effort. Regular joint exercises can be conducted in the protection shipping, from the Southeast Asian straits to the Japanese islands and South Korea. Such exercises can develop and train the region's nations in all domains of maritime warfare—for instance, antisubmarine and antisurface warfare. The participating nations would be showing both capability and will, and if China responded with belligerent passive-aggressiveness, it will merely be providing live training opportunities. Ideally, this will not occur, and China will respect and observe the rights of free passage and the various economic zones. Indeed, China has as much at stake in them as any nation, increasingly dependent as it is on the freedom of the seas for imported resources.

Change for the better in East Asia has been illustrated by the transformation of Vietnam, a nation that at the conclusion of the Vietnam War could barely sustain its population at the poverty level. Today, it has rejected the Marxist-Leninist model and pursues a state-capitalist economy. Nothing is more symbolic of change than the $1.3 billion investment made by Intel outside Ho Chi Minh City. Vietnam's ninety million people are now at a new level of prosperity and growth, one perhaps unthinkable at the time of another symbolic memory, the departure of the last US helicopter from the empty Saigon embassy in 1975. Vietnam can become a close ally and major trading partner with the United States and be integrated with the other Asian nations in a new Asian maritime strategy. The United States should be energetic in implementing the new strategy, which would combine US national interests, with an internationalist maritime policy. The sea is both the means and the end in a modern US Asian strategy.

Let us now address the Russia of Vladimir Putin. Russia has clearly violated the norms of international behavior by its annexation of the Crimea and its destabilization in eastern Ukraine. Russia's avowed objectives are not difficult to ascertain, whatever the pleadings of its leader. Several basic observations need to be made. Without its oil and gas production and export, the Russian economy would be in even worse shape than at present. The oligarchic nature of the ruling United Russia party, the roles of small economic elites, and the Russian Mafia, plus the nature of Vladimir Putin's background as a former KGB operative as well as his personality and political style, add up to a recipe for long-term failure. At some point opposition groups and the Russian masses may coalesce an effective alternative, and the huge personal wealth accumulated by a tiny minority may come to haunt them, but how and when are difficult to predict. Meanwhile, two fundamental facts need to be stated. First, Russia's gross domestic product is less than that of the state of California. Second, Russia has nuclear weapons. Without them, where would Russia be in the international order? Without nuclear weapons or its oil and gas, it is unlikely that Russia would have a leading place.

We saw in the earlier chapters that the Soviet navy was a serious challenge to the whole NATO edifice and that the US and Royal Navies kept it in check, by and large. However, we also acknowledged that the Berlin Wall did not come down too soon, given the technical strides that the Soviets appear to have been making and their ship and submarine build rates. Glasnost and perestroika changed all that once Mikhail Gorbachev became general secretary of the Central Committee of the Communist Party of the Soviet Union in March 1985. How far Vladimir Putin wishes to put the clock back remains to be seen—indeed, whether that could be done at all is an open question.

On the strategic-missile-submarine side, the Russians have, after a moribund period following the collapse of the Soviet Union, begun to rebuild their SSBN fleet, with four *Borei*-class SSBNs in the fleet and, according to the Russian News Agency Tass, another eleven expected to be built by 2020. The three remaining Delta III SSBNs and six Delta IVs will be gone by the 2020s. The Russians are building the *Yasen*-class SSGN, with eight ordered so far, and an SSN class that is (at this writing) to begin building in 2016, with perhaps fifteen to be completed by 2035. News reports state that after the improved-Kilo batch of six for the Black Sea Fleet is completed, the Russians will build a new air-independent improved *Lada* class—perhaps fourteen to eighteen over a fifteen-year period, with most commissioned in the 2020s.

Safety is a huge issue. Since 2000 the Russians have had seven major nuclear-submarine accidents. The worst of these was the loss of the SSGN *Kursk,* which exploded and sank with the loss of all hands. Russia's submarines, until the recent resurgence, were on average older than thirty years. However, with its remaining more-capable submarines and new SSNs and SSBNs, together with its nuclear-capable bombers and land-based missiles, Putin's Russia can send unwelcome messages to the West. For example, moving nuclear weapons near to the Polish border, or certainly into the Crimea, would be seen by NATO as aggressive.

The Russian surface navy is not in good shape, with perhaps too-grandiose plans for aircraft carriers, frigates, corvettes, and large destroyers on the order of 15,000 tons. It also envisions modernization for the *Kirov* and *Slava* cruiser classes and the *Udaloy* destroyers, though the *Sovremennyi*-class destroyers will be retired. In spite of the French *Mistral*-class amphibious-ship debacle, the Russians may build two or three 14,000–16,000-ton amphibious ships, along with four *Ivan Gren*–class amphibious ships in each of the Black Sea and Baltic Fleets. All of the above is very much dependent on Russian yard capacity and finances. If it all did happen, by about 2030, the Russian navy could be back in business. To date the Russians have fallen behind in almost every surface program. The overall picture is reasonably clear: the Russian navy will concentrate on strategic deterrence, the SSBN force, and coastal defense, leaving the future of blue-water navy, a legacy of the Cold War, to be determined.

The question for the West and specifically the United States is how to counter and modify Russian aggressive moves, short of direct confrontation. Where does the maritime side play in this? Sanctions and diplomacy have impacted Russia, though the former have negative economic implications as well for the West, particularly European nations dependent on Russian energy sources. Western naval power in the Baltic and Black Seas, forward-deployed presence of multinational naval forces, together with classic diplomacy, can send a clear message that aggression will not be rewarded. A US Navy and US Marine Corps MEF surged into either sea or both, supported by the NATO navies, would not only represent intent and deterrence but show solidarity of purpose and the clear military ability to stop aggression in its tracks. A further incursion into Ukraine by Russian or surrogate forces or a threat to the Baltic States can be met with an unequivocal display of naval and marine/amphibious power. US air wings, and in the future British ones, forward deployed and persistent, can pose a capability like that at Inchon in the Korean War.

A large and flexible amphibious force landed from the sea, at short notice, without requirements for shore support, can also, along with diplomacy, send a message. This would be a classic display of naval expeditionary warfare, based on three main tenets: forward, persistent presence; flexibility in terms of the mix of naval forces; and maneuver from the sea at times and places of one's choosing. These abiding principles will be addressed in our final chapter.

The Sea in Future Strategy

The Future Partnership of the United States Navy and Royal Navy

W orld events since September 11, 2001, have shaken the resolve of many nations, particularly within NATO, whose members have become somewhat disenchanted with out-of-area operations and other operations that have gone sadly out of kilter. Iraq, Afghanistan, and Libya come immediately to mind; each of these reflect the lack of wide-ranging strategic thinking about not just the how and what but the why. Cultural differences and sectarian rifts within the Muslim world were largely ignored in a somewhat heedless and headlong dash to seek reprisal for 9/11, the work of what initially was a small terrorist organization with limited resources. This observation raises the abiding questions of what strategy is, how it can it be developed and then implemented. Historically, naval forces have been one of the most valuable implements in the strategic armory; they represent a golden thread running through American and British history. We will revert to this theme momentarily, but first we have to address the hard facts and realities of the present and the future, so as not to let the past become prologue through the reinvention of failure. Lessons learned are invaluable today.

The United Kingdom went to the polls in May 2015 and elected a Conservative government, led by David Cameron, for the following five years. In November 2016, the United States will vote for its next president. Since the 2015 election the United Kingdom has been undergoing a Strategic Defense and Security Review (SDSR), a follow-on to predecessor reviews in 1998 (updated in 2003 by the *Delivering Security in a Changing World* white paper), and 2010 (October 19). Concurrently will come major decisions on how the United Kingdom will fund the replacement of its four *Vanguard*-class SSBNs, the stand-alone British nuclear deterrent. Exactly the same scenario applies to the United States: critical decisions about how the US Navy will pay for replacing the *Ohio*-class SSBN. The timing of the two replacement programs is interwoven. The United Kingdom and the Royal Navy are dependent on the US government and Navy for technical assistance—specifically, the Office of the Principal Executive Officer (PEO) Submarines, the Strategic Systems Project Office (SP), and the industrial base that supports the PEO and SP.

These are hugely costly at a time (2016) when the US Navy is bringing into service USS *Gerald R. Ford* (CVN 78), the first of the new aircraft-carrier class. At $13 billion this is the US Navy's most expensive ship, as well as the largest ship ever commissioned. The second of class, USS *John F. Kennedy* (CVN 79), will be commissioned in 2020, with others to follow at approximately five-year intervals. A total of ten *Ford*-class carriers are planned; construction is likely continuing to about 2058, a daunting and impressive prospect from our present vantage point. Likewise, the Royal Navy will be commissioning its two new carriers, the largest ships (at 60,000 tons) ever built by the Royal Navy, HMS *Queen Elizabeth* and HMS *Prince of Wales,* flying the Lockheed Martin F-35 aircraft. Also, the *Virginia*-class SSN and *Astute*-class SSN will continue to be built, with continuing upgrades. If we add destroyers, upgrades to Aegis cruisers and destroyers, new amphibious ships, new multipurpose ships for the Royal Navy and maintenance of its amphibious lift, one thing becomes clear: both nations are investing in their navies heavily, in terms both of gross national product and distribution of defense budgets. Where does all this fit into both nations' grand strategies? How will these navies, practically and pragmatically, individually and collectively, fit into the strategic tapestry?

The United Kingdom's previous SDSRs have been heavily criticized for their failure to spell out a rational national strategy, one predicated on clearly defined and national-security interests. How do these national interests rationalize force-structure and budgetary decisions? Many analysts have seen prior SDSRs as merely dividing up the funding pie between the three British armed services, each of which in recent years has borne cuts, certainly since the 2008 global financial crisis. The process was more about accommodation and compromise than thought-through, hardheaded, and well articulated strategic priorities.

The US Navy has been more fortunate, perhaps largely owing to the organizational and political factors that we discussed at the beginning of this book. Still, and in spite of weaknesses that the Royal Navy has endured since the changes in the United Kingdom's defense organization in the 1960s, it is important to note that today the Royal Navy is acquiring two new carriers, their air wings, and new nuclear attack submarines and is planning a SSBN replacement and new surface ships. This seems quite rosy. What force level does the Royal Navy require if it is to be a major partner of the US Navy? This comes back to one word: strategy.

The US Navy document "A Cooperative Strategy for 21st Century Seapower," signed by the Secretary of the Navy, Ray Mabus, and the three sea-service chiefs (the Chief of Naval Operations, the Commandant of the Marine Corps, and the Commandant of the Coast Guard), issued in March 2015, and published in a special section of the U.S. Naval Institute *Proceedings* in April 2015, is explicit. It clearly defines a US maritime strategy. A former Chief of Naval Operations, Admiral Gary Roughead, has stressed the need for a new US strategy for the Arctic, a new economic and resource frontier that conjoins multiple nations. He wisely recognizes that strategic aspects are one element of a broad set of vital national economic and security interests. The point here is that the United States is addressing interests in the strategic context, not in a piecemeal or ad hoc way. In 2014 the European Union issued a Maritime Security Strategy, and the United Kingdom issued a National Strategy for Maritime Security. Both of these showed positive trends, a revitalization of the maritime domain in grand strategy. Furthermore, the American Chief of Naval Operations and the British First Sea Lord have jointly issued a vision for deeper cooperation in the next fifteen years, how best to work together to pursue mutual strategic interests. Their declaration is a good starting point for our analysis and discussion.

At the heart of this analysis is the core concept of "strategy" itself. There can be many definitions, perhaps in the eye of the beholder. Nonetheless, it is essential that we have a framework; otherwise our future strategy may be built on shifting sands. There are two separate concepts: the ways and means to implement strategic goals, and the core strategic goals themselves. The latter is about what it is that we are trying to achieve and why, while the former is about how to do it—and it is easy to slip into the how without fully analyzing the why. We can address "naval power" and its characteristics, and the individual benefits for example of various naval capabilities, forward persistent presence, maneuver, flexibility to use the sea commons, overwhelming combined force, logistics, and so forth. This is not strategy but well understood and defined aspects of multiple naval means: surface, subsurface, air, space, amphibious, nuclear deterrence, and special forces. Strategy is fundamentally about what the United States and the United Kingdom want to do, and why, in order to protect and enhance their well defined perceptions and written statements of their national interests. Once those interests are defined and prioritized, it behooves both nations to consider "how to create the environment and means with which to both control and achieve favorable outcomes," however these may be defined. Influencing and controlling the behavior of others, whether state players or other actors, good or bad, in the best interests of the United States and the United Kingdom are the natural corollaries to what both countries define as their top priorities.

Admiral Sir George Zambellas, the First Sea Lord, and Admiral Jonathan Greenert, former Chief of Naval Operations, have done a sterling job in their joint paper, *Combined Seapower: A Shared Vision for Royal Navy–United States Navy Cooperation*. It is the way ahead for both navies, together and in unison, for at least the next fifteen years. What may need more emphasis is the question of what indeed the core national strategic interests are. Both admirals have brilliantly articulated the "how," with a fine shopping list of operational and technical issues, force mixes, exercises, joint training, forward-deployed joint and combined operations, intelligence, and personnel exchanges. They have clearly defined the absolute necessity for protecting, and controlling when necessary, the sea lines of communication and seaborne trade. But both countries' political, public, and media elites need to hear why the two combined navies are the best means to advance the national interests while restricting and, if necessary, denying any potential adversaries the same ability. The right words are vital in this debate: that sea power in its myriad US–UK combined format will offer both countries' leaderships the optimal means, together with diplomatic and economic means, to achieve favorable outcomes.

The substance of strategic expeditionary naval diplomacy and warfare, its core, characteristic value, is its ability to signal, influence, deter, and, at worst case, provide the full range of measured force to meet all known and projected military-political-economic contingencies. This is the key lesson of naval history, and grand strategy.

Maneuvering a fleet, of whatever composition, scenario, or local tactical situation, is predicated on the measured application of both implied and actual force. A full US–UK battle force of surface, subsurface, air, space, and special forces, grouped with a large amphibious force (which can include a MEF, with its organic air group), enables penetration and occupation of the most challenging threat region with extraordinary lethal force. The combined strength of a US–UK naval task force would make it, therefore, not just formidable but an instrument of strategic power. The history of the last fifteen years is a sad reflection on the fallacy of committing land forces to situations that were strategically untenable. Historically the United States and the United Kingdom have committed large armies, essentially "people's armies" led by career professionals, only in the face of the most threatening odds. Large standing armies, eating up national treasure, offer no strategic value unless the intent is to overrun, like Adolf Hitler, neighbors with brutal force. The "On and From the Sea" strategy offers a much more diverse and affordable set of strategic options, with forward presence and maneuverability crucial as instruments of not just national power but diplomatic signaling. The essence of maritime strategy resides therefore in these innate characteristics, put simply by one famous example. When asked if Napoleon could invade England, Admiral John Jervis responded, "I do not say they [the French] cannot come, I only say they cannot come by sea." This summarizes a critical strategic point, and within it lies the strategy that led to Napoleon's demise and to the end of French conquests during the Napoleonic era. As in countless scenarios in the past, the navies of the United States and the United Kingdom can launch forces onto land in measured and strategically placed ways when necessary, while controlling the seas and air above. Once the strategic advantages of combined US-UK naval forces are fully articulated, it becomes axiomatic that the maritime domain becomes the single best arena for protecting and enhancing the vital national interests of the United States and the United Kingdom.

The "Statement of Intent Regarding Enhanced Cooperation on Carrier Operations and Maritime Power Projection" (signed by the British secretary for defense and the American secretary of defense in January 2012) is a means to an end, but it is not a strategy. The strategic concepts described above call for a resolute statement of joint national resolve to use the sea and naval forces as "the primary means" to secure the vital national interests of the United States and the United Kingdom. The latter, with a lower gross national product and hence less available investment for defense, may have to transfer resources from the army budget to the Royal Navy. The great traditions and core capabilities of the British Army can be preserved, with perhaps a much larger reserve army and a reduced permanent, career force level. Resources will have to be found for the Royal Navy, and this is the most likely, perhaps only, practical outcome. It may be that the US Army too will have to be significantly reduced, in order to fund not just the *Ohio*-class SSBN replacement but also the forward presence and logistics sustainment that the new strategy dictates.

The "shared vision" for the US Navy and the Royal Navy, articulated by their two fine leaders, is a fitting end to our study. We end on a most positive note—that the cooperation and historical links of both navies will not only endure but be enhanced with new energy and vision, reflecting the hallmark of both navies: that people are the single most important factor and that there is no substitute for good leadership. Both the United States Navy and the Royal Navy are in highly capable hands.

Fear God and Dread Nought.

Source Notes

INTRODUCTION

Reference is made to key observations in Sir Michael Howard's autobiography, *Captain Professor: A Life in War and Peace* (2006), and to his *Liberation or Catastrophe? Reflections on the History of the 20th Century* (2007). Sir Michael is the founding father of the Department of War Studies, King's College, London. Besides his distinguished academic career he served in World War II in the British Army, winning the Military Cross for gallantry. His careful analysis of the value of studying the past in relation to current and future military events and strategic concepts reflects decades of research and is an invaluable source for stimulating thought about twenty-first-century strategy.

CHAPTER 1. Organizational Change and Strategic Priorities Impact the US Navy and the Royal Navy

The Naval Institute Press published in 1986 a set of collected essays and analyses, edited by James George, on how a range of key factors had shaped naval thinking and strategy regarding the Soviet navy and the navies of the Warsaw Pact. The Soviet and other communist navies remain primary sources for the thinking in the mid-1980s and key data relating to the reactions of the United States and the United Kingdom to the growth of Soviet naval power. Sir James Cable was a distinguished retired British diplomat who had a lifelong passion for the Royal Navy and naval strategy, writing *Britain's Naval Future* in 1983 (Naval Institute Press). Sir James and your author, when he worked for British Intelligence, met regularly at Sir James' Club in London for lunch over several years to discuss his book and ideas as to where the Royal Navy and its greatest ally, the US Navy, should be headed. A man who should have been a naval officer but instead spent his career in key British embassies dealing with the Soviet Union and its allies, Sir James had a brilliant insight into both the naval past and future. Parallel to the thinking of Sir James was the fine work of Ken Booth, who worked in academe in both the United States and the United Kingdom. Croom Helm published his *Navies and Foreign Policy* in 1977, at the height of the Cold War. When Booth's work is coupled with that of Sir Laurence Martin, a bedrock view of strategic naval issues from a 1970s vantage point emerges. Sir Laurence was one of your author's key mentors in the late 1960s, when he was the professor of war studies at King's College, London. Martin's *Arms and Strategy,* published in 1973 by Weidenfeld & Nicholson, and his *Sea in Modern Strategy,* published in 1967 by Chatto & Windus for the Institute for Strategic Studies, are seminal studies on naval thinking in the second half of the twentieth century.

CHAPTER 2. Limited War in the Nuclear Era

Reference is made very early on to Bernard Brodie's key works on nuclear theory and their impact on strategy. There are three major works, *Strategy in the Missile Age* (Princeton University Press, 1959), *The Future of Deterrence in U.S. Strategy* (University of California Press, 1968), and *War and Politics* (Macmillan, 1973). The quotation on page 40 is from *Strategy in the Missile Age.* Brodie remains the father of nuclear strategic thinking. The chapter also makes detailed references to work performed by your author in the 1980s for the US Department of Defense and Department of the Navy. These include two major studies: *Preliminary Overview of Soviet Merchant Ships in Anti-SSBN Operations and Soviet Merchant Ships and Submarine Masking,* and *SSBN Port Egress and the Non-Commercial Activities of the Soviet Merchant Fleet: Concepts of Operation and War Orders for Current and Future Anti-SSBN Operations.* Both these analyses contain detailed information on the strategic implications of Soviet attempts to thwart the efficacy of the primary US nuclear deterrent, the strategic missile submarine.

CHAPTER 3. The Technology Race Is On

There is a plethora of excellent data in *The Soviet and Other Communist Navies,* edited by James George, published by the Naval Institute Press in 1986. Your author has a chapter in this book. The fine detail in this chapter is taken from a unique unpublished US government study led by your author: *Soviet Submarine Warfare Strategy Assessment and Future US Submarine and Anti-Submarine Warfare Technologies.* This voluminous study contains more unclassified information on the technological aspects of the naval Cold War and the Soviet Union's emergent capabilities than most likely any other available study. This work is complemented by the data from a seminal article published by your author: "Soviet Submarine Prospects 1985–2000," in *The Submarine Review,* January 1986. Together these works contain a unique set of data that if augmented by standard publications—such as the Naval Institute's *Ships and Aircraft of the US Fleet,* by Norman Polmar, and *Jane's Fighting Ships* annual publications—constitute a powerful source and overview of the technological race and issues.

CHAPTER 4. The 1960s

In the mid-1970s the US Navy assembled a group of specialists to research and publish at different classification levels studies of where the Soviet navy was headed in its overseas operations, bases, and political-military objectives. Your author was part of this team. The unclassified product was comprehensively published in *Soviet Naval Diplomacy,* edited by B. Dismukes and J. McConnell, 1979. There is a chapter on the "June War, 1967," by Dr. Anthony Wells. The quotation on page 94 is from *The 1967 June War: Soviet Naval Diplomacy and the Sixth Fleet—A Reappraisal.* In addition, much more detailed research was carried out by your author on US, UK, and Soviet naval and intelligence operations in the Mediterranean; the unclassified results may be read in *The 1967 June War.* Much later your author followed up on his earlier work by a research paper that was published by the US Naval Institute *Proceedings* in 2005 as an article, "They Did Not Die in Vain: USS *Liberty* Incident—Some Additional Perspectives." It details the attack on the USS *Liberty,* the spy ship that was attacked by Israeli force on June 8, 1967. Subsequent to this the USS *Liberty* Alliance and the USS *Liberty* Veterans Association created a website of all available key declassified *Liberty*-related documents: usslibertydocument-center.com. It is the most comprehensive set of research documents that have been accessed by both specialist scholars and lay persons. Your author succeeded Admiral Thomas Moorer (late former chairman of the Joint Chiefs of Staff and Chief of Naval Operations) and Rear Admiral Clarence "Mark" Hill as the third chairman of the USS *Liberty* Alliance and was instrumental, with Commander Thomas Schaaf, USN (Ret.), in creating this website. The site includes highly sensitive declassified Central Intelligence Agency and National Security Agency documents, some with redactions. The reports and other personal papers of key personnel represent a unique research collection.

CHAPTER 5. The US Navy and Royal Navy as Key Echelons of American and British Intelligence

This chapter places some reliance on two sources mentioned earlier, George's *Soviet and Other Communist Navies* and your author's "Soviet Submarine Prospects 1985–2000," both of which contain crucial material about the key changes that were occurring. However, the highly detailed material in this chapter was derived from three unique sources that contain the most reliable evidence. The article "The Soviet Navy in the Arctic and North Atlantic," Dr. Anthony Wells, was the result of several years of research and operational involvement at an all-source level, distilled into this unclassified article. The same applies to the US government paper *NATO and US Carrier Deployment Policies;* it provides data and insights into key carrier operations at the height of the Cold War. Perhaps the most revealing document is *Sea War '85 Scenario;* this document provides details of the thinking behind the strategy, tactics, and operations for a major naval war against the Soviet Union and its allies in 1985 through the lens of intelligence data in the mid-1970s. Together the above documents and their core material offer a unique look at this chapter's topics. The quotation on page 101 is from Ben McIntyre, "Bond: The Real Bond," *Times* (London), April 5, 2008.

CHAPTER 6. The Soviets Shift Gears and Make Serious Challenges at the Time of the Walker Spy Ring

This chapter is the first to rely heavily on the personal papers, notes, and firm recollections of Dr. Anthony Wells for the period 1966–2015. They address, for instance, certain disagreements on intelligence data that arose between the United States and the United Kingdom after the Walker spy ring was exposed. These personal sources are supported by published material in George's *Soviet and Other Communist Navies* and your author's "Soviet Submarine Prospects 1985–2000." Much more detailed and weighty evidence is derived from three sources with which the author was involved: *Presence and Military Strategies of the USSR in the Arctic* provides unique insights into the strategic value of the Arctic and under-ice operations; the detailed and technically complex *The Application of Drag Reduction and Boundary Layer Control Technologies in an Experimental Program* offers highly reliable and historically valuable insight and data into key technical issues that the US and UK intelligence communities were addressing in the 1980s; and perhaps the most detailed and comprehensive data can be found in *Soviet Submarine Warfare Strategy Assessment and Future US Submarine and Anti-Submarine Warfare Technologies*. The latter contains uniquely presented material that was used by the US Department of Defense and the US Navy, in conjunction with the Royal Navy and the UK Ministry of Defense, to plan far ahead for meeting the Soviet challenge.

Chapter 7. A Real Shooting War at Sea

The personal papers, notes, and recollections of the author play heavily in this chapter. During this crucial operation the author was head of special programs in one of the UK's key intelligence directorates and worked closely with all the major US intelligence agencies and the US Navy. Many of the insights and much of the data recounted cannot be found in the other source material used in this chapter, including One *Hundred Days: The Memoirs of the Falklands Battle Group Commander,* by Admiral Sandy Woodward; *The Battle for the Falklands,* Max Hastings and Simon Jenkins; and *The Official History of the Falklands Campaign,* Sir Lawrence Freedman. Within the Private Papers Collection is a record of intelligence operations and technology from 1960 to 2015. In addition to Admiral Woodward's memoir the author used *No Picnic: 3 Commando Brigade in the South Atlantic 1982,* by Julian Thompson, a highly readable and accurate account of the Royal Marines in the Falklands. The life of the British Chief of the Defense Staff in 1982, Admiral of the Fleet Lord Lewin, can be explored in detail in the very fine biography *Lewin of Greenwich, The Authorized Biography of Admiral of the Fleet Lord Lewin,* by Richard Hill. Your author also wrote Admiral Woodward's obituary for the US Naval Institute *News,* reflecting on his overall career achievements and on why he was so successful in the South Atlantic campaign: "A Tribute to Admiral Sir John 'Sandy' Woodward." For a very good and comprehensive set of Falklands campaign photographs, do look at the Sunday Express Magazine's *War in the Falklands: The Campaign in Pictures.* For the famous interview with John Nott, see *BBC Newsnight,* October 1982 (YouTube). The interview seems to have been filmed on the 5th.

Chapter 8. The Changing Tide

This chapter relies heavily on the personal papers and notes in the document collection of Dr. Anthony R. Wells, for the period 1960–2015. This primary source material is supplemented by reliable and accurate secondary sources, of which the major ones are *Ships and Aircraft of the U.S. Fleet,* Norman Polmar (a series); *Guide to the Soviet Navy,* Polmar (a series); *Submarine Design and Development,* Norman Friedman; and *Anti-Submarine Warfare,* Rear Admiral J. R. Hill, RN (Ret.). Rear Admiral Hill was also the author of the fine biography of Admiral of the Fleet Lord Lewin, referenced in chapter 7's notes. *Jane's Fighting Ships* for 1960–2015 is a detailed and accurate source. While working for British Intelligence your author regularly met with Captain John Moore, RN (Ret.), the longtime editor of *Jane's Fighting Ships,* who too had worked for operational intelligence when in uniform. Another highly reliable and accurate source that your author used in this chapter and elsewhere is *The Military Balance,* published by the International Institute for Strategic Studies in London. This source is highly reliable and provides data that is not comprehensively referenced in most secondary sources.

CHAPTER 9. The 1990s

This chapter benefits from the author's personal involvement as technical director of Fleet Battle Experiments Alpha and Bravo, in the Third Fleet, US Pacific Fleet, and from his direct working involvement with two lead agencies of US intelligence. Dr. Wells' personal papers, notes, and recollections play heavily, along with reliable published material. The latter includes "Real Time Targeting: Myth or Reality," "Transformation: Some Insights and Observations for the Royal Navy from across the Atlantic," *NATO and US Carrier Deployment Policies, Sea War '85 Scenario,* and *Overview Study of the Maritime Aspects of the Nuclear Balance in the European Theater.* The author uses material from one of the videos made during one of the key Fleet Battle Experiments, which changed the way the way the US Navy operates: *Limited Objective Experiment ZERO,* as well as *Asymmetric Warfare Test, Training and Experimentation: Joint Video.* This video must be seen as showing how forward-looking the US Navy was during the last decade of the twentieth century and shortly before 9/11.

CHAPTER 10. Conflicts, Minor Wars, and the World-Changing Event of 9/11

This chapter reflects work performed by the author for the US intelligence community and the US Navy post-9/11, including notes and papers in his private collection. Material is used from unclassified, published, open-source material by the author, notably: "US Naval Power and the Pursuit of Peace in an Era of International Terrorism and Weapons of Mass Destruction"; and "Royal Navy at the Crossroads: Turn the Strategic Tide—A Way to Implement a Lasting Vision." In addition the author used and recommends two very good secondary sources: *Intelligence in War,* by John Keegan, a must-read by an author in a class of his own; and *Wars in Peace,* edited by Adrian L. Johnson. The latter, a collection of papers, provides reliable facts and general overviews, though perhaps it is limited in the quality of its analysis and lacks insider knowledge and experience. By contrast, John Keegan occupies the intellectual high ground and, though not current with the latest intelligence, he offers something well beyond the value of the latest National Intelligence Estimates.

Chapter 11. The New Challenge in the Middle East, the Rise of China, and a Possible Challenge from Russia

This chapter relies heavily on the author's work for the US intelligence community and his extensive travel in the Middle East and East Asia during this period, coupled with his research and published unclassified material in the public domain. The latter includes the following: "Royal Navy at the Crossroads," "A Strategy in East Asia That Can Endure," "The United States Navy, Jordan, and a Long Term Israeli-Palestinian Security Agreement," "Jordan, Israel, and US Need to Cooperate for Missile Defense," and "The Future of ISIS: A Joint US-Russian Assessment." Up-to-date, open-source technical material was obtained from *Jane's Fighting Ships,* 2014–15.

Chapter 12. The Sea in Future Strategy

The concluding chapter encapsulates many of the ideas and much of the data from the preceding chapters relating to future US Navy and Royal Navy strategic issues. The author has studied the maritime strategic dimensions in depth and published relevant articles in three major naval journals: "The Royal Navy Is Key to Britain's Security Strategy," "The Survivability of the Royal Navy and a New Enlightened British Defense Strategy," and "Admiral Sir Herbert Richmond: What Would He Think, Write and Action Today?" The latter article is of particular interest, because Admiral Sir Herbert Richmond (1871–1946) was one of the key founders of *The Naval Review* in the United Kingdom and is often described as "perhaps the most brilliant naval officer of his generation," or the "British Mahan." He led an intellectual revolution in the Royal Navy, stressing in particular the study of naval history. After a distinguished naval career he became the Vere Harmsworth Professor of Imperial and Naval History at Cambridge (1934–36) and the Master of Downing College, Cambridge (1934–46). In the centenary year of *The Naval Review* your author wrote a definitive article in its pages on what Admiral Richmond may think today about strategic issues and the use of naval power.

Bibliography

Booth, K. *Navies and Foreign Policy.* London: Croom Helm, 1977.

Brodie, Bernard. *The Future of Deterrence in U.S. Strategy.* Oakland: University of California Press, 1968.

———. *Strategy in the Missile Age.* Princeton, NJ: Princeton University Press, 1959.

———. *War and Politics.* New York: Macmillan, 1973.

Cable, James. *Britain's Naval Future.* Annapolis, MD: Naval Institute Press, 1983.

Cocker, M. P. *Royal Navy Submarines 1901–1982.* London: Frederick Warre, 1982.

Compton-Hall, Richard. *Subs versus Subs: The Tactical Technology of Underwater Warfare.* London: David & Charles, 1988.

Dismukes, B., and J. McConnell. *Soviet Naval Diplomacy.* Oxford, UK: Pergamon, 1979.

Freedman, Sir Lawrence. *Official History of the Falklands Campaign.* Volumes 1 & 2. London: Routledge, 2005.

———. *Strategy.* Oxford, UK: Oxford University Press, 2013.

Friedman, Norman. *Submarine Design and Development.* London: Conway Maritime, 1984.

George, James, ed. *The Soviet and Other Communist Navies.* Annapolis, MD: Naval Institute Press, 1986.

Greenert, Jonathan, and Sir George Zambellas. *Combined Seapower: A Shared Vision for Royal Navy–United States Navy Cooperation.* London and Washington, DC: Joint publication by the Ministry of Defense, London, and the Department of the Navy, Washington DC, Unclassified, December 11, 2014.

Hastings, Max, and Simon Jenkins. *The Battle for the Falklands.* New York: W. W. Norton, 1983.

Hill, Rear Admiral J. R. *Anti-Submarine Warfare.* Annapolis, MD: Naval Institute Press, 1985.

———. *Lewin of Greenwich. The Authorized Biography of Admiral of the Fleet Lord Lewin.* London: Cassell, 2000.

————, ed. *Oxford Illustrated History of the Royal Navy.* Oxford, UK: Oxford University Press, 1995.

Hinsley, F. H. *British Intelligence in the Second World War.* London: Her Majesty's Stationery Office, 1979.

Howard, Sir Michael. *Captain Professor: A Life in War and Peace.* New York: Continuum, 2006.

————. *Liberation or Catastrophe: Reflections on the History of the 20th Century.* London: A&C Black, 2007.

International Institute for Strategic Studies (IISS). *The Military Balance Collection.* London: IISS, various years.

Ireland, Bernard. *War at Sea 1897–1997.* With Eric Grove. London: Harper Collins & Janes, 1997.

Jane's Fighting Ships. London: Jane's, 1960–2015.

Johnson, Adrian L., ed. *Wars in Peace.* London: Royal United Service Institution, 2014.

Kegan, John. *Intelligence in War.* New York: Vintage Books & Random House, 2002.

Martin, Sir Laurence. *Arms and Strategy.* London: Weidenfeld & Nicholson, 1973.

————. *Sea in Modern Strategy.* London: Chatto & Windus, 1967.

Miller, Franklin C. *The Vital Place of Nuclear Weapons in 21st Century U.S. National Security.* Tokyo: Report of the International Commission on Nuclear Non-Proliferation and Disarmament, 2009.

Nguyen, Hung P. *Submarine Detection from Space: A Study of Russian Capabilities.* Annapolis, MD: Naval Institute Press, 1993.

Polmar, Norman. *The Ships and Aircraft of the US Fleet.* Annapolis, MD: Naval Institute Press, 1984.

Sainsbury, A. B. *The Royal Navy Day by Day.* London: Ian Allen, 1993.

Stefanick, Thomas. *Strategic Antisubmarine Warfare and Naval Strategy.* Lexington: Lexington Books, 1987.

Sunday Express Magazine. *War in the Falklands: The Campaign in Pictures.* London: George Weidenfeld & Nicholson, 1982.

Thompson, Julian. *No Picnic: 3 Commando Brigade in the South Atlantic 1982.* New York: Hippocrene Books, 1985.

Wells, Anthony. "Admiral Sir Herbert Richmond: What Would He Think, Write and Action Today?" *Naval Review* Centenary Edition (February 2013).

————. *The Application of Drag Reduction and Boundary Layer Control Technologies in an Experimental Program: Report for the Chief Naval Architect.*

Barrow-in-Furness, UK: Vickers Shipbuilding and Engineering Ltd., January 1986.

———. *Distributed Data Analysis with Bayesian Networks: A Preliminary Study for the Non-Proliferation of Radioactive Devices.* With Dr. Farid Dowla and Dr. G. Larson. Livermore, CA: Lawrence Livermore National Laboratory, 2003.

———. *Fiber Reinforced Pumice Protective Barriers: To Mitigate the Effects of Suicide and Truck Bombs—Final Report and Recommendations.* With Professor Vistasp Kharbari, Professor of Structural Engineering, University of California, San Diego. Washington, DC: Naval Air Systems Command, Department of the Navy, August 2006.

———. "The Future of ISIS: A Joint US-Russian Assessment." With Dr. Andrey Chuprygin. *Naval Review* (May 2015).

———. "Jordan, Israel, and US Need to Cooperate for Missile Defense." U.S. Naval Institute *News* (March 2013).

———. *Limited Objective Experiment ZERO.* Washington, DC: Naval Air Systems Command, Department of the Navy, July 2002.

———. *NATO and Carrier Deployment Policies: Formation of a New Standing Naval Strike Force in NATO.* Washington, DC: Center for Naval Analyses, Department of the Navy, April 1977.

———. *NATO and US Carrier Deployment Policies.* Washington, DC: Center for Naval Analyses, Department of the Navy, February 1977.

———. "A New Defense Strategy for Britain." U.S. Naval Institute *Proceedings* (March 1987).

———. *The 1967 June War: Soviet Naval Diplomacy and the Sixth Fleet—A Reappraisal.* Professional Paper 204. Washington, DC: Center for Naval Analyses, Department of the Navy, 1977.

———. *Operational Factors Associated with the Software Nuclear Analysis for the UGM-109A Tomahawk Submarine-Launched Land Attack Cruise Missile Combat Control System Mark 1.* Washington, DC: Department of the Navy, 1989.

———. *Overview Study of the Maritime Aspects of the Nuclear Balance in the European Theater. US Department of Energy Study for the European Conflict Analysis Project.* Washington, DC: US Department of Energy, October 1986.

———. Personal Papers and Notes 1966–2015. Wells Collection, Archives, Middleburg, VA.

———. *Preliminary Overview of Soviet Merchant Ships in Anti-SSBN Operations and Soviet Merchant Ships and Submarine Masking.* SSBN Security

Program, US Navy Contract N00016-85-C-0204. Washington, DC: Department of the Navy, 1986.

———. *Presence and Military Strategies of the USSR in the Arctic.* Quebec: Laval University Press for Quebec Center for International Relations, 1986.

———. "Real Time Targeting: Myth or Reality." U.S. Naval Institute *Proceedings* (August 2001).

———. "Royal Navy at the Crossroads: Turn the Strategic Tide—A Way to Implement a Lasting Vision." *Naval Review* (November 2010).

———. "The Royal Navy Is Key to Britain's Security Strategy." U.S. Naval Institute *Proceedings* (December 2010).

———. *Sea War '85 Scenario.* With Captain John L. Underwood, USN. Washington, DC: Center for Naval Analyses, Department of the Navy, April 1977.

———. "The Soviet Navy in the Arctic and North Atlantic." *National Defense* (February 1986).

———. "Soviet Submarine Prospects 1985–2000." *Submarine Review* (January 1986).

———. *Soviet Submarine Warfare Strategy Assessment and Future US Submarine and Anti-Submarine Warfare Technologies.* Washington, DC: Defense Advanced Research Projects Agency, US Department of Defense, March 1988.

———. *SSBN Port Egress and the Non-Commercial Activities of the Soviet Merchant Fleet: Concepts of Operation and War Orders for Current and Future Anti-SSBN Operations.* SSBN Security Program, US Navy Contract N136400. Washington, DC: Department of the Navy, 1986.

———. "A Strategy in East Asia That Can Endure." U.S. Naval Institute *Proceedings* (May 2011). Reprinted *Naval Review* (August 2011).

———. *Submarine Industrial Base Model: Key Industrial Base Model for the US Virginia Class Nuclear Powered Attack Submarine.* With Dr. Carol V. Evans, Principal Executive Officer Submarines. Washington, DC: Naval Sea Systems Command, Department of the Navy, n.d.

———. "The Survivability of the Royal Navy and a New Enlightened British Defense Strategy." *Submarine Review* (January 2011).

———. *Tactical Decision Aid: Multi Intelligence Capability for National, Theater, and Tactical Intelligence in Real Time across Geographic Space and Time.* Washington, DC: Department of the Navy and US National Intelligence Community, May 2012.

———. "They Did Not Die in Vain: USS *Liberty* Incident—Some Additional Perspectives." U.S. Naval Institute *Proceedings* (March 2005).

————. "Transformation: Some Insights and Observations for the Royal Navy from across the Atlantic." *Naval Review* (August 2003).

————. "A Tribute to Admiral Sir John 'Sandy' Woodward." U.S. Naval Institute *News* (August 2013).

————. "The United States Navy, Jordan, and a Long Term Israeli-Palestinian Security Agreement." *Submarine Review* (Spring 2013).

————. "US Naval Power and the Pursuit of Peace in an Era of International Terrorism and Weapons of Mass Destruction." *Submarine Review* (October 2002).

————. USS Liberty *Document Center,* ed. With Thomas Schaaf. [A document website produced by SiteWhirks, Warrenton, Virginia. This site receives regular updates.]

————. *Weapon Target Centric Model. Preliminary Modules and Applications.* Two Volumes. Washington, DC: Principal Executive Officer Submarines, Naval Sea Systems Command, Department of the Navy, August 2007.

Woodward, Admiral Sir John "Sandy." *One Hundred Days: The Memoirs of the Falklands Battle Group Commander.* With Patrick Robinson. Annapolis, MD: Naval Institute Press, 1992.

Index

About the Author

ANTHONY WELLS was born in Coventry, England. He is the only living person to have worked for British Intelligence, served in the Royal Navy and on exchange with the US Navy as a British citizen, and worked for US intelligence and the US Navy as a US citizen. He was educated at Durham University, King's College, London, and the London School of Economics. He was trained at Britannia Royal Naval College, Dartmouth, and the School of Maritime Operations.